MOTION TRACKING AND GESTURE RECOGNITION

Edited by **Carlos M. Travieso-González**

Motion Tracking and Gesture Recognition
http://dx.doi.org/10.5772/65236
Edited by Carlos M. Travieso-González

Contributors

Yang Zhao, Huan Tan, Lynn DeRose, Shazrinizam Shaharan, Donncha Ryan, Paul Neary, Houssam Salmane, Yassine Ruichek, Louahdi Khoudour, Volkan Kilic, Wenwu Wang, Jiande Sun, Yufei Wang, Jing Li, Enea Cippitelli, Ennio Gambi, Susanna Spinsante, Grazia Cicirelli, Tiziana D'Orazio

Published by InTech
Janeza Trdine 9, 51000 Rijeka, Croatia

Publishing Process Manager Mirena Calmic
Technical Editor SPi Global
Cover InTech Design team

First published July, 2017
Printed in Croatia
Legal deposit, Croatia: National and University Library in Zagreb

Additional hard copies can be obtained from orders@intechopen.com

Motion Tracking and Gesture Recognition, Edited by Carlos M. Travieso-González
p. cm.
Print ISBN 978-953-51-3377-3
Online ISBN 978-953-51-3378-0

For EU product safety concerns:
IN TECH d.o.o., Prolaz Marije Krucifikse Kozulić 3, 51000 Rijeka, Croatia,
info@intechopen.com or visit our website at intechopen.com.

Meet the editor

Carlos M. Travieso-González received his MSc degree in 1997 in Telecommunication Engineering at Polytechnic University of Catalonia (UPC), Spain, and his PhD degree in 2002 at the University of Las Palmas de Gran Canaria (ULPGC, Spain). He is an associate professor from 2001 in ULPGC, teaching subjects on signal processing and learning theory, and he got the positive accreditation from the Spanish government to be a full professor. His research lines are biometrics, biomedical signals, data mining, classification system, signal and image processing, and environmental intelligence. He has participated on different international and Spanish research projects, some of them as head researcher. He has up to 360 publications, as coauthor of books and book chapters, coeditor of proceeding books, guest editor on JCR-ISI international journals, coauthor of patents, and coauthor on JCR-ISI journal papers and conference papers. He has been a reviewer in different JCR-ISI indexed journals and TPC member on international conferences. He will be IEEE-IWOBI 2017 general chair and was COCOMED 2017 general cochair, IEEE-IWOBI 2015 general chair, InnoEducaTIC 2014 general chair, IEEE-IWOBI 2014 general chair, IEEE-INES 2013 general chair, NoLISP 2011 general chair, JRBP 2012 general chair, and IEEE-ICCST 2005 cochair.

Contents

Preface

Due to the rise of technological devices and smartphones, the visualization of multimedia content has become a routine. Every day, a large number of images or videos can be viewed and/or sent, which are already part of our daily lives. This does not go unnoticed for technological advances, where the researchers focus their efforts to turn that multimedia content into something more. Extracting information from videos and images can be very useful, since you can automatically get more information from the simple visualization.

In fields with security, medicine, and communication of humans, new and advanced techniques can be applied to facilitate or give more information to multimedia contents. A great number of tools are being developed in this sense, and in this book, works of high quality are presented, developed on a scientific methodology, giving validation to the present proposals. They have focused on motion tracking and gesture recognition. Therefore, it will be a very attractive reading for the reader.

Motion Tracking and Gesture Recognition is composed of seven chapters, which have been divided into two sections, motion tracking and gesture recognition. The section "Motion Tracking" has four chapters. Motion tracking is observed by a hand-tracking system for surgical training, an approach based on detection of dangerous situation by the prediction of moving objects, an approach based on human motion detection results and preliminary environmental information to build a long-term context model to describe and predict human activities, and a review about multispeaker tracking on different modalities. The section "Gesture Recognition" has three chapters. Gesture recognition is shown by a gait recognition approach using Kinect sensor, a study of different methodologies for studying gesture recognition on depth images, and a review about human action recognition and the details about a particular technique based on a sensor of visible range and with depth information.

As an editor of this book, I would like to thank the authors, their effort, and dedication that they have made to achieve some works of great quality. The sum of this effort has produced this book, which has become an inescapable read for all those who want to know the latest advances in tracking video and gesture recognition.

Carlos M. Travieso-González
University of Las Palmas de Gran Canaria,
Spain

Section 1

Motion Tracking

Chapter 1

Motion Tracking System in Surgical Training

Shazrinizam Shaharan, Donncha M Ryan and

Paul C Neary

Additional information is available at the end of the chapter

http://dx.doi.org/10.5772/intechopen.68850

Abstract

Introduction: Simulation technology is evolving and becoming the focus of attention in surgical training. The development of this technology in assessing open surgical skills is far behind when compared to minimally invasive surgery (MIS) training. Surgical skills such as suturing and tying surgical knots are assessed by an observational tool. It is labour-intensive and time-consuming. Therefore, we explored the potential use of motion tracking system as a non-observational assessment tool for basic surgical skills.

Methods: We established a motion tracking system using a device called the Patriot™ (Polhemus Inc., Colchester, VT) and software created by our co-supervisor which generates numerical metrics. We validated this system and applied it to the proficiency-based skill assessment.

Results: The Patriot™ system was able to differentiate between the different levels of expertise (construct validity) and demonstrated significant correlation with the classical assessment tool (concurrent validity) in open surgical skills. We demonstrated the potential application of this system in mapping of trainees' surgical proficiency.

Conclusion: Overall, we have established the validity of motion tracking in assessing the fluidity of the hands when completing fundamental surgical skills. Our research took a step forward beyond the validation paradigm by demonstrating its potential application in the surgical training programme.

Keywords: surgical skill, motion tracking, motion analysis, surgical skill assessment, construct validity, non-observational tool

1. Introduction

1.1. The challenges in healthcare and surgical training

The nature of surgical training is consistently evolving in the past decade along with continuous changes in the healthcare system worldwide. The modern healthcare system has been pressurized by the current law that involves a restricted number of working hours. The legal working hours per week can be as low as 48 hours in the European countries [1] and 80 hours in North America [2]. These working mandates are deemed necessary to guard against human errors that may be related to stress and fatigue in a high-pressured working environment. In addition, there is also an increasing popularity in reporting medico-legal cases in the current media. High profile medical reports such as the Kennedy Report (UK) [3] and the Institute of Medicine (US) report 'To Err is Human' [4] have highlighted surgical errors that turned the spotlight immediately on the adequacy of surgical training and, by extension, the quality of surgical trainees [5]. These current changes in healthcare system could be continued to cause negative impact upon the surgical training of many aspiring surgeons.

Historically, surgical training has been based on the apprenticeship model throughout many years. The trainee surgeons are taught on how to perform procedures by senior surgeons with on-the-job training. Therefore, the training is opportunistic and the trainees were expected to demonstrate their skills in the operating theatre under supervision of their consultants. This was coined by William Halstead who exemplified the training approach as 'see one, do one and teach one' [6]. The traditional teaching method is largely relying upon variable cases that the trainees encounter during their daily work routine. Typically, junior doctors learn from their seniors and more experienced colleagues and their consultants. The skill level of consultants is perceived as the proficiency level and therefore, the desired precision in surgical training. The trainees are expected to reach the proficiency level that would allow them to perform surgical procedures in the real operating theatre. However, it is a challenge to assess surgical skills and obtain an objective proficiency level.

This training model is less favourable in the current climate of healthcare system. Due to the restriction, the trainees have limited opportunities to gain competencies, and therefore the training period is prolonged. As a direct consequence of these challenges, interest in laboratories with formal curricula, specifically designed to teach surgical skills, has increased dramatically [7]. The attention has been shifted towards training in a simulation lab using inanimate bench models, animals (cadaveric or live), hybrid or virtual reality (VR) simulators. In United Kingdom, the use of live animals is not permitted under the current law, unlike in Europe, United States and other countries [8].

Therefore, simulation technology has gained its popularity among surgical training institution worldwide. With the advancement of laparoscopic and minimally invasive surgery (MIS) and steep learning curve in this specialty, a burst of simulators became available in the market for over a decade ago. Some examples of validated virtual reality (VR) simulators available in laparoscopy are MIST VR, LapSim, LapMentor and Xitact LS500 [9]. The trainees are able to practice their skills in hand-eye co-ordination, intracorporeal suturing and procedures such as laparoscopic cholecystectomy and appendicectomy by using these simulators. In general, the laparoscopic instruments used are fitted with sensors that allow the cameras to track their movement. The simulator then displays a two-dimensional graphic of an operative field such as the internal organs on a computer screen. From this, the simulators are able to track and quantify the movement that would be converted into meaningful metrics such as path length, smoothness and economy of movement. These metrics provide an objective automated measurement of technical skill proficiency instantaneously.

The advancement of simulation technology has allowed training bodies such as The Society of American Gastrointestinal and Endoscopic Surgeons (SAGES) to develop training models for both laparoscopic and endoscopic skills. In the recent years, surgical training institutions have been incorporating simulators in surgical skills assessment and trainees' selection process. We found that only 56% of the studies in the literature employed simulator-generated objective metrics in the laparoscopic skills assessment either exclusively or combined with other assessment tools [10], unlike other industries, such as the aviation industry, which are more advanced in the simulation technology.

The MIS and laparoscopic surgery is only a branch of surgical specialties. In general, the progression of simulator development has tended to target minimally invasive surgery (MIS) [11]. However, open surgery remains the foundation of all surgical specialties. The surgical trainees are expected to master technical skills in open surgery before they are allowed to progress to more complex surgical procedures such as MIS and microsurgery. Examples of technical skills in open surgery include hand knot tying, suturing skill, repair of nerve or tendon and open hernia repair. The surgeon's ability to tie knots securely is of paramount importance as loosening of surgical knots, during or after tying, can compromise the outcome of a surgical procedure [12].

Despite its importance, the training of open surgical techniques is largely depending on inanimate bench models. The trainees would practice surgical skills on bench models such as skin pads and saphenofemoral junction model from Limbs and Things™ (Bristol, United Kingdom) and laparotomy model from Simulab Corporation (Seattle, WA). This is in contrast with MIS or laparoscopic surgery simulators. Typically, in order to assess their competency in this skill, a trainee will perform a specific procedure such as excision of sebaceous cyst using an inanimate model and an observer who has extensive experience in the field such as a consultant or a senior registrar will watch the trainees and assess their skills using observer-dependent assessment tools. This can be done either by face-to-face or video recording [13].

The classic observational assessment tool for open surgical skills is the objective structured assessment of technical skills (OSATS) (**Figures 1** and **2**). It was coined by Professor Reznick and his research team in Canada [14]. It is based on observation and completing two sets of checklists. The first checklist consists of important steps in a specific procedure and trainees are assessed whether they have taken all these steps or not. The second checklist is the global rating scale (GRS) which examines the global performance of the trainees by using five-point Likert scale. It assesses the fluidity and efficiency of movement during completion of a surgical task.

Checklist For Skin Suturing

Name: JR/Student Years of Training:

Instructions to candidates

Suture the clean incised wound with interrupted sutures

Item		Done correctly	Not don correctl
1.	Selects appropriate suture, needle holder and forceps.	1	0
2.	Needle loaded ½ to 2/3 from tip.	1	0
3.	Bite distance from the skin edge-5mm.	1	0
4.	Angle at which bite taken - 900	1	0
5.	Single attempt while taking bites in the skin	1	0
6.	Movement occurs at wrist	1	0
7.	Forceps used to hold skin or s/c tissues (minimum use)	1	0
8.	Whether takes bites from both skin edges in one go/separately	1	0
9.	Equal bites on both sides	1	0
10.	Whether needle touched with hand	1	0
11.	Number of knots taken	1	0
12.	Knot is square or not.	1	0
13.	Knot is too tight or too loose.	1	0
14.	Suture breaks or not	1	0
15.	Knot is on the incision line or on one side	1	0
16.	Distance of cutting the suture from the knot	1	0
17.	Suture board moves or not	1	0
18.	Skin edges are everted or inverted	1	0
19.	Inter sutural distance - 0.5 to 1cm.	1	0
	Maximum Total Score	(19)	
	Total Score Examiner		

Figure 1. A sample of task-specific checklist from OSATS [15].

The observational assessment tool requires the recruitment of expert surgeons to assess trainees. This proves to be labour-intensive and time-consuming. One would argue that there could be human bias or favouritism when scoring trainees using this type of assessment. Data in several studies suggested that unblinded raters give higher scores than blinded raters (as would be expected if knowledge of a learner subconsciously influences a rater's behaviour) [16]. Therefore, surgical training is moving away from the observer-dependant assessment tools but towards more objective and quantifiable analysis of the technical skills. This would allow the assessment of the trainees' skill level and measure their reached precision according to their corresponding training years.

1.2. Open surgical skills

Open surgical skills are fundamental in surgery. The skills involve hand dexterity using surgical instruments. Thomas Morstede stated more than 500 years ago that surgeons should 'be dextrous, have steady untrembling hands, and clear sight' [17]. A good surgeon is perceived as having a greater economy and precision of hand and instrument movement [18].

Open surgical skills vary from simple technique, such as hand knot tying and suturing, to more complex procedures, such as tendon or nerve repair, laparotomy and vessel anastomosis. All of the surgical trainees are required to master the open basic surgical skills, particularly in suturing and hand knot tying skill. A good technique would ensure that the wound

GLOBAL RATING SCALE OF OPERATIVE PERFORMANCE

Please circle the number corresponding to the candidate's performance in each category, irrespective of training level

Respect for Tissue :				
1 Frequently used unnecessary force on tissue or caused damage by inappropriate use of instruments	2	3 Careful handling of tissue but occasionally caused inadvertent damage	4	5 Consistently handled tissue appropriately with minimal damage
Time and Motion :				
1 Many unnecessary moves	2	3 Efficient time/motion but some unneccessary moves	4	5 Clear economy of movement and maximum efficiency
Instrument Handling :				
1 Repeatedly makes tentative or awkward moves with instruments by inappropriate use of instruments	2	3 Competent use of instruments but occasionally appeard stiff or awkward	4	5 Fluid moves with instruments and no awkwardness
Knowledge of Instruments :				
1 Frequently asked for wrong instrument or used inappropriate instrument	2	3 Knew names of most instruments and used appropriate instrument	4	5 Obviously familiar with the instruments and their names
Flow of Operation :				
1 Frequently stopped operating and seemed unsure of next move	2	3 Demonstrated some forward planning with reasonable progression of procedure	4	5 Obviously planned course of operation with effortless flow from one move to the next
Use of Assistants :				
1 Consistently placed assistants poorly or failed to use assistants	2	3 Appropriate use of assistants most of time	4	5 Strategically used assistants to the best advantage at all time
Knowledge of Specific Procedure :				
1 Deficient knowledge. Needed specific instruction at most steps	2	3 Knew all important steps of operation	4	5 Demonstrated familiarity with all aspects of operation

Figure 2. The global rating scale (GRS) of operative performance.

edges are approximated neatly without causing any gaping if the sutures are loose or skin necrosis if the sutures are too tight. The trainees would hone their skills by practising on bench models as shown in **Figures 3** and **4**.

The movement of the hands and fingers has to be precise and economical to ensure that the procedure runs smoothly with minimum complication. However, the assessment of dexterity, smoothness and economy of hand movement using surgical instruments has been subjective and several attempts have been made to quantify dexterity, but many of these are unsatisfactory [19]. Many have associated dexterity with the time taken to complete a surgical task. It is a crude assessment and it is a poor measurement of technical skills. Although operative speed is a desirable surgical quality to lower the time spent under anaesthesia, it fails to assess the quality of surgical performance [20].

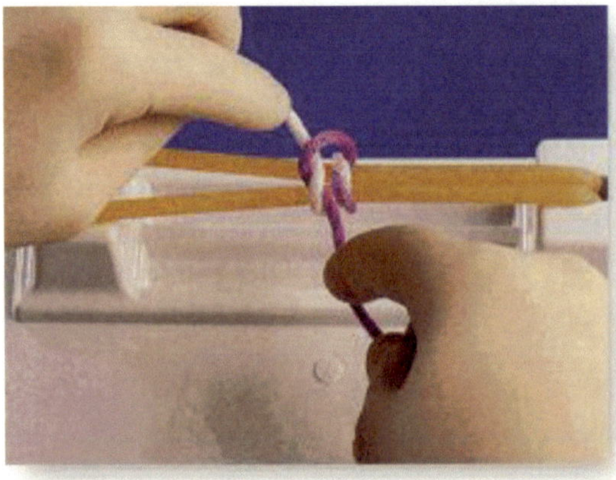

Figure 3. A standard surgical knot tying task performed using the knot tying training jig from Limbs and Things™ (Bristol, UK).

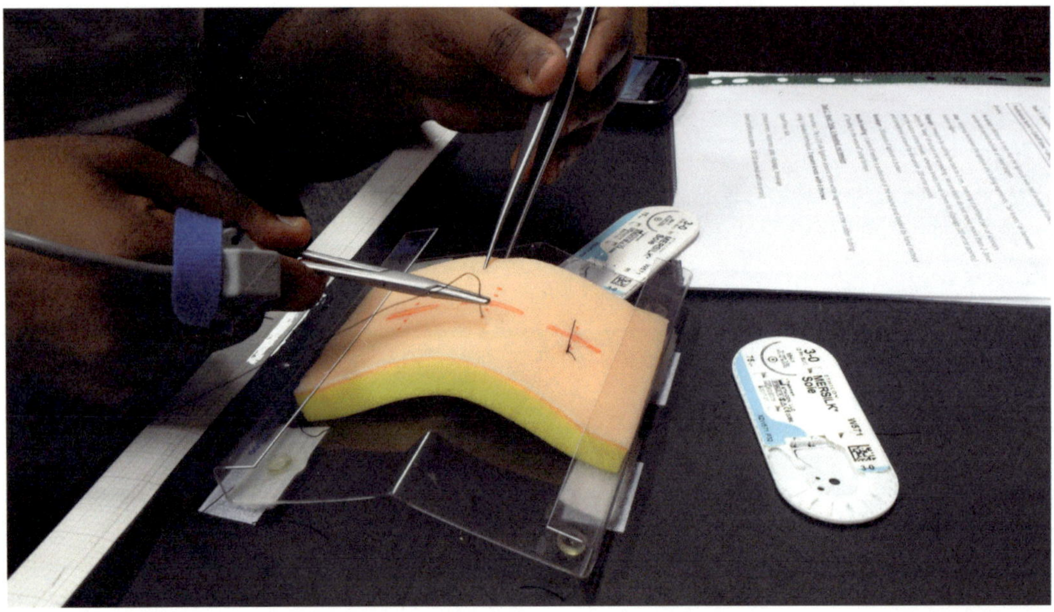

Figure 4. A trainee performing a simple interrupted suturing task using skin pads with simulated wound edges.

The objective assessment of open surgical skills is slow to evolve, unlike MIS and laparoscopic surgical training. We require an assessment tool that could quantify the hand motion and provide an objective scale on the performance when completing a surgical task. Therefore, we explored the potential use of motion analysis in assessing open surgical skills. It would be a non-observational assessment tool that is automated and objective.

2. Materials and methods

2.1. Participants demographics

All medical students in pre-clinical years (Years 1–3) from the Royal College of Surgeons in Ireland (RCSI), basic surgical trainees (Years 1 and 2) and consultant surgeons were invited to participate in our study. This allowed us to divide the participants into three different subject groups: novice, trainees and experts. It was made clear that the participation is voluntary. Ethical approval was granted by Research Ethics Committee of RCSI.

Figure 5 showed the demographics of participants in this study.

	Expert	Trainee	Novice
Hand Knot Tying Skill	n=5	n=28	n=25
Gender			
Male	5	16	17
Female	0	12	8
Dominant Hand			
Right	5	25	22
Left	0	3	3
Suturing Skill	n=10	n=35	n=27
Gender			
Male	9	21	18
Female	1	14	9
Dominant Hand			
Right	5	34	24
Left	0	1	3

Figure 5. Participants demographics.

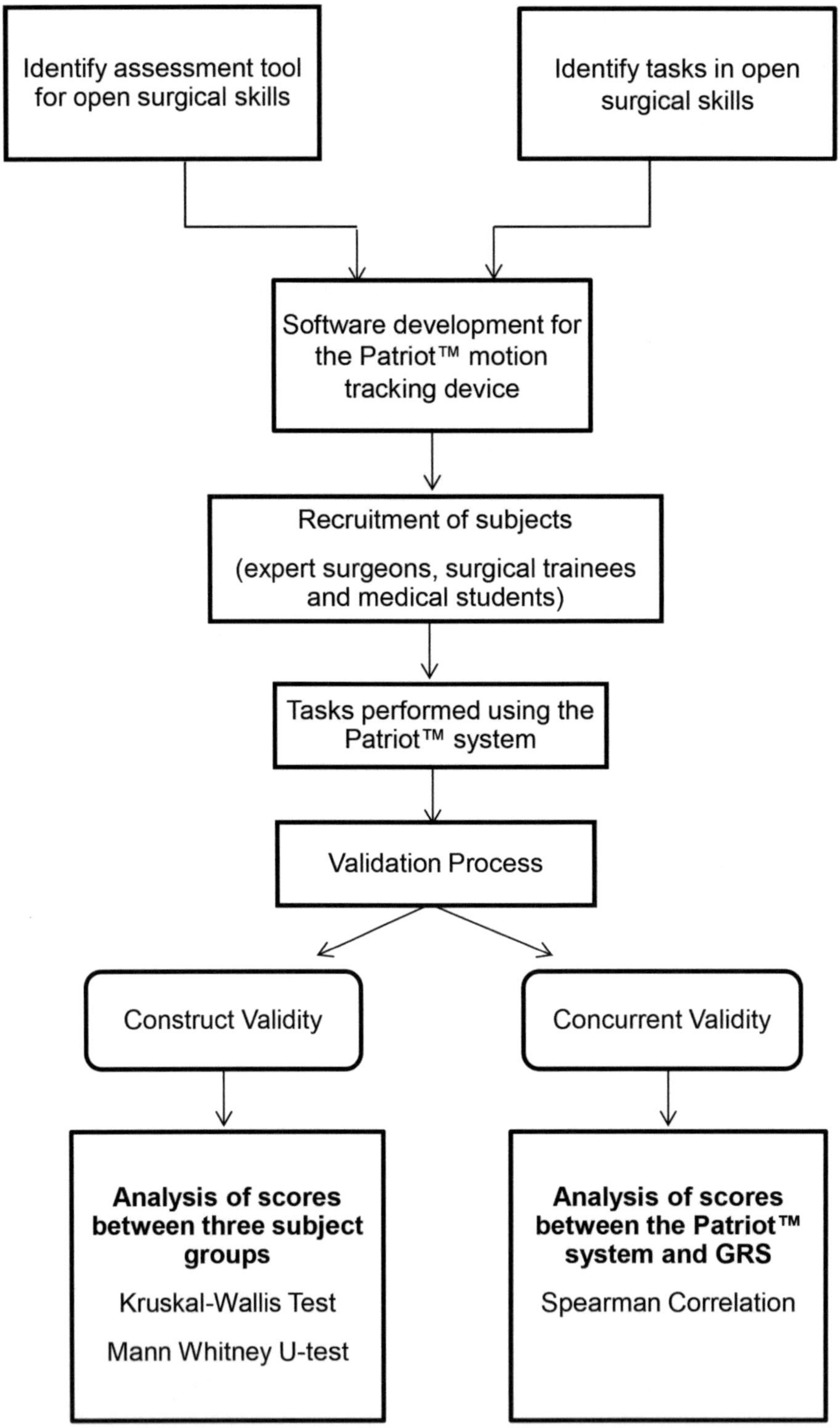

Figure 6. Flow diagram of the experiment process.

2.2. Basic surgical skills assessment

Inanimate bench models are used in this study. The bench models were from Limbs and Things™ (Bristol, UK) which include the knot tying trainer jig, skin pads, skin pad jig and cyst pads. All participants were required to perform two fundamental tasks. Below are the tasks involved and their description.

Task 1: One-handed knot tying skill

The participants were required to perform surgical knots using the one-handed technique. They were given a standardised length of 2/0 Mersilk (Ethicon) suture tie. The surgical knots were performed on the knot tying trainer jig.

Task 2: Suturing simple interrupted technique

The participants were required to perform simple interrupted sutures on a simulated wound. This task was performed on skin pads (Limbs and Things, Bristol, UK). A 3/0 Mersilk suture (Ethicon) and surgical instruments were provided.

The participants' performances were assessed using observational tool (GRS) and non-observational tool (motion tracking device). The data allowed us to analyse the validity of motion tracking device as an assessment tool in comparison with the well-established GRS scoring system. During the experiment, videos were recorded in anonymous fashion. Each video was labelled by a random code generator so that the assessor could not identify the level of experience of each participant. The participants also had a sensor attached to their right index finger to track hand motion and this will be discussed in detail in the next section.

As for observational assessment, two assessors were selected to assess each video using the GRS. The assessors were expert surgeons with greater than 10 years of consultant experience and are involved in teaching and educating surgical trainees in Ireland. The experiment process is outlined in **Figure 6**.

3. Motion analysis in surgical skill assessment

3.1. The role of motion analysis

Surgical specialties have initiated a trend towards a more objective and quantifiable measure of technical skill proficiency [21]. In minimally invasive surgery (laparoscopy and endoscopy), simulators have been developed with the ability to quantify the associated skills with specific metrics including total path length, movement efficiency and smoothness. Motion smoothness in handling surgical tools is an essential skill that surgical residents must acquire before independently operating on patients [22].

The use of motion analysis has been pioneered in gait analysis [23]. It is used in tracking the movement of body parts. These methods usually make use of markers located on body articulations to garner movement information from a particular limb [18]. Its application is evident in various areas including sports such as golf, training an apprentice in spray painting and also in diagnostic simulators such as ultrasound simulation [24]. Undoubtedly, one of the most promising technological tools in medical training are the simulators for the acquisition of clinical skills using motion sensors [25]. The surgical arena has used this technology to try and quantify surgical performance. Motion analysis allows assessment of surgical dexterity using parameters that are extracted from movement of the hands or laparoscopic instruments [26]. The motion analysis provides parameters that measure the precision of hand motion when performing surgical skills. Hence, surgical competencies, particularly in surgical trainees, can be ascertained by using these parameters.

Lord Ara Darzi and his researchers [27] pioneered the use of an electromagnetic motion tracking device in surgery, called the Imperial College Surgical Assessment Device (ICSAD). This is the combination of a commercially available electromagnetic tracking system (Isotrak, Polhemus Inc, Colchester, VT) and a bespoke computer software program [28]. This motion analysis device uses an alternating current electromagnetic system with passive receiver attached to the dorsum of the hand over the mid-shaft of the third metacarpal [29]. It measures the time taken, the number of movements and the path length. All of these metrics have been shown to change with experience in laparoscopic surgery [30] and in open surgery (bowel anastomosis and vein patch insertion) [18].

We used a commercially available motion tracking device called The Patriot™ from Polhemus Inc., Colchester, VT. This device utilises electromagnetic technology and tracks 6 degrees of freedom (6DOF) measurements of the sensor's movement. In our study, we attached the sensor on to the participants' right index finger. **Figure 7** showed the airplane image that indicates the sensor. It will move to the position and orientation of the right index finger. The retrieved position and orientation are displayed as numbers in six columns (upper part of screenshot), from left to right, positions in X-, Y- and Z-axis and orientation in yaw, pitch and roll. The Patriot™ collects these raw data which in turn convert to a set of meaningful metrics using our bespoke software.

3.2. Construct validity of motion analysis in surgical skills assessment

Every evaluative tool needs to provide invaluable information on what it measures or examines and that the conclusions drawn from the tool are dependable. A validated assessment device should be able to differentiate level of surgical skills according to the level of competency and this is classified as construct validity. One inference of construct validity is the extent to which a test discriminates between various levels of expertise [31]. Mason et al. [32] have reviewed the published evidence as it relates to motion analysis and the assessment of surgical performance. This systematic review reported construct validity of ICSAD and other forms of motion analysis devices such as ProMIS augmented reality simulator and Hiroshima University Endoscopic Surgical Assessment Device (HUESAD) in assessing laparoscopic skills.

Our research further assessed the use of a novel electromagnetic tracking system in basic surgical skill tasks by using our own in-house computer software with a finger sensor. **Figures 8** and **9** showed the standard set up for knot tying task and suturing task, respectively, with the Patriot™ motion tracking device. Our in-house software was designed to generate the classic metrics that are time and total path length (TPL). In addition, new metrics were developed:

http://dx.doi.org/10.5772/intechopen.68850

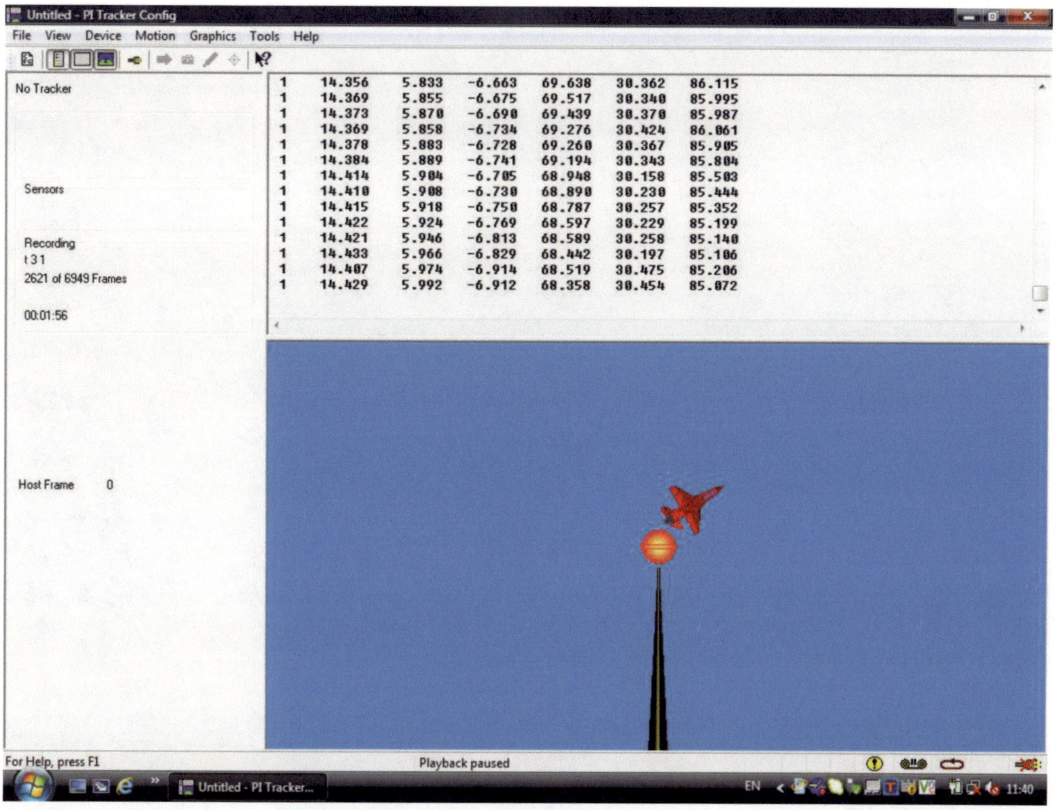

Figure 7. A screenshot of the PiMgr software.

average deviation distance from X-, Y- and Z-axis and average distance from centre of the bench model. The centre of the bench model is labelled as a point of interest (POI), as we believe that hand motion is most efficient when the hands are at certain distance away from the centre of the workstation. Subjectively, when performing a certain task in open surgery, such as tying surgical knots or suturing, a novice would have unnecessary movement of their hands which include moving hands further away from the field of surgery. This is thought to be inefficient in view of the economy of the hand movement.

Our results demonstrated construct validity for both fundamental skills which were one-handed knot tying task (**Figure 10**) and the simple interrupted suturing skill (**Figure 11**) for the metrics of time, total path length, point of interest and deviation from the Z-axis.

The box and whiskers plot shows a significant difference between experts, trainees and novices ($p < 0.001$). This was analysed using Kruskal Wallis statistical test. The horizontal lines within boxes are the median. The boxes and whiskers represent interquartile range and range, respectively. The dot represents outlier.

The novel parameters were able to differentiate subjects according to level of experience along with the validated metrics as reported in literature [18, 33]. This implies that a surgical novice

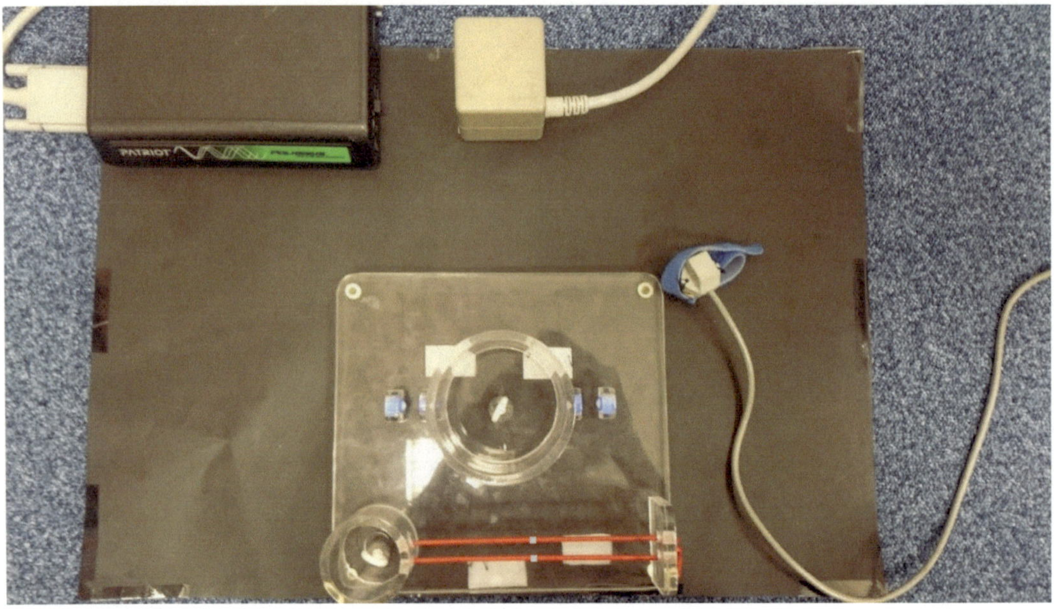

Figure 8. Knot tying model with the Patriot™ motion tracking device.

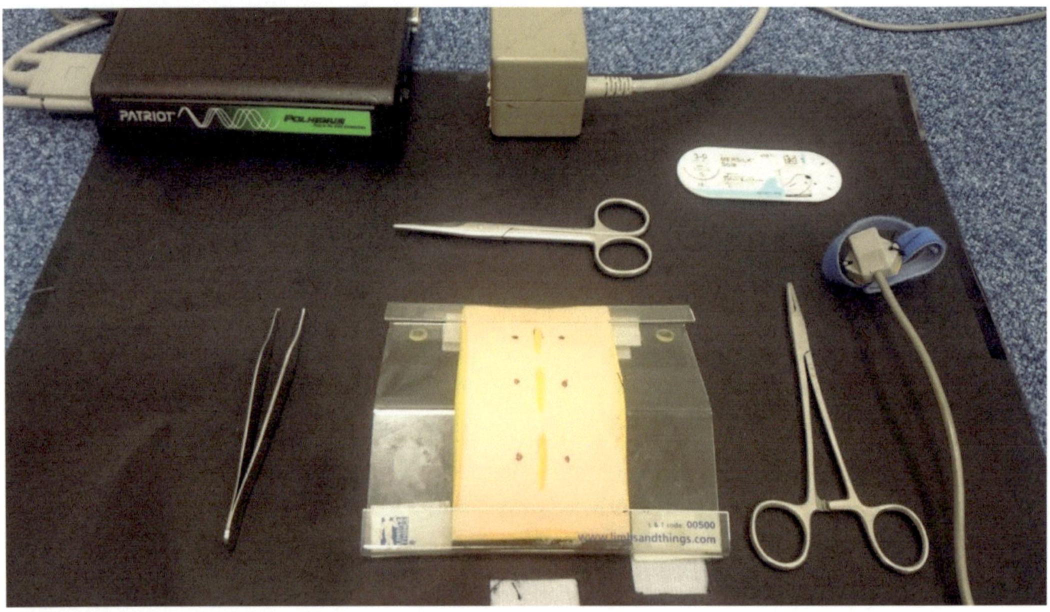

Figure 9. Simple interrupted suturing model and instruments with the Patriot™ motion tracking device.

moved his or her hand further away from the virtual Z-axis and mid-point of the workstation than experts or surgical trainees, as seen subjectively in the video recordings. Therefore, it is postulated that this pattern of movement is less efficient. The lack of significant change in X- and Y-axis may reflect the standard suture tie length used in this experiment. This limits the movement of the hand in these axes.

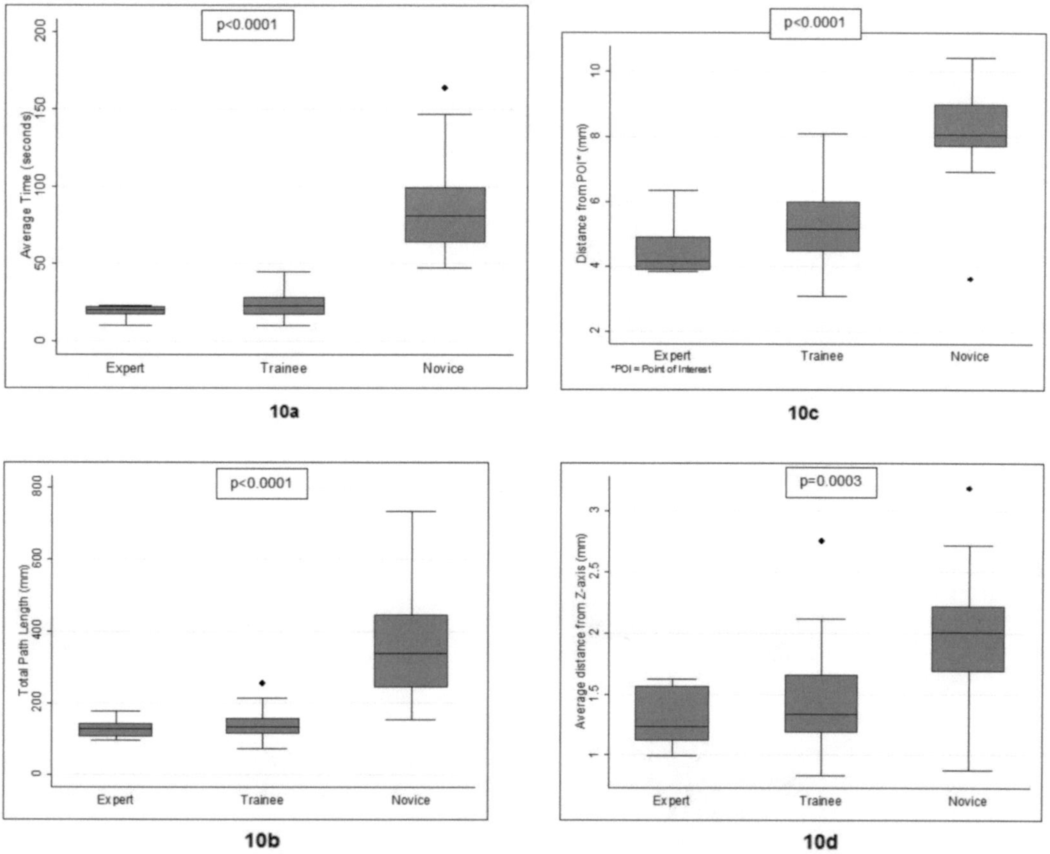

Figure 10. Distribution of the time taken (a) and total path length (b), average distance from the POI (c) and Z-axis (d) between the three subject groups in completing one-handed knot tying skill.

3.3. Concurrent validity of motion analysis in surgical skills assessment

A further validation of the motion analysis device was required to prove that it is a robust assessment tool. It is important that the metrics from motion analysis have a good correlation with the gold standard assessment tool, which is the global rating scale (GRS), as mentioned previously. This would prove the concurrent validity of this novel device.

Datta et al. [34] revealed that there was a strong correlation between number of hand movements analysed using the ICSAD and the GRS in suturing vein patch on an inanimate model (Spearman coefficient of −0.587, $p < 0.01$). In another study by Ezra et al. [33], concurrent validity was demonstrated between these two assessment tools in microsurgery suturing task. The metrics used in this study were path length, hand movements and time.

In our chapter, for the one-handed knot tying skill, our results demonstrated a significant correlation between all the metrics generated by the Patriot™ motion tracking device and the items of the GRS scoring tool. The only parameter that failed to demonstrate a significant relationship was deviation from the x-axis and 'respect for tissue'. For the simple interrupted

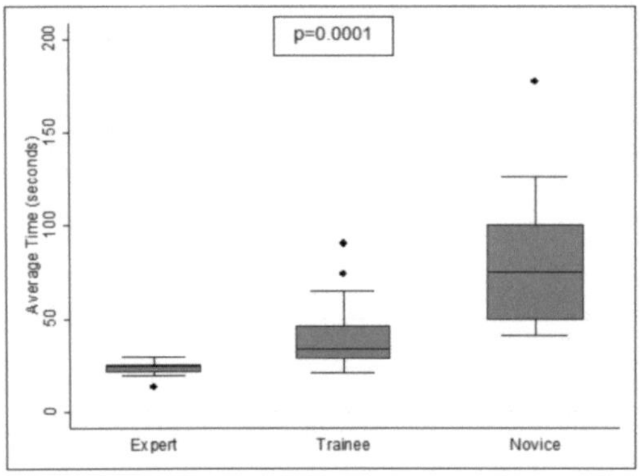

Figure 11a

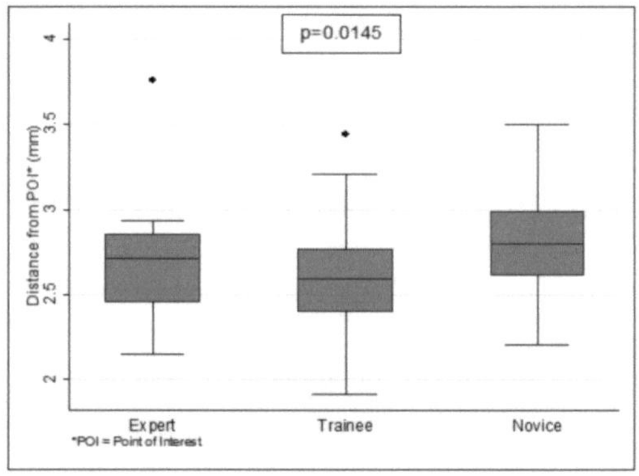

Figure 11c

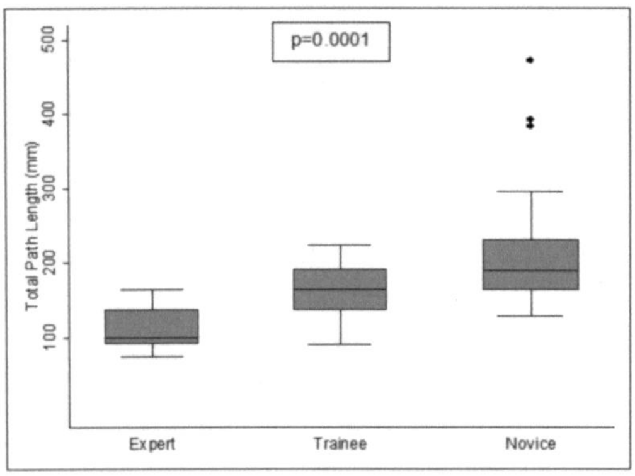

Figure 11b

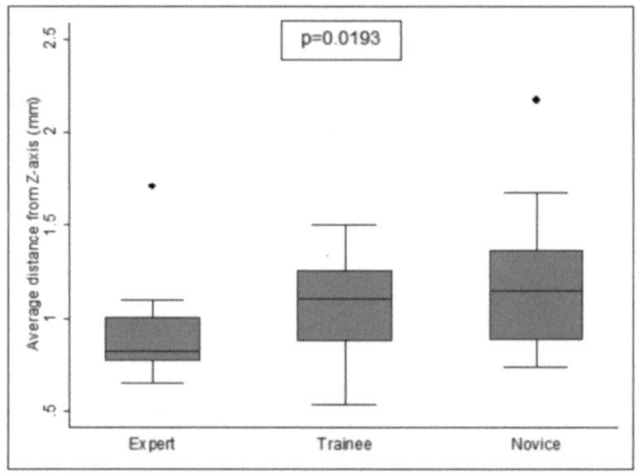

Figure 11d

Figure 11. Distribution of the time taken (a), total path length (b), average distance from the POI (c) and Z-axis (d) between the three subject groups in completing simple suturing task.

suturing skill, we found a significant correlation between time, total path length and deviation from the z-axis and the total GRS score.

However, the metrics from Patriot™ motion tracking system failed to show a more convincing correlation with the scale assessing tissue handling. This may be explained by the fact that the 'respect for tissue' component on the GRS is a very subjective parameter. This is reflected in the poor inter-rater reliability of the GRS scoring system. Apart from this, the metrics correlated well with the GRS items especially items involving motion and flow of operation. We could safely suggest that the Patriot provides more objective score than the observer-dependant scale.

4. Application of motion analysis in surgical training

The use of motion tracking and analysis in assessing surgical skills has been described mainly in laparoscopic skills [11, 35]. There is a lack of literature that describes the integration of such technology in surgical training curricula across the globe, despite a myriad of validation studies.

The surgical trainees learn fundamental basic skills at an early stage. Open basic skills remains to be the principal skills across all surgical specialties. Therefore, any aspiring surgeons are expected to be proficient in these skills before they can proceed to perform simple procedures such as excision of skin or subcutaneous lesion or more complex procedures such as repair of tendon or nerve. The trainees would require direct guidance and abundance of practice in order to be proficient in these skills, as the saying goes 'practice makes perfect'. By having an expert or supervisor to observe them consistently during practice session is not feasible when clinical work takes priority. Therefore, motion analysis system would be necessary to provide an automated system that allows the trainees to practice and record their performance in their own time.

Proficiency-based training has been described as learning environments in which the trainee progresses from less to more technically demanding skills and tasks only after achieving predefined criteria [36, 37]. One widely available simulation-based assessment and certification program is the fundamentals of laparoscopic surgery (FLS) developed by the Society of American Gastrointestinal and Endoscopic Surgeons (SAGES) and now administered by SAGES and the American College of Surgeons [38]. The FLS program incorporates tasks from the McGill Inanimate System for Training and Evaluation of Laparoscopic Skills (MISTELS) program, including laparoscopic suturing, and uses well-described, low-fidelity inanimate models [39]. The proficiency scores were determined by a group of experts in the skills and the trainees or users are required to reach these predetermined scores before they could proceed to the next level or task. These proficiency scores act as an aim for the trainees to achieve and subsequently motivate them to keep practising until a high standard of surgical skills is accomplished. In order to do this, an automated objective measurement is much desirable, as it does not require any expert surgeons or observers to monitor and assess the performance.

We applied the concept of proficiency-based training by using the validated metrics from the Patriot™ motion tracking system. We determined the proficiency goals or desired precision for each of these metrics in knot tying and suturing skills. This was achieved by gathering the experts' scores from the motion analysis and calculating the proficiency target as follows:

$$\text{Proficiency level} = \text{Mean score of the expert surgeons} + 1 \text{ standard deviation.} \quad (4.1)$$

The performance of surgical trainees in Years 1 and 2 of the surgical training programme was assessed using the Patriot™ device. Their scores were then analysed against these predetermined proficiency goals. Our intention was to have an objective automated tool that can be integrated into the national training curricula as part of the training module. This will help the trainees to practise and eventually achieve the desired precision or performance in the most fundamental skills in surgery.

Figure 12 showed a sample of trainees' performance in suturing which was mapped out against the proficiency target. The dashed line represents the proficiency level of 143.6 mm. The diamond shape points below the dashed line are the trainees who have shorter path length and considered as proficient in their skill (n = 13, 52%). The round shape points above the dashed line are the trainees with longer path length and did not reach proficiency level (n = 22.48%).The performance graph is very useful when there is a group of surgical trainees

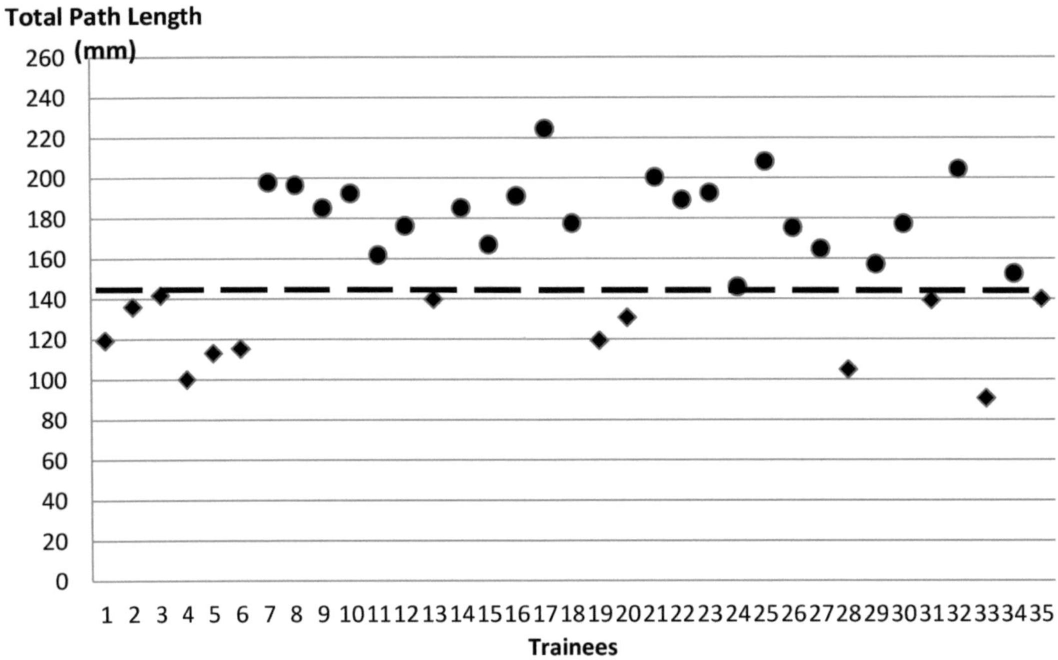

Figure 12. The total path length (TPL) of all the trainees in the study who performed simple interrupted suturing skill.

assessing their suturing technique and they are able to compare their reached precision with the desired precision.

The main advantage of motion analysis system in surgical training is that it is capable of producing automated objective scoring system and does not require a group of observers to assess the performance in any particular surgical skills. In our study, the Patriot™ motion analysis system has shown a promising potential in a learner-oriented proficiency curriculum [40]. By providing an objective and numerical rating, trainees could benchmark and aim to improve their score through enhancement of surgical skill [41]. As surgical educators, this assessment tool is useful in identifying any surgical trainees who are underperform according to the proficiency standard at an early stage of their training years. A remedial session can be offered to these surgical trainees and their training module can be customized for them in order to be able to reach proficiency as required. The motion analysis system can be used continuously by the trainees during practice session and also in any departmental assessment settings.

The learning curve in surgical skills is steep. The trainees are required to improve their skills or reached precision over time and progress in their surgical training. They are expected to practice the skills, preferably in the simulation lab until they achieve the desired precision. The training programmes are designed to teach the trainees skills that are appropriate to their levels. The early part of the learning curve is associated with a higher complication rate [42]. The improvement in their reached precision in the simulation lab will allow them to perform procedures on patients in real operating room with confidence. They will also progress to a more complex procedure such as tendon repair, vessel anastomosis and bowel resection.

Motion analysis provides an objective measurement of the skills that can be used to map out the learning curve. In order to reach proficiency in the learning curve, using time only as a metric is not reliable. It measures how fast someone completes a task. This does not include how efficient it was performed. Therefore, it is regarded as an adjuvant tool to assess surgical technical skills due to its unique properties including non-observer dependent, automated and feasibility.

4.1. Limitation of motion analysis and future research

The main limitation of motion analysis is that its inability to detect surgical errors. Hand-tracking data appear to confirm that skilled individuals demonstrate a shorter path length, make fewer movements and take less time to perform an operation, but with the caveat that this improved performance is not accompanied by an increase in error [43]. In minimally invasive surgical training such as laparoscopic skills, the technology in VR simulators such as LapSim and LapMentor is more advanced than open surgical skills training. These simulators are programmed to identify any surgical errors as well as analysing the movement of the instruments.

Therefore, this vital limitation of motion analysis may be overcome by incorporating an assessment of the end-product following a completion of surgical task. For instance, the quality of the surgical knots can be assessed by a force gauge device in order to ensure that the knots do not slip under certain tension. It is important that the surgical knots are secure as knot slippage in a real operating setting can cause catastrophic bleeding which leads to morbidity towards patients.

This shortcoming highlights that the surgical competency is multimodal and there is no single solution for surgical assessment. We propose that surgical educators should incorporate motion analysis and assessment of the end-product quality when assessing surgical techniques. Further research should be focused on creating an all-in-one package in assessing surgical competency that would be objective, automated and most importantly independent from any observers.

Another limitation of motion analysis is that its use in the real operating setting. All the studies in the literature showed the use of motion analysis system in a simulation lab [10]. The fundamental assumption of simulation-based training is that the skills acquired in simulated settings are directly transferable to the operative setting [44]. The current motion tracking devices that are readily available use electromagnetic field to track sensors on the hands. These devices are sensitive to surrounding metal objects such as electronic machines, metal bars or large electrical cables in the walls that can cause erratic reading. These metal objects are certainly present in all real operating theatres in the hospitals. In addition, the sensors on the devices are attached via cables, which potentially could interfere with the sterility of the operating field. Due to these limitations, it is not feasible to utilize these devices in assessing surgical skills in a real operating theatre. Therefore, a new invention of a system that is wireless and not susceptible to the surrounding metal objects is much desired.

5. Summary

Open surgical skill training requires an assessment tool that is independent, automated and objective. The validity of motion analysis in assessing fundamental surgical skills has been proven and showed positive results. It has demonstrated its potential use in a proficiency-based training as a step away from the traditional method of surgical training. The future of simulation-based surgical training in open surgical skills appears promising and it will finally shape the pathway towards creating top quality surgeons in the current climate of healthcare system.

Author details

Shazrinizam Shaharan[1]*, Donncha M Ryan[1] and Paul C Neary[2]

*Address all correspondence to: shaharas@gmail.com

1 Royal College of Surgeons in Ireland, Dublin, Republic of Ireland

2 Trinity College, Dublin, Republic of Ireland

References

[1] European Union, Employment Rights and Work Organisation. 2013. Available from: http://europa.eu/legislation_summaries/employment_and_social_policy/health_hygiene_safety_at_work/c10418_en.htm 2013 and http://eur-lex.europa.eu/homepage.html [Accessed: 25 November 2013]

[2] Accreditation Council for Graduate Medical Education. Common Program Requirements. 2011. Available from: http://www.acgme.org/acWebsite/dutyHours/dh_dutyHours CommonPR.pdf [Accessed: 25 November 2013]

[3] Kennedy I. Learning from Bristol: The Report of the Public Enquiry into Childrens Heart Surgery at the Bristol Royal Infirmary 1984-1995. 2001. Available from: http://www.bristol-inquiry.org.uk/2001

[4] Kohn L, Corrigan J, Donaldson M. To Err is Human: Building a Safer Health System. Washington DC: Institute of Medicine; 1999

[5] Carroll SM, Kennedy AM, Traynor O, Gallagher AG. Objective assessment of surgical performance and its impact on a national selection programme of candidates for higher surgical training in plastic surgery. Journal of Plastic, Reconstructive & Aesthetic Surgery. 2009;**62**(12):1543-1549

[6] Cameron JL. William Stewart Halsted. Our surgical heritage. Annals of Surgery. 1997;**225**(5):445-458. PubMed PMID: 9193173. Pubmed Central PMCID: PMC1190776. Epub 1997/05/01. eng

[7] Reznick R, MacRae H. Teaching surgical skills – changes in the wind. New England Journal of Medicine. 2006;**355**:2664-2669

[8] Sarker SK, Patel B. Simulation and surgical training. International Journal of Clinical Practice. 2007;**61**(12):2120-2125

[9] Schijven M, Jakimowicz J. Simulators, first experiences. Minimally Invasive Therapy & Allied Technologies. 2003;**12**(3):151-154

[10] Shaharan S, Neary P. Evaluation of surgical training in the era of simulation. World journal of Gastrointestinal Endoscopy. 2014;**6**(9):436-447. PubMed PMID: 25228946. Pubmed Central PMCID: 4163726

[11] Neary PC, Boyle E, Delaney CP, Senagore AJ, Keane FB, Gallagher AG. Construct validation of a novel hybrid virtual-reality simulator for training and assessing laparoscopic colectomy; results from the first course for experienced senior laparoscopic surgeons. Surgical Endoscopy. 2008;**22**(10):2301-2309. PubMed PMID: 18553207. Epub 2008/06/17. eng

[12] Alzacko SM, Majid OW. "Security loop" tie: A new technique to overcome loosening of surgical knots. Oral Surgery, Oral Medicine, Oral Pathology, Oral Radiology, and Endodontics. 2007;**104**(5):e1–e4. PubMed PMID: 17964468. Epub 2007/10/30. eng

[13] Jensen AR, Wright AS, McIntyre LK, Levy AE, Foy HM, Anastakis DJ, et al. Laboratory-based instruction for skin closure and bowel anastomosis for surgical residents. Archives of Surgery. 2008;**143**(9):852-858

[14] Martin JA, Regehr G, Reznick R, MacRae H, Murnaghan J, Hutchison C, et al. Objective structured assessment of technical skill (OSATS) for surgical residents. The British Journal of Surgery. 1997;**84**(2):273-278

[15] Shindholimath VV GA, Srivastava A, Aggarwal S, Seenu V, Chumber S, Bal S, Guleria S, Parshad R, Dhar A. Teaching and assessment of surgical skills through simulation in surgical training. Indian Journal of Surgery. 2003;**65**:483-487

[16] Hatala R, Cook DA, Brydges R, Hawkins R. Constructing a validity argument for the Objective Structured Assessment of Technical Skills (OSATS): A systematic review of validity evidence. Advances in Health Sciences Education: Theory and Practice. 2015;**20**(5) 1149-1175. PubMed PMID: 25702196. Epub 2015/02/24. eng

[17] Kirkpatrick JJ, Naylor IL. The qualities and conduct of an English surgeon in 1446: As described in a manuscript attributed to Thomas Morstede. Annals of the Royal College of Surgeons of England. 1997;**79**(3):225-228. PubMed PMID: 9196347. Pubmed Central PMCID: PMC2502902. Epub 1997/05/01. eng

[18] Datta V, Mackay S, Mandalia M, Darzi A. The use of electromagnetic motion tracking analysis to objectively measure open surgical skill in the laboratory-based model. Journal of The American College of Surgeons. 2001;**193**(5):479-485. PubMed PMID: 11708503. Epub 2001/11/16. eng

[19] Kirby TJ. Dexterity testing and residents' surgical performance. Transactions of the American Ophthalmological Society. 1979;**77**:294-307. PubMed PMID: 545827. Pubmed Central PMCID: PMC1311706. Epub 1979/01/01. eng

[20] Shah J, Buckley D, Frisby J, Darzi A. Reaction time does not predict surgical skill. The British Journal of Surgery. 2003;**90**(10):1285-1286. PubMed PMID: 14515301. Epub 2003/09/30. eng

[21] Hayter MA, Friedman Z, Bould MD, Hanlon JG, Katznelson R, Borges B, et al. Validation of the imperial college surgical assessment device (ICSAD) for labour epidural placement. Canadian Journal of Anesthesia. 2009;**56**(6):419-426

[22] Ghasemloonia A, Maddahi Y, Zareinia K, Lama S, Dort JC, Sutherland GR. Surgical skill assessment using motion quality and smoothness. Journal of Surgical Education. 2017 Mar-Apr;**74**(2):295-305. PubMed PMID: 27789192. Epub 2016/10/30. eng.

[23] Biryukova EV, Roby-Brami A, Frolov AA, Mokhtari M. Kinematics of human arm reconstructed from spatial tracking system recordings. Journal of Biomechanics. 2000;**33**(8):985-995. PubMed PMID: 10828329. Epub 2000/06/01. eng

[24] MOTION(TM) PII. 2008. http://polhemus.com/motion-tracking/case-studies#patriot [Accessed: 2 May 2015]

[25] Juanes JA, Gomez JJ, Peguero PD, Ruisoto P. Digital environment for movement control in surgical skill training. Journal of Medical Systems. 2016;**40**(6):133. PubMed PMID: 27091754. Epub 2016/04/20. eng

[26] van Hove PD, Tuijthof GJ, Verdaasdonk EG, Stassen LP, Dankelman J. Objective assessment of technical surgical skills. The British Journal of Surgery. 2010;**97**(7):972-987. PubMed PMID: 20632260. Epub 2010/07/16. eng

[27] Taffinder N, Smith S, Mair J, Russell R, Darzi A. Can a computer measure surgical precision? Reliability, validity and feasibility of the ICSAD. Surgical Endoscopy. 1999;**13**(suppl 1):81

[28] Darzi A, Datta V, Mackay S. The challenge of objective assessment of surgical skills. American Journal of Surgery. 2001;**181**:484-486

[29] Bann SD, Khan MS, Darzi AW. Measurement of surgical dexterity using motion analysis of simple bench tasks. World Journal of Surgery. 2003;**27**(4):390-394. PubMed PMID: WOS:000182421900003. English

[30] Torkington J, Smith SG, Rees BI, Darzi A. Skill transfer from virtual reality to a real laparoscopic task. Surgical Endoscopy. 2001;**15**(10):1076-1079

[31] Moorthy K, Munz Y, Sarker SK, Darzi A. Objective assessment of technical skills in surgery. The British Medical Journal. 2003 Nov 1;**327**(7422):1032-7

[32] Mason JD, Ansell J, Warren N, Torkington J. Is motion analysis a valid tool for assessing laparoscopic skill? Surgical Endoscopy and Other Interventional Techniques. 2013;**27**(5):1468-1477

[33] Ezra DG, Aggarwal R, Michaelides M, Okhravi N, Verma S, Benjamin L, et al. Skills acquisition and assessment after a microsurgical skills course for ophthalmology residents. Ophthalmology. 2009;**116**(2):257-262

[34] Datta V, Chang A, Mackay S, Darzi A. The relationship between motion analysis and surgical technical assessments. American Journal of Surgery. 2002;**184**(1):70-73

[35] Smith SG, Torkington J, Brown TJ, Taffinder NJ, Darzi A. Motion analysis. Surgical Endoscopy. 2002;**16**(4):640-645

[36] Stefanidis D, Korndorffer Jr JR, Markley S, Sierra R, Scott DJ. Proficiency maintenance: Impact of ongoing simulator training on laparoscopic skill retention. Journal of The American College of Surgeons. 2006;**202**(4):599-603. PubMed PMID: 16571429. Epub 2006/03/31. eng

[37] Aggarwal R, Grantcharov TP, Eriksen JR, Blirup D, Kristiansen VB, Funch-Jensen P, et al. An evidence-based virtual reality training program for novice laparoscopic surgeons. Annals of Surgery. 2006;**244**(2):310-314. PubMed PMID: 16858196. Pubmed Central PMCID: PMC1602164. Epub 2006/07/22. eng

[38] Vassiliou MC, Feldman LS. Objective assessment, selection, and certification in surgery. Surgical Oncology. 2011;**20**(3):140-145

[39] Scott DJ, Goova MT, Tesfay ST. A cost-effective proficiency-based knot-tying and suturing curriculum for residency programs. Journal of Surgical Research. 2007;**141**(1):7-15. PubMed PMID: WOS:000247488500002. English

[40] Shaharan S, Nugent E, Ryan DM, Traynor O, Neary P, Buckley D. Basic surgical skill retention: Can patriot motion tracking system provide an objective measurement for it? Journal of Surgical Education. 2016 Mar-Apr;**73**(2):245-9. PubMed PMID: 26572096. Epub 2015/11/18. eng

[41] Saleh GM, Lindfield D, Sim D, Tsesmetzoglou E, Gauba V, Gartry DS, et al. Kinematic analysis of surgical dexterity in intraocular surgery. Archives of Ophthalmology. 2009;**127**(6):758-762. PubMed PMID: WOS:000266772300006

[42] Buckley CE NE, Ryan D, Neary P. Chapter 7: Virtual Reality – A New Era in Surgical Training. Virtual Reality in Psychological, Medical and Pedagogical Applications. Intech; 2012. Available from: URL: http://www.intechopen.com/books/virtual-reality-in-psychological-medicaland-pedagogical-applications/virtual-reality-a-new-era-insurgical-training.

[43] Gallagher AG, Satava RM, Shorten GD. Measuring surgical skill: A rapidly evolving scientific methodology. Surgical Endoscopy and Other Interventional Techniques. 2013;**27**(5):1451-1415

[44] Sturm LP, Windsor JA, Cosman PH, Cregan P, Hewett PJ, Maddern GJ. A systematic review of skills transfer after surgical simulation training. Annals of Surgery. 2008;**248**(2):166-179

Chapter 2

Layered Path Planning with Human Motion Detection for Autonomous Robots

Huan Tan, Yang Zhao and Lynn DeRose

Additional information is available at the end of the chapter

http://dx.doi.org/10.5772/intechopen.68145

Abstract

Reactively planning a path in a dynamic and unstructured environment is a key challenge for mobile robots and autonomous systems. Planning should consider factors including the long-term and short-term prediction, current environmental situation, and human context. In this chapter, we present a novel robotic path-planning method with human activity information in a large-scale three-dimensional (3D) environment. In the learning stage, this method uses human motion detection results and preliminary environmental information to build a long-term context model with a hidden Markov model (HMM) to describe and predict human activities in the environment. In the application stage, when a robot detects humans in the environment, it first uses the long-term context model to generate impedance areas in the environment. Then, the robot searches each area of the environment to find paths between key locations, such as escalators, to generate a Reactive Key Cost Map (RKCM), whose vertexes are those key locations and edges are generated paths. The graphs of all areas are connected using the key nodes in the subgraphs to build a global graph of the whole environment. Finally, the robot can reactively plan a path based on the current environmental situation and predicted human activities. This method enables robots to navigate robustly in a large-scale 3D environment with regular human activities, and it significantly reduces computing workload with proposed RKCM.

Keywords: motion detection and tracking, path planning, mobile robot navigation

1. Introduction

Autonomous and intelligent navigation in a dynamic and unstructured environment is a critical capability for mobile robots and autonomous systems. It integrates lots of technologies from sensing, environmental modeling, object tracking, planning, decision making, control, and so on, to deal with the challenges from a dynamic and uncertain environment, so that robots are capable of planning paths to avoid moving obstacles and human beings in a real-world environment.

Lots of researchers have proposed various methods of addressing path-planning problems, which have been applied successfully in various domains. However, most of those methods targeted at finding a path-planning solution in a two-dimensional (2D) environment, or an oversimplified three-dimensional (3D) environment. As more and more mobile robots and autonomous systems are placed in buildings to provide services for human beings, an emerging and interesting problem is how to plan paths for robots to navigate effectively across floors in a multistorey building.

Consider a multistorey building with multiple elevators or escalators on the same floor. If we ask a robot to deliver a box from the first floor to the fifth floor in the building, there will be multiple paths for the robot to navigate via the elevators or the escalators. For example, the robot can take the elevator to go to the fifth floor directly and then go to the destination. Or if the fifth floor is very crowded with people, it can use the elevator on the first floor to go to the second floor, and then go to another elevator at a different location on the second floor to reach the destination on the fifth floor. Then, it becomes a practical and important problem to choose which elevators the robot should take, based on the dynamic environment and human context information.

Additionally, the final state on one floor is the initial state of the next floor, toward which the robot is navigating. While the cost function on each floor can be minimized locally based on some criteria, how to minimize the global cost is also an interesting question that we need to answer. Since there will be people walking in a building, the environment is changing constantly, and thus the cost of moving from one location to another location varies based on timing, business schedule, and other factors. The scenario described above can be extended to other industrial domains, such as transporting in rail yard (multiple 2D environment), health-care service robotics (hybrid 2D environment), and aerial service robotics (full 3D path planning).

The motivation of this chapter is to propose a solution to address the two major problems mentioned above. First, we present a method of building a global graph to describe the environment, which takes human motion in the environment into consideration. Human motion can be detected and its 2D spatial distribution can be estimated by the state-of-the-art radio tomographic imaging (RTI) technology. Then, we use a hidden Markov model (HMM) to represent a long-term context model. In the application stage, when humans are detected, we use the long-term context model to predict the short-term activities of humans in the environment. Then, we build Reactive Key Cost Maps (RKCMs) for all the floors using the predicted human activities.

Second, we present a hierarchy planning framework for robots to find a path to minimize the global cost. This method considers the whole map as a graph, and the adjacent subgraphs for corresponding floors are connected using elevator or stairs, which are also associated with costs. By planning on the higher layer of the global graph, we can optimize the global cost.

http://dx.doi.org/10.5772/intechopen.68145

The rest of the chapter is organized as follows: Section 2 summarizes previous work on indoor human detection and motion planning, Section 3 explains our methodology in detail, Section 4 uses some experimental results to validate our proposed methodology, and Section 5 proposes some future work and summarized this paper.

2. Motivation

In a Veteran Affairs (VA) hospital, thousands of surgical tools are transported between the operating rooms and the sterilization facilities every day. Currently, the logistics of the perioperative process is labor intensive, with medical instruments being processed manually by people. This manual process is inefficient and could lead to improper sterilization of instruments. A systematic approach can dramatically improve surgical instrument identification and count, sterilization, and patient safety.

A fully automated robotic system involves multiple mobile and static robots for both manipulation and transportation. The overall robotic system is shown in **Figure 1**. A key task throughout the sterilization process is to move robots in the hospital from one location to another location while avoiding hitting any obstacles including assets and people. It is a typical indoor robot navigation task. However, due to the dynamic human activities in a hospital, we need to address two challenges: one is to detect and track human motion and activities in the hospital, and the other is to plan the motion trajectories for robots to navigate through multiple floors.

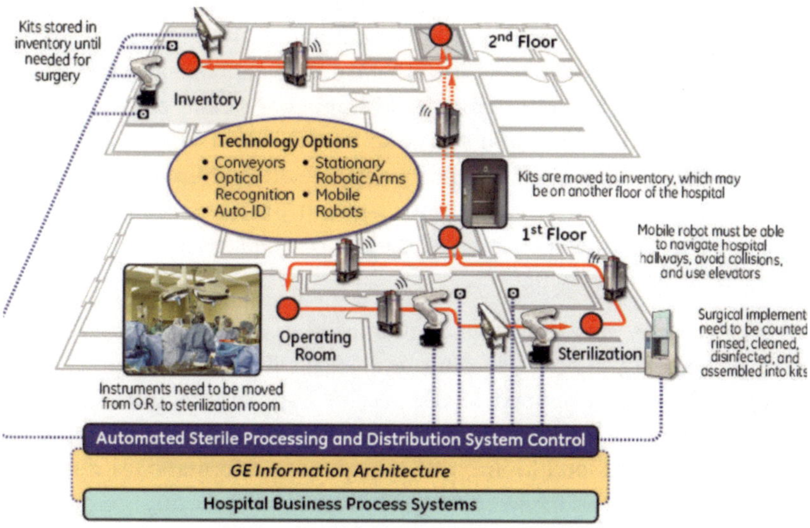

Figure 1. Overall robotic system.

3. Related work

Robot navigation is one of the most important topics in robotics; many sensors and techniques have been studied in the past few decades [1]. Odometer and inertial sensors such as accelerometer and gyroscope have been used for dead reckoning, that is, relative position estimation. For absolute position measurements, various systems have been developed using sensors such as magnetic compasses, active beacons, and global positioning system (GPS) chips. Combining relative and absolute position measurements, GPS-aided inertial navigation systems have achieved satisfying performance for many outdoor robotic applications. However, accurate and robust localization is still an open problem in the research community for an indoor environment and GPS-denied situation.

As wireless devices and networks become more pervasive, radio-based indoor localization and tracking of people becomes a practical and cost-effective solution. Extensive research has been performed to investigate different wireless devices and protocols such as ultra-wide band (UWB), Bluetooth, Wi-Fi, and so on to locate people carrying radio devices at indoor or GPS-denied environments [2–4]. A few recent studies even measure and model the effect of the human body on the antenna gain pattern of a radio [5, 6], and use the model and the effect to jointly track both the orientation and position of the person wearing a radio device such as an radio-frequency identification (RFID) badge [6, 7]. However, all these methods require people to participate in the motion capture and tracking system by carrying devices with them all the time.

With respect to motion planning, there are some existing methods that use the historical human activity data to assist robotic motion planning. A well-known example is the planning engine in the Google Map, which relies on crowd-sourced user data [8, 9]. However, we are targeting on robot motion planning at indoor environments [10, 11], where we cannot collect human activity data from Google Map or GPS. We also cannot expect that everyone in a building can hold a device for us to collect the human-associate data [12]. A natural and noncooperative method [13] is to obtain such data by actively detecting and tracking human activities in the environment without mounting any sensors on human bodies, and that is the basic innovation point and contribution of our method proposed in this book chapter. The technology we used in this book chapter successfully helps us build a model to describe human activities in the environment.

For robots to interact with human beings, human motion detection and tracking is a critical problem to solve. Recently, a novel sensing and localization technique called radio tomographic imaging (RTI) was developed to use received signal strength (RSS) measurements between pairs of nodes in a wireless network to detect and track people [14]. Various methods and systems have been developed to improve the system performance at different situations. For example, a multichannel RTI system was developed by exploring frequency diversity to improve the localization accuracy [15]. A variance-based RTI (VRTI) was developed to locate and track moving people even through nonmetal walls [16, 17]. Further, to locate stationary and moving people even at non–line-of-sight (NLOS) environments, kernel distance-based RTI (KRTI) was developed that uses the histogram distance between a short-term and a long-term

RSS histogram [18]. The state-of-the-art RTI technology has been used to locate and track people in buildings, but we are not aware of any research effort in using RTI to assist human robot interaction and robot path planning.

RTI technology could help us describe human activities in the environment, especially in buildings. The next step is to use appropriate methods to represent the information obtained [19]. When building a model of describing human activities, some researchers focused on building a mathematical field model, for example, Gaussian Mixture Model (GMM) [20]. Given a position, the model returns a density of humans in the environment. Some researchers use nodes to represent humans. One well-accepted and popular method is hidden Markov model (HMM) [21]. Both discrete [21] and continuous HMMs [22] have been proposed to describe states and transitions. In our system, we choose to use discrete HMM to simplify the model and reduce the computing time when the robot is moving. Lots of literatures can be found in this paper for using HMMs in robotics research [23]. In our method, we used HMMs, but we describe human activities using the costs, not the nodes. Our contribution is to successfully integrate the human detection results into an HMM and reduce the number of nodes in the HMMs for robotic path planning.

Based on the representation model that we chose, a motion-planning algorithm is used to enable robots to find a path from the current location to the target position by searching the reachable space and finding a path to satisfy task constraints [24]. The path-planning process can be done in a configuration space or a task space. Current path-planning methods are categorized into three types [24, 25]: (1) roadmap [26], which samples the configuration of a task space and finds a shortest or an optimal path to connect the sampled points; (2) potential field [27], which generates a path in the configuration or a task space by moving a particle attracted by the goal and repelled by impedance areas; and (3) strategy searching [28], which searches the policy or strategy database to find a solution that describes the path.

4. Methodology

The proposed system includes several subsystems such as robot navigation, human activity and motion detection, long-term context model, and so on. The overall system architecture is shown in **Figure 2**. We explain each subsystem in detail in this section.

First, we need to detect human activities in the environment. The detection result is used for building a long-term context model in the learning stage and predicting the current human activities in the environment in the application stage. Most of human activities could be simplified as human motions and locations if we do not want to consider what humans are doing. In the human detection part, we choose to use the KRTI technology to record the locations of humans in the environment. The locations are recorded together with timing information to construct a hidden Markov model, which is stored as our long-term context model, after the model is learnt and built. In the application stage, whenever a human is detected in the environment, robots use the context model to predict the human's activity in the future a few minutes/hours depending on the use cases. The descriptions of current and

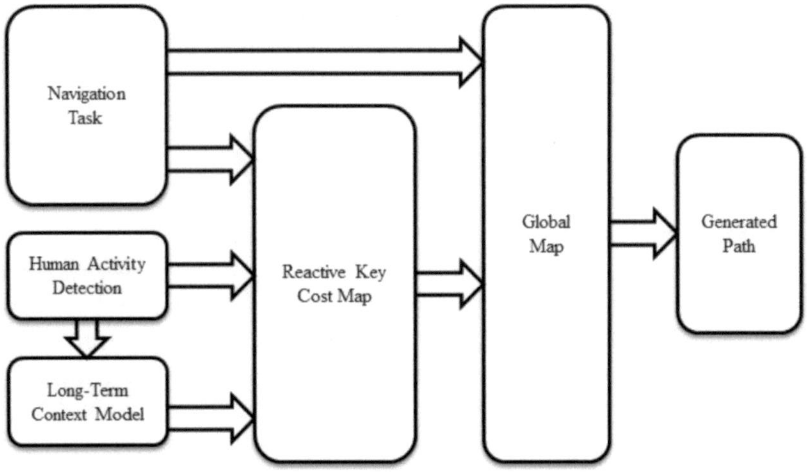

Figure 2. System architecture.

predicted humans' activities are combined to generate impedance areas. The impedance areas will be used to generate Reactive Key Cost Maps describing the cost between the key locations including elevators and the stairs. All the RKCMs are connected by elevators and stairs, where robots can use to move from one floor to another. The connected graph is the global graph describing the current paths and connections in the multifloor environment.

When a target is defined in the cost map, which does not belong to elevators and the stairs, we add the target location to the graph and use a Gaussian model to compute the cost of moving from key locations to the target location. The robot then tries to search a shortest path from its current location to the target location in the global graph. Please notice that the path maps are changing all the time, because the information on the heat map changes continuously based on the current and predicted human activities, which are detected by our indoor localization sensors.

4.1. Human motion and activity detection

This part is the first step of the whole system. All the following analysis, planning, and decision making are based on the detection results coming from this step. The input of this step is the locations detected by the sensors, and the output of this step is different in the learning stage and the application stage. In our system, we propose to use kernel distance-based radio tomographic imaging (KRTI) to detect human beings and track their positions in the environment. First, we give a simple introduction to the KRTI system.

4.1.1. Human motion detection and tracking

Assume we have a wireless network with L links. For each link, received signal strength (RSS) is measured at the receiver from the transmitter, and we use q_l to denote the histogram of the RSS measurements recorded during a calibration period, and use p_l to denote the RSS histogram in a short time window during the online period. Then, we can calculate the kernel distance between two histograms q_l and p_l for each link as [18]

$$d_l(p_l, q_l) = {p_l}^T K p_l + {q_l}^T K q_l - 2{p_l}^T K q_l \tag{1}$$

where K is a kernel matrix from a kernel function such as a Gaussian kernel.

Let $d = [d_0, \cdots d_{L-1}]^T$ denote a kernel distance vector for all L links of a wireless network, and let $x = [x_0, \cdots, x_{M-1}]^T$ denote an image vector representing the human motion and presence in the network area. Then, the previous RTI work has shown the efficacy of a linear model $\boldsymbol{W}$ to relate RSS measurements with the image vector $\boldsymbol{x}$ [14, 16, 17]:

$$d = Wx + n \tag{2}$$

where $\boldsymbol{n}$ is a vector representing the measurement noise and model error.

Finally, a KRTI image $\hat{x}$can be estimated from the kernel distance vector d using the generalized least-squares solution [17, 18]:

$$\hat{x} = (W^T {C_n}^{-1} W + {C_x}^{-1})^{-1} W^T {C_n}^{-1} d \tag{3}$$

where C_x is the covariance matrix of $\boldsymbol{x}$, and C_n is the covariance matrix of $\boldsymbol{n}$. More details of the KRTI formulation can be found in Ref. [18].

4.1.2. Modeling stage of human activity detection

In the learning stage, the goal is to build a heat map describing long-term human activities. The process is to put the sensor in the environment for a long and meaningful time and record the human locations with temporal information. In our experience, the duration of this process depends on the situational environment and the requirements of applications. Normally, we put the sensors in the environment for one whole week to collect weekly based data. The reason is that we find the daily human activities to be largely different and the weekly human activities have some trackable patterns. **Figure 3** displays an example of detected human activities in a small environment.

To simplify the modeling process, we use Gaussian Mixture Model (GMM) [29] to model the locations. The 'hot' locations are described as Gaussian models whose centers are the peak points of activities that happen every day. It is easy to understand that those peak points are some public spaces in the environment. Mathematically, the location of each Gaussian model is described as

$$G_k(j) = \{(x, y), \sigma\} \tag{4}$$

where k represents the kth floor, j is the index number of the Gaussian model on the kth floor, (x, y) is the location of the center of the Gaussian model w.r.t. the local coordinates of the kth floor, and σ is the variance.

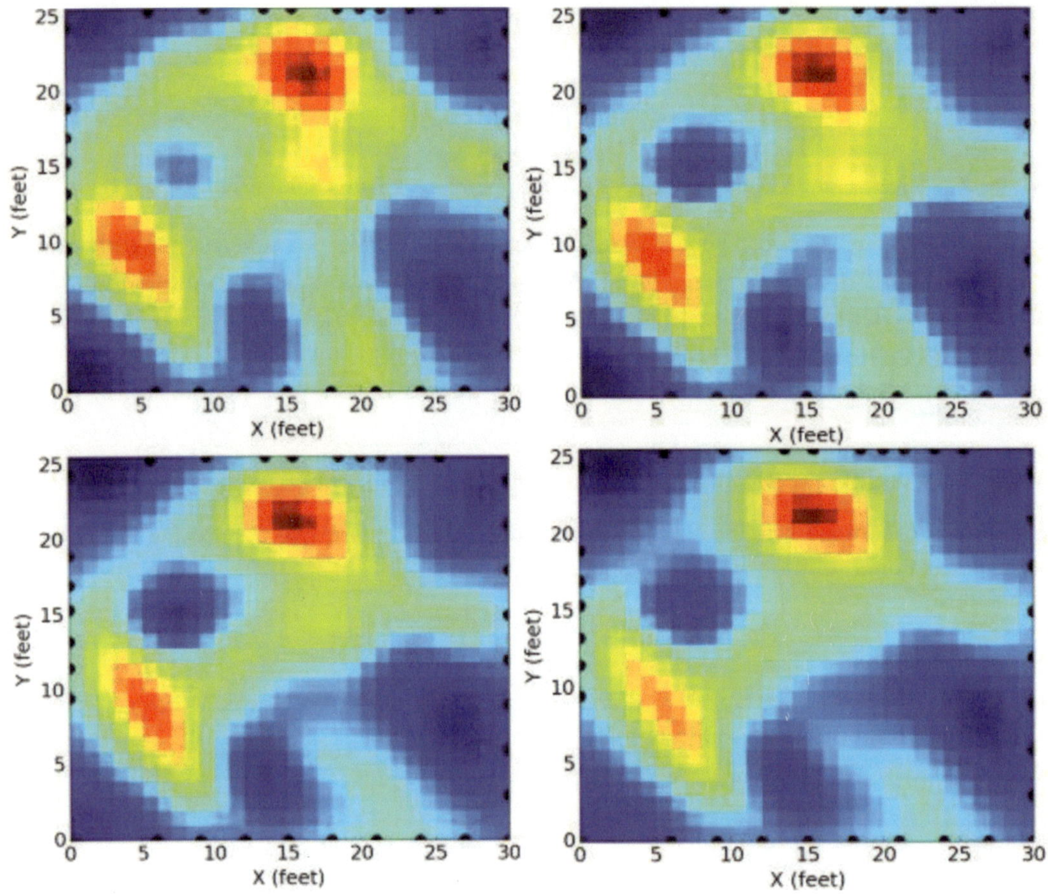

Figure 3. Human motion detection.

Then, based on the temporal information, a Hidden Markov Model [30] can be built. The HMM model describes the relationship between each location, especially when a human is within an area described using Gaussian model, where he/she will move to.

Assuming on kth floor, we have N Gaussian models and is monitored from the starting time: t_1, and the current state q_t is S_i at time t. The probability of the transition from $q_t = S_i$ to $q_{t+1} = S_j$ at time $t + 1$ is

$$P\left(q_{t+1} = G_k(j)|q_t = G_k(i), q_{t-1} = G_k(p), \ldots, q_1 = S_l\right) = P\left(q_{t-1} = G_k(j)|q_t = G_k(i)\right), 1 \leq i, j \leq N \tag{5}$$

The state transition matrix is defined as A, where

$$a_{ij} = P\left(q_{t+1} = G_k(j)|q_t = G_k(i)\right), 1 \leq i, j \leq N \tag{6}$$

Then, the observation matrix defined as B is given by

http://dx.doi.org/10.5772/intechopen.68145

$$b_{ik} = P\left(o_k | q_t = G_k(i)\right), 1 \le i \le N, 1 \le k \le M \tag{7}$$

It means that the measured value is v_k at time t while the current state is $G_k(i)$.

The initial state distribution is defined as

$$\pi_i = P\left(q_1 = G_k(i)\right) 1 \le i \le N \tag{8}$$

The complete Hidden Markov Model then is defined as

$$\lambda = (A, B, \pi) \tag{9}$$

Then, this model describes the transition between two locations based on the observations. As mentioned in Ref. [20], the Bayesian method is used to determine the number of states in a HMM model by minimizing the equation:

$$BIC = -2L_f + n_p \log(T) \tag{10}$$

where L_f is the likelihood of the model given the observed demonstration, n_p is the number of the independent parameters in the model, and T is the number of observations. The model, which has the smallest value according to Eq. (10), will be chosen.

An example of a HMM built for our system is shown in **Figure 4**.

4.1.3. *Application stage of human activity detection*

Given an observation O_k, the nearest Gaussian model is computed:

$$l = \operatorname{argmin} ||O_k - G_k(i)|| \tag{11}$$

which is used to define the current state $G_k(i)$.

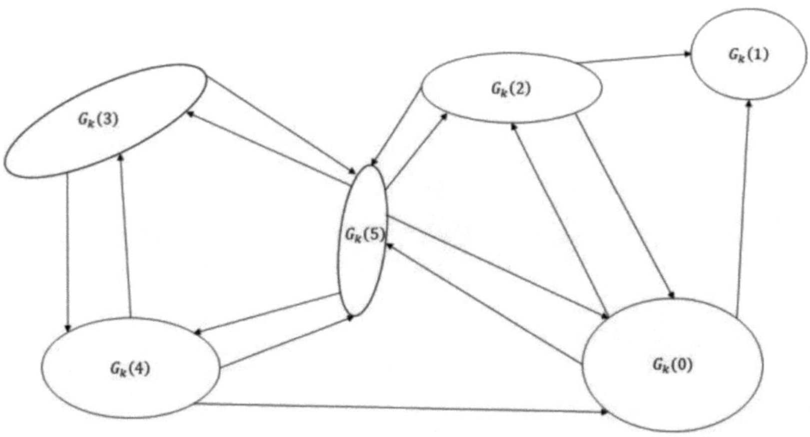

Figure 4. Example of HMM of human activities.

The most probable area where the human will move to is determined by the equation:

$$m = P\left(q_{t+1} = G_k(j) | q_t = G_k(i)\right) \tag{12}$$

then the area covered by $G_k(l)$ and $G_k(m)$ will be masked as high-impedance area in the map in the next step.

One important thing we want to mention is that there are lots of people moving in a business building. Then from the detection side, there will be lots of areas masked as high-impedance areas.

4.2. Reactive Key Cost Map

After we have the high-impedance areas obtained from the application stage of human activity detection, the next step is to use a map or a graph, which is associated with costs between two key locations, to describe the current environmental information. In our method, Gaussian models are used to describe human activities at hot locations in the environment. However, we do not need to use all of them in the global shortest path searching. What we care about is the cost between key locations, not all the locations. The key locations in our definition are (1) elevators and stairs, which connect two floors and (2) target locations, which may not be the hot locations we detected in the above sections but the robot needs to move to.

We segment the free space of a static map into grids. Then, we overlay the high-impedance areas to the static grid-based map as shown in **Figure 5**.

The cost of moving from one grid to an adjacent free grid is always 1, and the cost of moving from one grid to an adjacent impedance grid is defined using the following equation:

$$c(i,j) = \eta * (\text{impedance}_{\text{current}} + 1) + (1 - \eta)\text{impedance}_{\text{history}}(t) \tag{13}$$

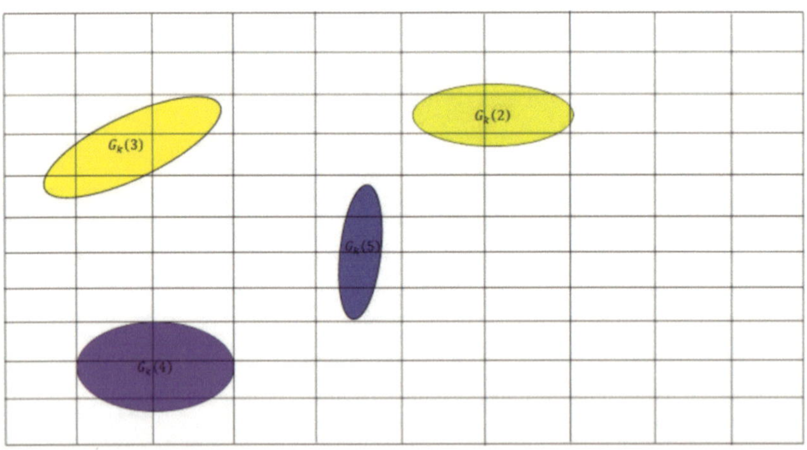

Figure 5. Map overlay.

$\text{impedance}_{\text{current}}$ is defined by the number of people. And $\text{impedance}_{\text{history}}$ is defined by the number of people detected at t from the historical data.

Using $c(i, j)$, we can build a *Reactive Key Cost Map* for each floor. As we mentioned earlier, we do not care about the path between each location, but it is necessary to find the cost of paths between key locations.

However, most of the time, a target location in a navigation task is a public space like a conference room, an office, and so on, which are not close to the key locations. So before we build our cost graph, we need to build one additional key location in the map. Then, we connect the closest neighbors to the target node. The cost is computed using the Gaussian impedance area:

$$c(i, t) = \text{impedance}(i) * N\left(x|x_i, \sum\right) \tag{14}$$

where x is the target location, x_i is the center of the Gaussian impedance area, and Σ is the variance matrix. **Figure 6** displays the cost map generated from **Figure 5**.

Then, we apply a shortest path-searching algorithm to find the shortest paths between all the key locations on each floor. In our system, we used A* algorithm [31], since the map is known and the heuristic and current cost are all known. Specifically, A* selects the path that minimizes

$$f(n) = g(n) + h(n) \tag{15}$$

where n is the last node on the path, $g(n)$ is the cost of the path from the start node to n, and $h(n)$ is a heuristic that estimates the cost of the cheapest path from n to the goal.

After the searching, a Reactive Key Cost Map is built and all the paths are described with cost, which is shown in **Figure 7**.

The next step is to connect all the maps of floors together and the connection points are elevators and stairs. This is a simple matching and connection process.

4.3. Path searching

After the maps of the whole building is built, path searching and planning can all be done in the global map.

Since we largely reduce the complexity of the map by building a Reactive Key Cost Map, the computing task on the path-searching part is not very difficult. We use Dijkstra's algorithm [32] to find a shortest path in a constructed directed map. Dijkstra's algorithm is a greedy searching algorithm to find a shortest path in a directed graph by repeatedly updating the distances between the starting node and other nodes until the shortest path is determined. Let the node at which we are starting be called the initial node. Let the distance of node Y be the distance from the initial node to Y. Dijkstra's algorithm will assign some initial distance values and will try to improve them step by step as follows:

1	1	1	1	1	1	1	1	1	1
1	1	1	1	1	$G_K(2)$	$G_K(2)$	1	1	K_2
1	$i_K(3)$	$i_K(3)$	1	1	$G_K(2)$	$G_K(2)$	$G_K(2)$	1	1
$i_K(3)$	$i_K(3)$	$i_K(3)$	1	1	$G_K(2)$	$G_K(2)$	1	1	1
$i_K(3)$	$i_K(3)$	1	1	$G_K(5)$	1	1	1	1	1
1	1	1	1	$G_K(5)$	1	1	1	1	1
1	1	1	1	$G_K(5)$	1	1	1	1	1
1	K_1	1	1	$G_K(5)$	1	1	1	1	1
1	$G_K(4)$	$G_K(4)$	1	1	1	1	1	1	1
1	$G_K(4)$	$G_K(4)$	1	1	1	1	1	K_3	1
1	$G_K(4)$	$G_K(4)$	1	1	1	1	1	1	1

Figure 6. Cost map with three key points.

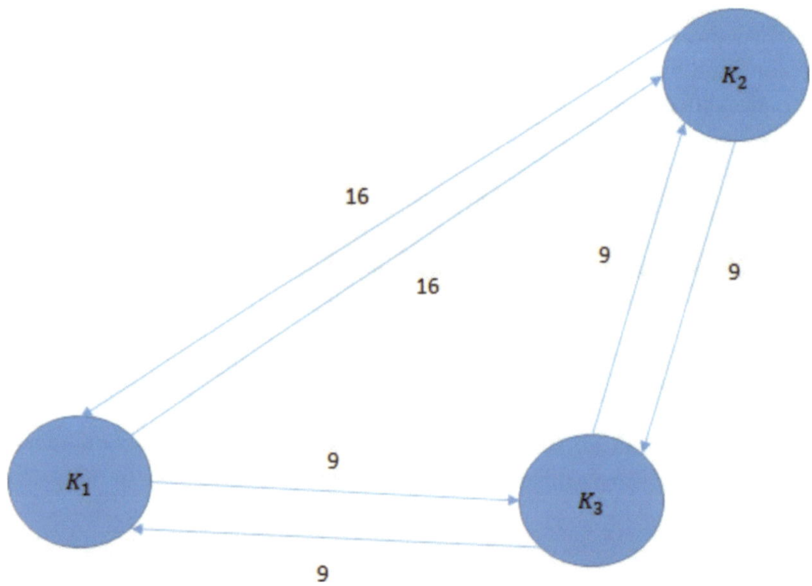

Figure 7. Example of Reactive Key Cost map.

1. Assign to every node a tentative distance value: set it to zero for our initial node and to infinity for all other nodes.
2. Mark all nodes unvisited. Set the initial node as current. Create a set of the unvisited nodes called the unvisited set consisting of all the nodes except the initial node.
3. For the current node, consider all its unvisited neighbors and calculate their tentative distances. For example, if the current node A is marked with a distance of six, and the edge connecting it with a neighbor B has length 2, then the distance to B (through A) will

be 8, the summation of the above two numbers. If this distance is less than the previously recorded tentative distance of B, then overwrite that distance. Even though a neighbor has been examined, it is not marked as "visited" at this time, and it remains in the unvisited set.

4. When we are done considering all the neighbors of the current node, mark the current node as visited and remove it from the unvisited set. A visited node will never be checked again.

5. If the destination node has been marked visited (when planning a route between two specific nodes) or if the smallest tentative distance among the nodes in the unvisited set is infinity (when planning a complete traversal), then stop. The algorithm has finished.

6. Select the unvisited node that is marked with the smallest tentative distance, and set it as the new "current node," then go back to step 3.

Using Dijkstra's algorithm, in a map, a shortest path can be generated from the "Starting" node to a destination node. In our testing, we found some issues when applying Dijkstra's algorithm in 3D path searching. Then, we simplify our case by confining that the global map can be represented as a 2D graph. This paper does not focus on proposing a novel planning algorithm, so improving the motion-planning algorithm is not the concentration.

5. Experiments and results

To evaluate our system, we need to have two types of evaluation. One is to make sure the path can be generated. We tested this part in a static environment assuming that the human motion and activities have been detected and remained the same for a certain amount of time. The second testing is to test the reactive planning. Assuming that humans are moving in the environment, then we generate a path plan reactively based on the current environmental situation. This part is to validate that the system is responsive quickly enough to deal with the uncertain and unexpected human activities in the environment. First, we describe how we perform experiments to evaluate our human motion-tracking system.

5.1. Human detection results and dataset of RTI localization

We use the TelosB motes [33] as our wireless nodes to form a wireless network as our testbed. We deploy nodes at static locations around an area of interest, as shown in **Figure 8**. All nodes are programmed with TinyOS program Spin [34] so that each node can take turns to measure the received signal strength from all the other nodes. A base station is connected to a laptop to collect pairwise RSS measurements from all nodes of the wireless network. Once we collect RSS from the network, we feed the RSS vector to our KRTI formulation as described in Section 4.1.1.

We describe our experiment in a controlled environment to evaluate our motion-tracking system. As shown in **Figure 8**, 34 TelosB nodes were deployed outside the living room of a

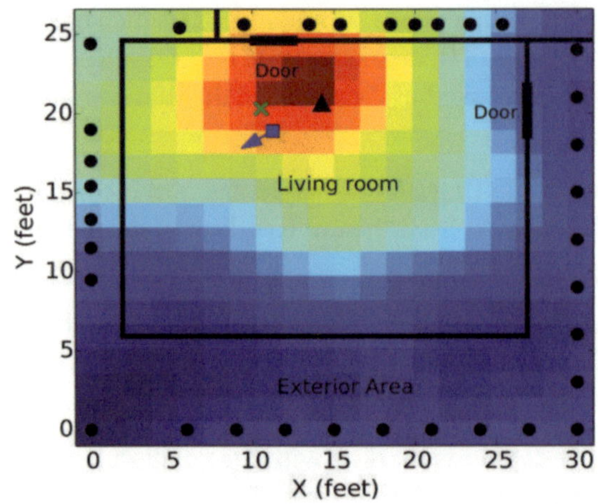

Figure 8. Experimental layout with reconstructed RTI image (anchor nodes shown as bullets, true person position shown as a cross, RTI position estimate shown as a triangle, and robot's orientation and position are shown as arrow and square for illustration purpose).

residential house. Before people started walking in the area, we collect pairwise RSS measurements between anchor nodes as our calibration measurements. During the online period, people walked around a marked path a few times in the living room, so that we know the ground truth of the locations of the people to compare with the estimate from RTI. The reconstructed KRTI image is shown in **Figure 8** with the black triangle indicating the location of the pixel with the maximum pixel value, which is the location estimate of a person. Note that KRTI can detect human presence by choosing a threshold of the pixel value based on the calibration measurements. KRTI is also capable of tracking multiple people, as shown in **Figure 3**. More details of the experiments and dataset can be found in Refs. [17, 18].

5.2. Simulation results

We tested our proposed algorithm in simulation. After detecting the human activities, the robot builds the heat map and the 2D RKCM of each floor. **Figure 9** displays three 2D graphs of three floors, which are labeled by shadowed circles. They are connected by stairs or elevators. The cost of moving from one floor to another floor using the elevators or stairs is manually defined as three in our graphs.

The distance matrix used for Dijkstra's searching algorithm is shown in Eq. (16). Each row represents the distance from one node to other nodes. The elements represent the distance values. Given a task of the start point i_1 on map 1 and the goal state k_3 on map 3, the robot finds a path from i_1 to k_3 as shown in **Figure 10**. The cost of the path is 25 which is the global minimum cost.

Comparing the time spent on movement and detection, the time of finding path based on RKCM can almost be ignored. There are lots of papers describing the algorithm complexities of Dijkstra's algorithm and other algorithms, where readers can refer to [32]

http://dx.doi.org/10.5772/intechopen.68145

$$\text{RKCM} = \begin{array}{c||ccccccccc|} i_1 & 0.0 & 16 & 9.0 & 0.0 & 0.0 & 0.0 & 0.0 & 0.0 & 0.0 \\ i_2 & 16 & 0.0 & 9.0 & 3.0 & 0.0 & 0.0 & 0.0 & 0.0 & 0.0 \\ i_4 & 9.0 & 9.0 & 0.0 & 0.0 & 3.0 & 0.0 & 0.0 & 0.0 & 0.0 \\ j_2 & 0.0 & 3.0 & 0.0 & 0.0 & 10 & 7.0 & 0.0 & 0.0 & 0.0 \\ j_4 & 0.0 & 0.0 & 3.0 & 10 & 0.0 & 6.0 & 0.0 & 0.0 & 0.0 \\ j_5 & 0.0 & 0.0 & 0.0 & 7.0 & 6.0 & 0.0 & 0.0 & 0.0 & 3.0 \\ k_1 & 0.0 & 0.0 & 0.0 & 0.0 & 0.0 & 0.0 & 0.0 & 15 & 20 \\ k_3 & 0.0 & 0.0 & 0.0 & 0.0 & 0.0 & 0.0 & 15 & 0.0 & 4.0 \\ k_5 & 0.0 & 0.0 & 0.0 & 0.0 & 0.0 & 3.0 & 20 & 4.0 & 0.0 \end{array} \quad (16)$$

We still use traditional online sense-plan-act algorithms when the robot is moving. However, the experiments here largely reduce the computing workload on the robot side. The robot knows in advance what is happening in the environment based on the HMM model built from historical data, then it uses the HMM to find a path which is optimal based on the historical

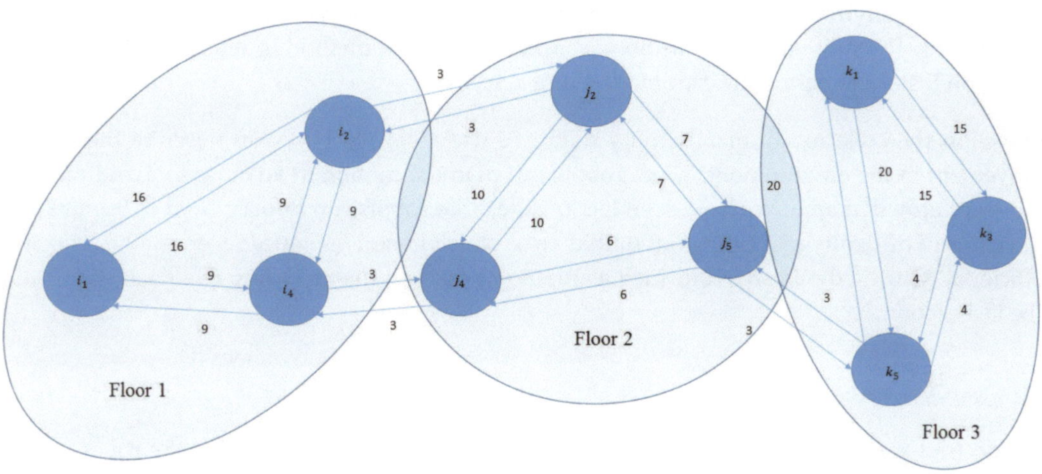

Figure 9. Reactive Key Cost map.

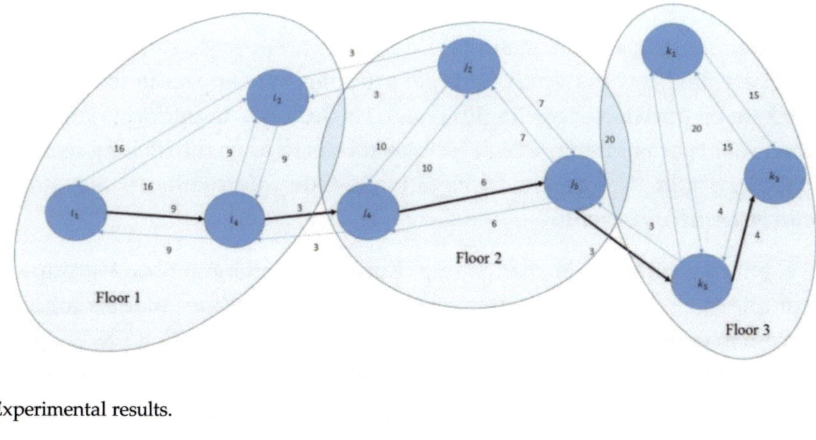

Figure 10. Experimental results.

information, under the assumption that the current situation is similar to the historical situation during the same time every day or every week.

5.3. Discussion

5.3.1. Discussion on the results

From the above experimental results, we can clearly see that our system builds the global graph using the monitored human activities and generates a shortest path for robots to move to the target locations.

In most indoor robotic navigation challenges, especially in crowded environment, researchers tend to equip robots with various sensors to make sure that they can detect everything in the environment. Then based on the comprehensive detection and recognition process, a smart decision-making mechanism can help robots to plan the motion, switch strategies, and move freely in the environment. This method enforces large workload on the online-computing component. The motivation of this book chapter is to find a method to reduce such workload based on historical data of human motion and activity.

Based on the collected human activity data, we use a simple HMM to describe the cost of movement in the environment. Then, robots can plan the motion in advance to avoid moving to a very crowded area. We have seen lots of cases that robots run into a crowd of human and have lots of difficulty in moving out of that area, which generates concerns on safety, cost, and efficiency. Our method can avoid such a situation based on the modeling results as seen from the last section.

5.3.2. Future work

We do find some situations that the system does not work very well. When the robot moves too fast, and the humans nearby are walking, the planning is not fast enough to reflect the current changes of the environment, and thus collision happens. We have not done much testing on this part and we plan to have more testing to make the system more robust in such situations.

Additionally, we cannot expect that static HMM model can provide satisfying information for robots to use. Every day, new patterns of human activities may appear in the environment and the model needs to be updated accordingly. Thus, it is desirable to perform data collection and modeling when robots are moving, which enables robots to have the lifelong learning capability. This capability could help robots to have up-to-date information to use and make the planning more efficient and useful.

Moving one robot in a building is challenging, but motion planning for a group of robots is even more complex [35, 36]. Sharing latest updated human activity models among robots is key to the success to realize coordinated and collaborated robotic motion planning. The critical technical problem is to design a method of fusing models into one for all the robots to use.

6. Conclusion

This book chapter proposes a hybrid method of planning paths in a global graph composed of subgraphs. We take the human activity into consideration to build a cost graph. This method significantly reduces the computing workload because it avoids planning in a global graph with lots of grids and possibilities. We also carry out experiments in simulation to validate our proposed method. The methods proposed in this chapter provide a solution to enable autonomous systems/robots to navigate effectively and robustly in human-existing multistorey buildings.

Author details

Huan Tan*, Yang Zhao and Lynn DeRose

*Address all correspondence to: huantan@ieee.org

GE Global Research Center, Niskayuna, New York, NY, USA

References

[1] Borenstein J, Everett H, Feng L, Wehe D. Mobile robot positioning-sensors and techniques. Naval Command Control and Ocean Surveillance Center RDT and E Div. San Diego, CA; 1997

[2] Patrick L, et al. ALPS: A bluetooth and ultrasound platform for mapping and localization. In: Proceedings of the 13th ACM Conference on Embedded Networked Sensor Systems. ACM; 2015

[3] Benjamin K, Pannuto P, Dutta P. PolyPoint: Guiding indoor quadrotors with ultra-wideband localization. In: Proceedings of the 2nd International Workshop on Hot Topics in Wireless. ACM; 2015

[4] Zheng Y, Wu C, Liu Y. Locating in fingerprint space: Wireless indoor localization with little human intervention. In: Proceedings of the 18th Annual International Conference on Mobile Computing and Networking. ACM; 2012

[5] Andrew H, Siddiqi S, Sukhatme G. An experimental study of localization using wireless Ethernet. In: Proceedings of the International Conference on Field and Service Robotics; 2003. pp. 201–206

[6] Yang Z, Patwari N, Agrawal P, Rabbat M. Directed by directionality: Benefiting from the gain pattern of active RFID badges. IEEE Transactions on Mobile Computing. 2012;**11**:865–877

[7] Fernando S, Jiménez AR, Zampella F. Joint estimation of indoor position and orientation from RF signal strength measurements. In: Proceedings of 2013 International Conference on Indoor Positioning and Indoor Navigation; October 2003. pp. 1–8

[8] Available from: https://developers.google.com/maps/

[9] Doherty ST, Lemieux CJ, Canally C. Tracking human activity and well-being in natural environments using wearable sensors and experience sampling. Social Science & Medicine. 2014;**106**:83–92

[10] Huan T, Mao Y, Xu Y, Kannan B, Griffin WB, DeRose L. An integrated robotic system for transporting surgical tools in hospitals. In: 2016 Annual IEEE Systems Conference (SysCon); Orlando, FL; 2016. pp. 1–8

[11] Huan T, Holovashchenko V, Mao Y, Kannan B, DeRose L. Human-supervisory distributed robotic system architecture for healthcare operation automation. In: Proceedings of 2015 IEEE International Conference on Systems, Man, and Cybernetics. Kowloon; 2015. pp. 133–138

[12] Christopher R, Tan H, Kannan B, DeRose L. Towards safe robot-human collaboration systems using human pose detection. In: Proceedings of 2015 IEEE International Conference on Technologies for Practical Robot Applications (TePRA); Woburn, MA; 2015. pp. 1–6

[13] Zhengyu P, Muñoz-Ferreras J-M, Tang Y, Roberto G-G, Li C. Portable coherent frequency-modulated continuous-wave radar for indoor human tracking. In: Proceedings of 2016 IEEE Topical Conference on Biomedical Wireless Technologies, Networks, and Sensing Systems (BioWireleSS); 2016. pp. 36–38

[14] Joey W, Patwari N. Radio tomographic imaging with wireless networks. IEEE Transactions on Mobile Computing. 2010;**9**:621–632

[15] Ossi K, Bocca M, Patwari N. Enhancing the accuracy of radio tomographic imaging using channel diversity. In: Proceedings of 2012 IEEE 9th International Conference on Mobile Adhoc and Sensor Systems (MASS); 2012

[16] Joey W, Patwari N. See-through walls: Motion tracking using variance-based radio tomography networks. IEEE Transactions on Mobile Computing. 2011;**10**:612–621

[17] Yang Z, Patwari N. Robust estimators for variance-based device free localization and tracking. IEEE Transactions on Mobile Computing. 2015;**14**:2116–2129

[18] Zhao Y, Patwari N, Phillips JM, Venkatasubramanian S. Radio tomographic imaging and tracking of stationary and moving people via kernel distance. In: Proceedings of 2013 ACM/IEEE International Conference on Information Processing in Sensor Networks; 2013

[19] Aggarwal JK, Ryoo MS. Human activity analysis: A review. ACM Computing Surveys (CSUR). 2011;**43**(3):16

[20] Calinon S, Guenter F, Billard A. On learning, representing, and generalizing a task in a humanoid robot. IEEE Transactions on Systems, Man, and Cybernetics, Part B (Cybernetics). 2007;**37**(2):286–298

[21] Tetsunari I, Tanie H, Nakamura Y. Keyframe compression and decompression for time series data based on the continuous hidden Markov model. In: Proceedings of 2003 IEEE/RSJ International Conference on Intelligent Robots and Systems; 2003. pp. 1487–1492

[22] Yongjin K, Kang K, Jin J, Moon J, Park J. Hierarchically linked infinite Hidden Markov Model based trajectory analysis and semantic region retrieval in a trajectory dataset. Expert Systems with Applications. 2017; **78**: 386–395

[23] Dariu GM. The visual analysis of human movement: A survey. Computer Vision and Image Understanding. 1999;**73**(1):82–98

[24] Kavraki LE, LaValle SM. Motion planning. In: Springer Handbook of Robotics. Springer. Eds: Bruno S and Oussama K. International Publishing; 2016. pp. 139–162

[25] Huan T. Applying an extension of estimation of distribution algorithm (EDA) for mobile robots to learn motion patterns from demonstration. In: Proceedings of 2015 IEEE International Conference on Systems, Man, and Cybernetics; Kowloon; 2015. pp. 2829–2834

[26] Minguez J, Lamiraux F, Laumond J-P. Motion planning and obstacle avoidance. In: Springer Handbook of Robotics. Springer Verlag Berlin Heidelberg. International Publishing; 2016. pp. 1177–1202

[27] Huan T, Erdemir E, Kawamura K, Du Q. A potential field method-based extension of the dynamic movement primitive algorithm for imitation learning with obstacle avoidance. In: 2011 IEEE International Conference on Mechatronics and Automation; Beijing; 2011. pp. 525–530

[28] Bayat B, Crasta N, Crespi A, Pascoal AM, Ijspeert A. Environmental Monitoring using Autonomous Vehicles: A Survey of Recent Searching Techniques. No. EPFL-REVIEW-225318. Elsevier; 2017

[29] Zivkovic Z. Improved adaptive Gaussian mixture model for background subtraction. In: Proceedings of the 17th International Conference on Pattern Recognition. Vol. 2; 2004. pp. 28–31

[30] Rabiner LR. A tutorial on Hidden Markov Models and selected applications in speech recognition. Proceedings of the IEEE. 1989;**77**(2):257–286

[31] González D, Pérez J, Milanés V, Nashashibi F. A review of motion planning techniques for automated vehicles. IEEE Transactions on Intelligent Transportation Systems. 2016;**17** (4):1135–1145

[32] Krüsi P, Furgale P, Bosse M, Siegwart R. Driving on point clouds: Motion planning, trajectory optimization, and terrain assessment in generic nonplanar environments. Journal of Field Robotics. 2016

[33] Memsic website. Available from: http://www.memsic.com/wireless-sensor-networks/TPR2420

[34] Sensing and Processing Across Networks (SPAN). Lab Spin website. Available from: http://span.ece.utah.edu/spin

[35] Huan T, Liao Q, Zhang J. An improved algorithm of multiple robots cooperation in obstacle existing environment. In: Proceedings of 2007 IEEE International Conference on Robotics and Biomimetics (ROBIO); Sanya; 2007. pp. 1001–1006

[36] Huan T. Imitation learning and behavior generation in a robot team. In: Ani Hsieh M, Chirikjian G, editors. Distributed Autonomous Robotic Systems, the 11th International Symposium, Springer Tracts in Advanced Robotics (STAR). Vol. 104; Springer Berlin Heidelberg; 2014. pp. 423–434

Chapter 3

Audio-Visual Speaker Tracking

Volkan Kılıç and Wenwu Wang

Additional information is available at the end of the chapter

http://dx.doi.org/10.5772/intechopen.68146

Abstract

Target motion tracking found its application in interdisciplinary fields, including but not limited to surveillance and security, forensic science, intelligent transportation system, driving assistance, monitoring prohibited area, medical science, robotics, action and expression recognition, individual speaker discrimination in multi-speaker environments and video conferencing in the fields of computer vision and signal processing. Among these applications, speaker tracking in enclosed spaces has been gaining relevance due to the widespread advances of devices and technologies and the necessity for seamless solutions in real-time tracking and localization of speakers. However, speaker tracking is a challenging task in real-life scenarios as several distinctive issues influence the tracking process, such as occlusions and an unknown number of speakers. One approach to overcome these issues is to use multi-modal information, as it conveys complementary information about the state of the speakers compared to single-modal tracking. To use multi-modal information, several approaches have been proposed which can be classified into two categories, namely deterministic and stochastic. This chapter aims at providing multimedia researchers with a state-of-the-art overview of tracking methods, which are used for combining multiple modalities to accomplish various multimedia analysis tasks, classifying them into different categories and listing new and future trends in this field.

Keywords: audio-visual tracking, multi-speaker tracking, deterministic, stochastic approaches

1. Introduction

Speaker tracking aims at localizing the moving speakers in a scene by analysing the data sequences captured by sensors or arrays of sensors. It gained relevance in the past decades due to its widespread applications such as automatic camera steering in video conferencing

[1], individual speaker discriminating in multi-speaker environments [2], acoustic beamforming [3], audio-visual speech recognition [4], video indexing and retrieval [5], human-computer interaction [6], and surveillance and monitoring [7] in security applications. There are numerous challenges, which make speaker tracking a difficult task including, but not limited to, the estimation of the variable number of speakers and their states, and dealing with various conditions such as occlusions, limited view of cameras, illumination change and room reverberations [8–10].

Using multi-modal information is one way to address these challenges since more comprehensive observations for the state of the speakers can be collected in multi-modal tracking as compared to the single-modal case, and the collection of the multi-modal information can be achieved by sensors such as audio, video, thermal vision, laser-range finders and radio-frequency identification (RFID) [11–13]. Among these sensors, audio and video sensors are commonly used in speaker tracking compared to others, because of their easier installation, cheaper cost and more data-processing tools [9, 14, 15].

Earlier methods in speaker tracking employ either visual-only or audio-only data, and each modality offers some advantages but is also limited by some weaknesses [16, 17]. Tracking with only video [16–18] offers robust and accurate performance when the camera field of view covers the speakers. However, it degrades when the occlusion between speakers happens, when the speakers go out of the camera field of view, or any changes on illumination or target appearance have occurred. Although audio tracking [19–21] is not restricted by these limitations, it has a tendency to non-negligible-tracking errors because of intermittency of audio data. In addition, audio data may be corrupted by background noise and room reverberations. Nevertheless, the combination of audio and video data may improve the tracking performance when one of the modalities is missing or neither provides accurate measurements, as audio and visual modalities are often complementary to each other which can be exploited to further enhance their respective strengths and mitigate their weaknesses in tracking.

Previous techniques were focused on tracking a single person in a static and controlled environment. However, theoretical and algorithmic advances together with the increasing capability in computer processing have led to the emergence of more sophisticated techniques for tracking multiple speakers in dynamic and less controlled (or natural) environments [22–24]. In addition, the type of sensors used to collect the measurements is advanced from single- to multi-modal.

In the literature, there are many approaches for speaker tracking using multi-modal information, which can be categorized into two methods as one is deterministic and data-driven while the other is stochastic and model-driven [25, 26]. Deterministic approaches are considered as an optimization problem by minimizing a cost function, which needs to be defined appropriately. A representative method in this category is the mean-shift method [27, 28], which defines the cost function in terms of colour similarity measured by Bhattacharyya distance. The stochastic and model-driven approaches use a state-space approach based on the Bayesian framework as it is suitable for processing of multi-modal information [29]. Representative methods are the Kalman filter (KF) [30], extended KF (EKF) and particle filter (PF) [31]. The PF approach is more robust for non-linear and non-Gaussian models as compared with the KF and EKF approaches since it easily approaches the Bayesian optimal estimate with a sufficiently large number of particles [11].

One challenge in the implementation of the PF to tracking problem is to choose an optimal number of particles [9, 32]. An insufficient number may introduce a particle impoverishment, while a larger number (than required) will lead to extra computational cost. Therefore, choosing the optimal number of particles is one of the issues that affect the performance of the tracker. To address this issue and to find the optimal number of particles for the PF to use, adaptive particle filtering (A-PF) approaches have been proposed in Refs. [9, 32–35]. Fox [34] proposed KLD sampling, which aims to bind the error introduced by the sample-based representations of the PF using the Kullback-Leibler divergence between maximum likelihood estimates (MLEs) of the states and the underlying distribution to optimize the number of particles. The KLD-sampling criterion is improved in Ref. [35] for the estimation of the number of particles, leading to an approach for adaptive propagation of the samples. Subsequent work [33] introduces the innovation error to estimate the number of particles by employing a twofold metric. The particles are removed by the first metric in case their distance to a neighbouring particle is smaller than a predefined threshold. The second metric is used to set the threshold on the innovation error in order to control the birth of the particles. These two thresholds need to be set before the algorithm is run. A new approach is proposed in Refs. [9, 32], which estimates noise variance besides the number of particles in an adaptive manner. Different from other existing adaptive approaches, adaptive noise variance is employed in this method for the estimation of the optimal number of particles based on tracking error and the area occupied by the particles in the image.

One assumption in the traditional PF used in multi-speaker tracking is that the number of speakers is known and invariant during the tracking. In practice, the presence of the speakers may change in a random manner, resulting in time-varying number of speakers. To deal with the unknown and variable number of speakers, the theory of random finite sets (RFSs) has been introduced, which allows multi-speaker filtering by propagation of the multi-speaker posterior [36–39]. However, the computational complexity of RFS grows exponentially as the number of speakers increases since the complexity order of the RFS is $O(M^{\Xi})$ where M is the number of measurements and Ξ is the number of speakers. The PHD filtering [40] approach is proposed to overcome this problem, as the first-order approximation of the RFS whose complexity scales linearly with the number of speakers since the complexity order of the PHD is $O(M\Xi)$. This framework has been found to be promising for multi-speaker tracking [36]. However, the PHD recursion involves multiple integrals that need to have closed-form solutions for implementation. So far, two analytic solutions have been proposed: Gaussian mixture PHD (GM-PHD) filter [41, 42] and sequential Monte Carlo PHD (SMC-PHD) filter [43, 44]. Applications of GM-PHD filter are limited by linear Gaussian systems, which lead us to consider SMC-PHD filter to handle non-linear/non-Gaussian problems in audio-visual tracking [15, 45].

Apart from the stochastic methodologies mentioned above, the mean-shift [28] is a deterministic and data-driven method, which focuses on target localization using representation of the target. The mean-shift easily convergences to peak of the function with a high speed and a small computational load. Moreover, as a non-parametric method, the solution of the mean shift is independent from the features used to represent the targets. On the other hand, the performance of the mean-shift is degraded by occlusion or clutter as it searches the densest (most similar) region starting from the initial position in the region of interest. In this sense, the mean-shift trackers may fail easily in tracking small- and fast-moving targets as the region of interest may not cover the targets, which results in a track being lost after a complete occlusion. Also, it is formulated for single-target tracking, so it cannot handle a variable number of targets. Therefore, several methods [14, 15, 46–49] have been proposed by integrating both deterministic and stochastic approaches to benefit their respective strengths which will be discussed in Section 4.

2. Tracking modalities

2.1. Visual cues

Visual tracking is a challenging task in real-life scenarios, as the performance of a tracker is affected by the illumination conditions, occlusion by background objects and fast and complicated movements of the target [50, 51]. To address these problems, several visual features, that is, colour, texture, contour and motion [52], are employed in existing tracking systems.

Using colour feature is a very intuitive approach and commonly applied in target tracking as the information provided by colour helps to distinguish between targets and other objects. Several approaches can be found in the literature which employs colour information to track the target. In Ref. [53], a colour mixture model based on a Gaussian distribution is used for tracking and segmentation, while in Ref. [58], an adaptive mixture model is developed. Target detection and tracking can be easily maintained using colour information if the colour of the target is distinct from those of the background or other objects.

Another approach for tracking is contour-based where shape matching or contour-evolution techniques [54] are used to track the target contour. Active models like snakes, geodesic-active contours, B-splines or meshes [55] can be employed to represent the contours. Occlusion of the target by other objects is the common problem in tracking. This problem can be addressed by detecting and tracking the contour of the upper body [56] rather than tracking the contour of the whole bodies, which leads to the detection of a new person as the upper bodies are often distinguishable from back and front view for different people.

Texture is another cue defined as a measure for surface intensity variation. Properties like smoothness and regularity can be quantified by the texture [57–59]. The texture feature is used with Gabor wavelet in Ref. [60]. The Gabor filters can be employed as orientation and scale-tunable edge and line detectors, and the statistics of these micro-features are mostly used to characterize the underlying texture information in a given region [61]. For improved detection and recognition, local patterns of image have gained attention recently. Local patterns are used in several application areas such as image classification and face detection since they offer promising results. In Ref. [62], the local binary patterns (LBPs) method is used to create a type of texture descriptor based on a grey-scale-invariant texture measure. Such a measure is tolerant to illumination changes.

Another cue used in tracking, particularly in indoor environments, is motion which is an explicit cue of human presence. One way to extract this cue is to apply foreground detection algorithms. A simple method for foreground detection is to compute the difference of two consecutive frames which gives the moving part of the image. Although it has been used in multi-modal-tracking systems [63], it fails when the person remains stationary since the person is considered part of background after some time.

The scale-invariant feature transform (SIFT) proposed in Ref. [64] has found wide use in tracking applications. SIFT uses local features to transform the image data into scale-invariant coordinates. Distinctive invariant features are extracted from images to provide matching between several views of an object. The SIFT feature is invariant to scaling, translation, clutter, rotation, occlusion and lighting which makes it robust to changes in three-dimensional (3D) viewpoint and illumination, and the presence of noise. Even a single feature has high matching rate in a large database because the SIFT features are generally distinctive. On the other hand, non-rigid targets [65] in noisy environments degrade the SIFT matching rate and recognition performance.

So far, several visual cues were introduced, and among them colour cues have been used more commonly in tracking applications due to their easy implementation and low complexity. Colour information can be used in the calculation of the histogram of possible targets at the initialization step as reference images which can be used in detection and tracking of the target. There are two common colour histogram models, RGB or HSV [66] in the literature and HSV is more preferable since it is observed to be more robust to illumination variation [9].

2.2. Audio cues

There are a variety of audio information that could be used in audio tracking such as sound source localization (SSL), time-delay estimation (TDE) and the direction of arrival (DOA) angle.

The audio source localization methods can be divided into three categories [67], namely steered beamforming, super-resolution spectral estimation and time-delay estimation. Beamformer-based source localization offers comparatively low resolution and needs a search over a highly non-linear surface [20]. Also, it is computationally expensive which may be limited in real-time applications. Super-resolution spectral estimation methods are not well suited for locating a moving speaker since it is under the assumption that the speaker location is fixed for a number of frames [68]. However, the location of a moving speaker may change considerably over time. In addition, these methods are not robust to modelling errors caused by room reverberation and mostly have high computational cost [20, 69]. The time-delay of arrival (TDOA)-based location estimators use the relative time delay between the wave-front arrivals at microphone positions in order to estimate the location of the speaker. As compared with the other two methods, the TDOA-based approach has advantages in the following two aspects. The first one is its computational efficiency and the second one its direct connection to the speaker location.

The problem of DOA estimation is similar to that of the TDOA estimation. To estimate the DOA, the TDOA needs to be determined between the sensor elements of the microphone array. Estimation of source locations mainly depends on the quality of the DOA measurements. In the literature, several DOA estimation techniques such as the MUSIC algorithm [70] and the coherent signal subspace (CSS) [71] have been proposed. The main differences between them are the way of dealing with reverberation, background noise and movement of the sources [20]. The following three factors influence the quality of the DOA estimation. The spectral content of the speech segment is considered as the first one which is used for derivation of the DOAs. The reverberation level of the room is the second one which causes outlier in the measurements because of the reflections from the objects and walls. The positions of the microphone array to the speakers and the number of simultaneous sources in the field are considered the third factor.

3. Audio-visual speaker tracking

Speaker tracking is a fundamental part of multimedia applications which plays a critical role to determine the speaker trajectories and analyse the behaviour of speakers. Speaker tracking can be accomplished with the use of audio-only, visual-only or audio-visual information.

Audio-only information based approaches for speaker tracking have been presented in [19, 20, 37, 72–74]. An audio-based fusion scheme was proposed in Ref. [20] to detect multiple speakers where the locations from multiple microphone arrays are estimated and fused to determine the state of the same speaker. Separate KFs are employed for all the individual microphone arrays for the location estimation. To deal with motion of the speaker and measurement uncertainty, the probabilistic data association technique is used with an interacting model.

One issue in Ref. [20] is that it cannot deal with the tracking problem for a time-varying number of speakers. Ma et al. [37, 72] proposed an approach based on random finite set to track an unknown and time-varying number of speakers. The RFS theory and SMC implementation are used to develop the Bayesian RFS filter, which tracks the time-varying number of speakers and their states. The random finite set theory can deal with a time-varying number of speakers; however, the maximum number of speakers that can be handled is limited as its computational complexity increases exponentially with the number of speakers. In that sense, a cardinalized PHD (CPHD) filter is proposed in Ref. [74], which is the first-order approximation of the RFS, to reduce the computational cost caused by the number of speakers. The positions of the speakers are estimated using TDOA measurements from microphone pairs by asynchronous sensor fusion with the CPHD filter.

A time-frequency method and the PHD filter are used in Ref. [73] to localize and track simultaneous speakers. The location of multiple speakers is estimated based on the time-frequency method, which uses an array of three microphones, then the PHD filter is employed to the localization results as post-processing to handle miss-detection and clutters.

Speaker tracking with multi-modal information has also gained attention, and many approaches have been proposed in the past decade using audio-visual information [2, 6, 23, 29, 75–81], providing the complementary characteristics of each modality. The differences among these existing works arise from the overall objective such as tracking either single or multiple speakers and the specific detection/tracking framework.

Audio-visual measurements are fused by graphical models in Ref. [23] to track a moving speaker in a cluttered and noisy environment. Audio and video observations are used jointly by computing their mutual dependencies. The model parameters are learnt using the expectation-maximization algorithm from a sequence of audio-visual data.

A hierarchical Kalman filter structure was proposed in Refs. [2, 80] to track people in a three-dimensional space using multiple microphones and cameras. Two independent local Kalman filters are employed for audio and video streams, and then the outputs of these two local filters are combined under one global Kalman filter.

Unlike [2, 80], particle filters are used in Ref. [81] to estimate the predictions from audio- and video-based measurements and audio-visual information fusion is performed at the feature level. In other words, the independent particle coordinates from the features of both modalities are fused for speaker tracking. These works [2, 23, 80, 81] have focused on the single-speaker case which cannot directly address the tracking problem for multiple speakers.

Two multi-modal systems are introduced in Ref. [75] for the tracking of multiple persons. A joint probabilistic data association filter is employed to detect speech and determine active speaker positions. Two systems are performed for visual features where a particle filter is applied first using foreground, colour, upper body detection and person region cues from multiple camera images and the latter is a blob tracker using only a wide-angle overhead view. Then, acoustic and visual tracks are integrated using a finite state machine. Unlike [75], a particle filtering framework is proposed in Ref. [29, 77] which incorporates the audio and visual detections into the particle filtering framework using an observation model. It has the capability to track multiple people jointly with their speaking activity based on a mixed-state dynamic graphical model defined on a multi-person state space. Another particle filter based multi-modal fusion approach is proposed in Ref. [78] where a single speaker can be identified in the presence of multiple visual observations. Gaussian mixtures model was adopted to fuse multiple observations and modalities. Compared to [29, 75, 77, 78], particle filtering framework is not used in Ref. [6]; instead, hidden Markov model based iterating decoding scheme is used to fuse audio and visual cues for localization and tracking of persons.

In Refs. [14, 76, 79], the Bayesian framework is used to handle the tracking problem for a varying number of speakers. The particle filter is used in Ref. [76], and observation likelihoods based on both audio and video measurements are formulated to use in the estimation of the weights of the particles, and then the number of people is calculated using the weights of these particles. The RFS theory based on multi-Bernoulli approximations is employed in Ref. [79] to integrate audio and visual cues with sequential Monte Carlo implementation. The nature of the random finite set formulation allows their framework to deal with the tracking problem for a varying number of targets. Sequential Monte Carlo implementation (or particle filter) of PHD filter is used in Ref. [14] where audio and visual modalities are fused in the steps of particle filter rather than using any data fusion algorithms. Their work substantially differs from existing works in AV multi-speaker tracking with respect to the capabilities for dealing with multiple speakers, simultaneous speakers, and unknown and time-varying number of speakers.

4. Tracking algorithms

In this section, a brief review of tracking algorithms is presented which covers the following topics: Bayesian statistical methods, visual and audio-visual algorithms and non-linear filtering approaches.

Recall that in Section 1, tracking methods are either stochastic and model-driven or deterministic and data-driven [25].

The stochastic approaches are based on the Bayesian framework which uses a state-space approach [82]. Representative methods in this category are the Kalman filter (KF) [30], extended Kalman filter (EKF) [83, 84] and particle filter (PF) [11]. The PF approach is more robust as compared to the KF and EKF approaches as it can approach the Bayesian optimal estimate with a sufficiently large number of particles [11]. It has been widely applied to speaker tracking problems [29, 76, 81]. The PF is used to fuse object shapes and audio information in Refs. [29, 81]. In Ref. [76], independent audio and video observation models are fused for simultaneous tracking and detection of multiple speakers. However, one challenge in PF is to choose an appropriate number of particles. While an insufficient number may lead to particle impoverishment (i.e. loss of diversity among the particles), a larger number (than required) will induce additional computational cost. Therefore, the performance of the tracker depends on the number of particles that are estimated as an optimal value.

The PHD filter [85] is another stochastic method based on the finite-set statistics (FISST) theory, which propagates the first-order moment of a dynamic point process. The PHD filter is used in many application areas after its proposal and some applications with speaker tracking are reported in Refs. [37, 73]. It has an advantage over other Bayesian approaches such as Kalman and PF filters, in that the number of targets does not need to be known in advance since it is estimated in each iteration. The issue in the PHD filter is that it is prone to estimation error in the number of speakers in the case of low signal-to-noise ratio [36]. The reason is that the PHD filter restricts the propagation of multi-target posterior to the first-order distribution moment, resulting in loss of information for higher order cardinality. To address this issue, the cardinality distribution is also propagated with PHD distribution in the cardinalized PHD (CPHD) filter which improves the estimation of the target number [36, 86] and state of the speakers [74]. However, additional distribution for cardinality requires extra computational load, which makes the CPHD computationally more expensive than the PHD filter. Moreover, the spawning of new targets is not modelled explicitly in the CPHD filter.

As a deterministic and data-driven method, the mean-shift [28] uses representation of the target for localization, which is based on minimizing an appropriate cost function. In that sense, a similarity function is defined in Ref. [32] to reduce the state estimation problem to a search in the region of interest. To obtain fast localization, a gradient optimization method is performed. The mean-shift works under the assumption that the representation of the target is sufficiently distinct from the background which may not be always true. Although the mean-shift is an efficient and robust approach, in occlusion and rapid motion scenarios [87, 88], it may fail when the target is out of the region of interest, in other words, the search area.

Many approaches have been proposed in the literature to address these problems in mean-shift tracking, which can be categorized into two groups. One group [87, 89–91] improves the mean-shift tracking by, for example, introducing adaptive estimation of the search area, iteration number and bin number. In the other group, the mean-shift algorithm is combined with other methods such as particle filter [46–49]. The stochastic and deterministic approaches are integrated under the same framework in many studies. Particle filtering (stochastic) is integrated with a variation approach (deterministic) in Ref. [25] where the 'switching search' algorithm is run for all the particles. In this algorithm, the momentum of the particles is compared with a pre-determined threshold value, and if it is smaller than the threshold, the deterministic search is run; otherwise, the particles are propagated in terms of a stochastic motion model.

The particle filtering and mean-shift are combined in Ref. [48] under the name of mean-shift embedded particle filter (MSEPF). It is inspired by Sullivan and Rittscher [25], but the mean shift is used as a variational method. It is aimed to integrate the advantages of the particle filtering and mean-shift method. The MSEPF has a capability to track the target with a small number of particles as the mean-shift search concentrates on the particles around local modes (maxima) of the observation. To deal with the possible changes in illuminations, a skin colour model is used and updated for every frame. As an observation model, colour and motion cues are employed. To use a multi-cue observation model, the mean-shift analysis is modified and applied to all the particles. Resampling (selective resampling) is, then, applied when the effective sample size is too small. The mean-shift and particle filtering methods are used independently in Ref. [46]. The estimated positions of the target obtained by these two methods are compared using the Bhattacharyya distance at every iteration and the best value is chosen as the estimated position of the target to avoid the algorithm from being trapped to a local maximum, and thus finding the true maximum beyond the local one.

A hybrid particle with a mean-shift tracker is proposed in Ref. [92] which works in a similar manner to that in Ref. [48]. Alternatively, [92] uses the original application of the mean-shift and performs the mean-shift process on all the particles to reach the local maxima. Moreover, an adaptive motion model is used to deal with manoeuvring targets, which have a high speed of movement. The kernel particle filter is proposed in Ref. [93] where small perturbations are added to the states of the particles after the mean-shift iteration to prevent the gradient ascent from being stopped too early in the density. Kernel radius is calculated adaptively every iteration and this method is applied to multiple target tracking using multiple hypotheses which are then evaluated and assigned to possible targets. An adaptive mean-shift tracking with auxiliary particles is proposed in Ref. [49]. As long as the conditions are met, such as the target remaining in the region of interest, and there are no serious distractions, the mean-shift is used as the main tracker. When sudden motions or distractions are detected by the motion estimator, auxiliary particles are introduced to support the mean-shift tracker. As the mean shift may diverge from the target and converge on the background, background/foreground feature selection is applied to minimize the tracking error. Even though this study is inspired by Sullivan and Rittscher [25], where the main tracker is a particle filter, in Ref. [49], the main tracker is the mean-shift. In addition, the switched trackers are used to handle sudden movements, occlusion and distractions. Moreover, to maintain tracking even when the target appearance is affected by illumination or view point, the target model is updated online.

In the literature, several frameworks have been proposed to combine the mean-shift and particle filters. However, it is still required to have an explicitly designed framework for a variable number of targets. Both the mean-shift and particle filter were derived for tracking only a single target. To address this issue, the PHD filter is found as a promising solution as it is originally designed for multi-target tracking. However, the PHD filter does not have closed-form solutions as the recursion of the PHD filter includes multi-dimensional integrals. To derive analytical solution of the PHD filter, the particle filter or sequential Monte Carlo (SMC) implementation [44] is introduced which leads to SMC-PHD filtering. In Ref. [14], the mean-shift is integrated with standard SMC-PHD filtering, aiming at improving computational efficiency and estimation accuracy of the tracker for a variable number of targets.

Besides the tracking methods explained so far, speaker tracking with multi-modal usage introduces a problem which is known as data association. Each measurement coming from multi-modality needs to be associated with an appropriate target. Data association methods are divided into two classes [94]. Unique neighbour is the first data association, and a representative method in this class is multiple hypothesis tracking (MHT). Here, each existing track is associated with one of the measurements. All-neighbours data association belongs to the second class which uses all the measurements for updating the entire track estimate, for example, the joint probabilistic data association (JPDA). In MHT, the association between a target state and the measurements is maintained by multiple hypotheses. However, the required number of hypotheses increases exponentially over time [95]. In JPDA, separate Gaussian distributions for each target [96] are used to approximate the posterior target distribution which results in an extra computational cost. Data association algorithms in target-tracking applications with Bayesian methods and the PHD filter can be found in [20, 97–100]. However, it is found that classical data association algorithms are computationally expensive which lead to the fusion of multi-modal measurements inside the proposed framework [8, 9, 29, 73, 80, 81, 83]. As in Refs. [8, 9], audio and visual modalities are fused in the steps of the visual particle filter.

Among the methods explained above, the PF, RFS, PHD filter and mean-shift are the main methods discussed throughout this chapter and the main concepts of the methods are presented below.

4.1. Particle filtering

The PF became widely used tools in tracking after being proposed by Isard et al. [31] due to its ability to handle non-linear and non-Gaussian problems. The main idea of the PF is to represent a posterior density by a set of random particles with associated weights, and then compute estimates based on these samples and weights [101]. The principle of the particle filter is illustrated in **Figure 1**. Ten particles are initialized with equal weights in the first step.

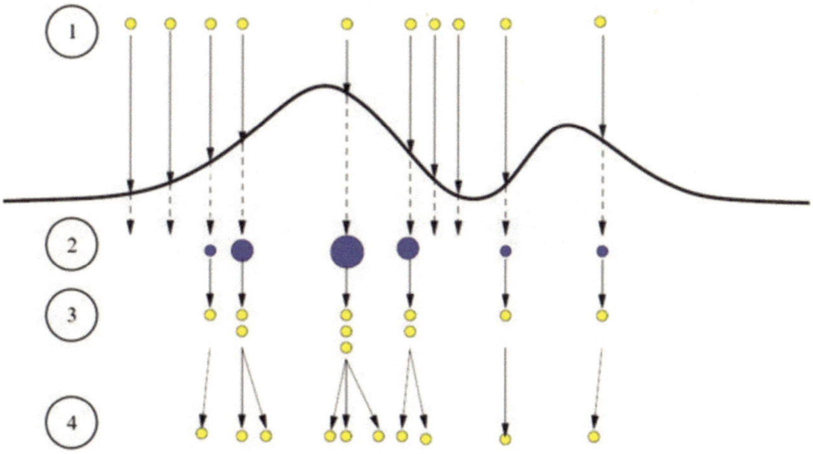

Figure 1. Steps of the particle filter. The first step is particle initialization with equal weights. The particles are weighted in the second step. After a resampling step is performed in the third step, the particles are distributed to predict the next state in the fourth step. This figure is adapted from Ref. [102].

In the second step, the particles are weighted based on given measurements, and as a result, some particles require small weights while others require larger weights represented by the size of the particles. The state distribution is represented by these weighted particles. Then, a resampling step is performed which selects the particles with large weights to generate a set of new particles with equal weights in the third step. In step four, these new particles are distributed again to predict the next state. This loop continues from steps two through four until all the observations are exhausted.

Although there are various extensions of the PF in the literature, the basic concept is the same and based on the idea of representing the posterior distribution by a set of particles.

4.2. Random finite set and PHD filtering

The generic PF is designed for single-target tracking. Multi-target tracking is more complicated than single-target tracking as it is necessary to jointly estimate the number of targets and the state of the targets. One multi-target tracking scenario is illustrated in **Figure 2a**, where five targets exist in state space (bottom plane) given at the previous time with eight measurements in observation space (upper plane). In this scenario, the number of measurements is larger than the number of targets due to clutter or noise. When the targets are passed to the current time, the number of targets becomes three and two targets no longer exist.

In that sense, the variable number of targets and noisy measurements need to be handled for reliable tracking in multi-target case. The RFS approach [36] is an elegant solution to address this issue. The basic idea behind the RFS approach is to treat the collection of targets as a set-valued state called the multi-target state and the collection of measurements as a set-valued observation, called multi-observation. So, the problem of estimating multiple targets in the presence of clutter and uncertainty is handled by modelling these set-valued entities as

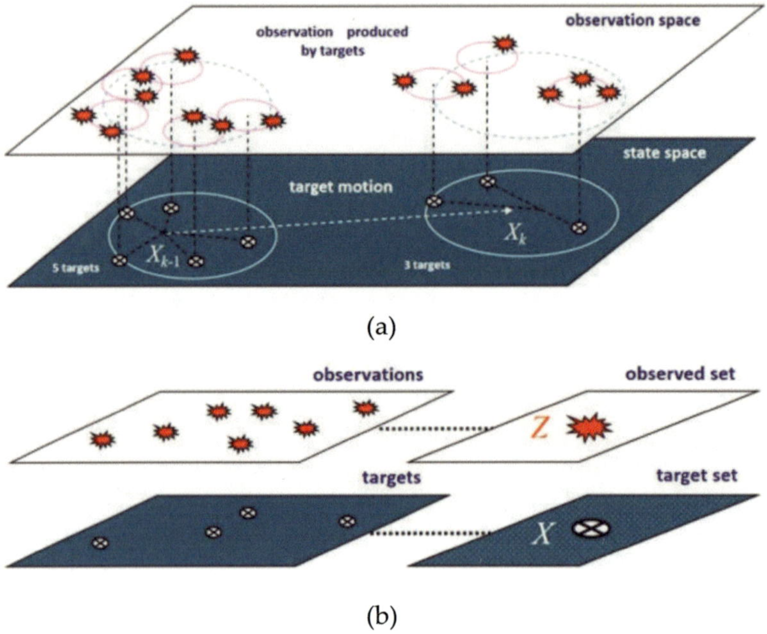

Figure 2. An illustration of the RFS theory in a multi-target tracking application. One possible multi-target tracking scenario is given in (a), and (b) represents the RFS approach to multi-target tracking. The figures are adapted from Ref. [103].

random finite sets [41]. The point here is to generalize the tracking problem from single target to multiple targets.

Figure 2b illustrates the RFS approach where all the targets are collected in one target set and all the measurements are considered as one measurement set. The RFS propagates the full multi-target posterior for multi-target filtering. The state model of the RFS incorporates individual target dynamics which are target birth, target spawn and target death. In addition, the observation model of the RFS incorporates the measurement likelihood as target detection uncertainty (miss-detection) and clutter (false alarm). These incorporations are implemented by assigning hypotheses, and all possible associations between hypotheses and measurement/targets need to be repeated at every time step, resulting in increased computational cost in the case of a high number of targets and measurements.

To alleviate the computational cost, the PHD filter is introduced which is a computationally cheaper alternative to the RFS. The PHD filter is the first-order approximation of the RFS and propagates only the first-order moments instead of the full multi-target posterior [44, 104]. The PHD filter function is denoted as the intensity $v(x)$ whose integral on any region of the state space gives the expected number of targets. The peaks of the PHD function point the highest local concentration of the expected number of targets, which can be used to provide estimates of individual targets [36]. The PHD filter is illustrated in **Figure 3** by a simple example [36] which corresponds to Eq. (1)

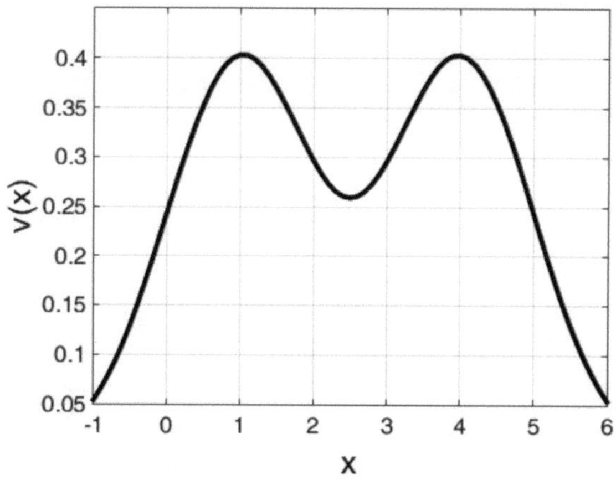

Figure 3. A simple example for the PHD filter. This figure is adapted from Ref. [36].

$$v(x) = \mathcal{N}_{\sigma^2}(x-a) + \mathcal{N}_{\sigma^2}(x-b) = \frac{1}{\sqrt{2\pi}\sigma}\left[\exp\left(-\frac{(x-a)^2}{2\sigma^2}\right) + \exp\left(-\frac{(x-b)^2}{2\sigma^2}\right)\right] \quad (1)$$

Figure 3 is plotted for Eq. (1) with $\sigma = 1$, $a = 1$ and $b = 4$. The peaks of $v(x)$ is near the target locations $x = 1$ and $x = 4$.

The integral of $v(x)$ computes the actual number of targets Ξ:

$$\Xi = \int v(x)dx = \int \mathcal{N}_{(\sigma)^2}(x-a)dx + \int \mathcal{N}_{(\sigma)^2}(x-b)dx = 1 + 1 = 2 \quad (2)$$

4.3. Mean-shift tracking

Different from stochastic approaches such as the PF, RFS and PHD filter, the mean-shift is a deterministic method [28]. The mean-shift can be defined as a simple iterative procedure that shifts each data point to the average of data points in its neighbourhood [105].

Common application areas are clustering [106], mode seeking [107], image segmentation [108] and tracking [109]. Simple implementation of the mean-shift method is illustrated in **Figure 4** where the purpose is to find the densest region of the distributed balls. The first step is to select an initial point with the region of interest as shown in **Figure 4a** where the circle indicates the region of interest centred on the initial point. In **Figure 4b**, the centre of the mass is calculated using the balls inside the region of interest. To get the distance and direction for shifting the initial point, the mean-shift vector is calculated in **Figure 4c**. The initial point is shifted to a new point together with the region of interest in **Figure 4d**. The centre of the mass is calculated again using the balls inside the region of interest which leads to new mass point in **Figure 4e**. The mean-shift vector is calculated to obtain the direction and distance for shifting and the region of interest is shifted to a new point as illustrated in **Figures 4f** and **g**, respectively. This iteration continues until the mean-shift method reaches the densest point in **Figure 4h**.

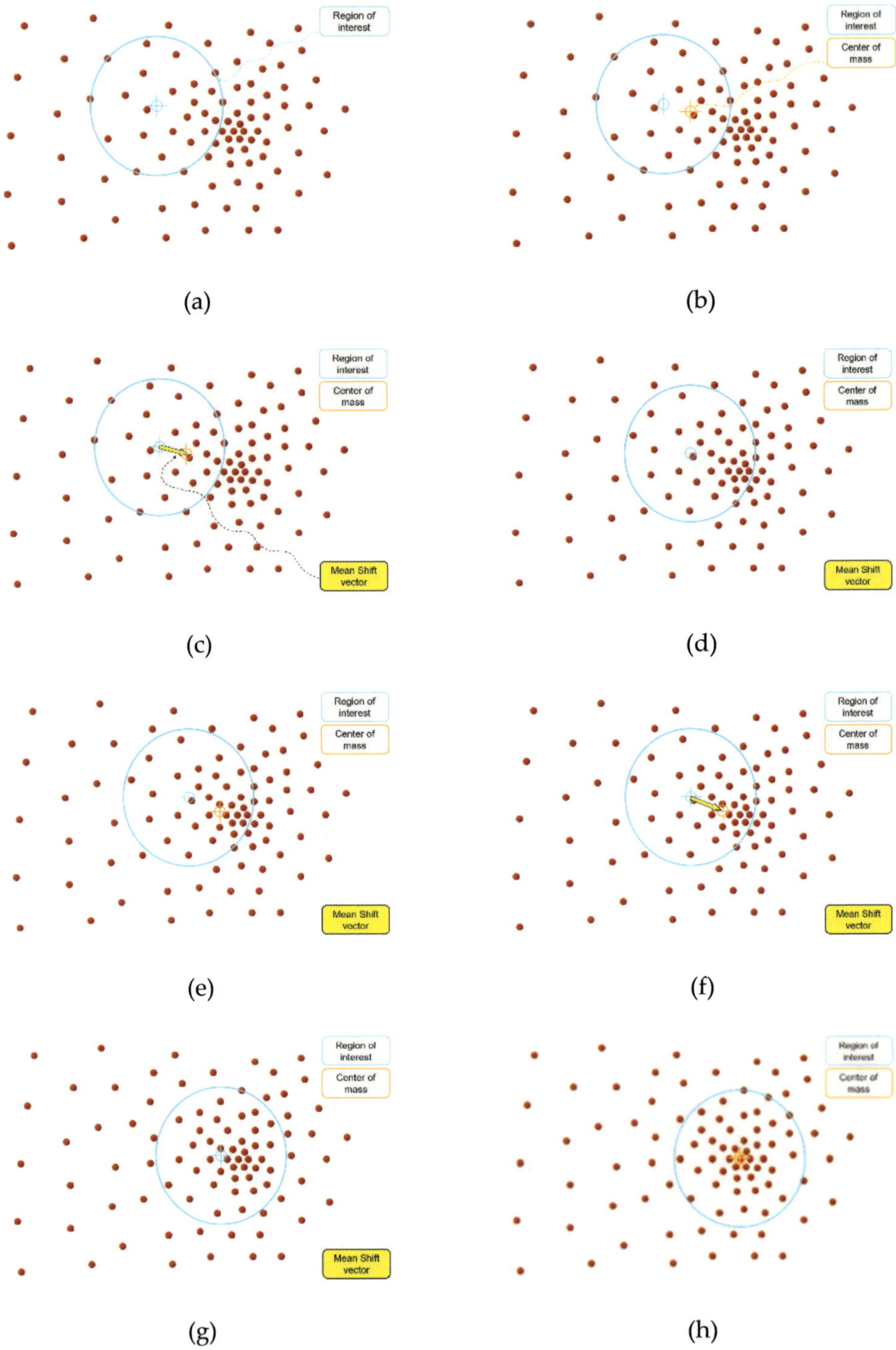

Figure 4. Simple descriptions of the mean-shift process. These figures are adapted from Ref. [110].

5. Relevant datasets

In order to perform a quantitative evaluation of the audio-visual tracker, both audio and video sequences are required. In that sense, several datasets are presented in the literature that combine multiple audio and video sources for tracking.

The augmented multi-party interaction (AMI) [111] corpus includes 100 h of meetings, which were recorded in English using three different rooms. Natural conversations are included in some of the meetings, and many others, in particular those using a scenario in which the participants play different roles in a design team, are also reasonably natural. The number of speakers in the natural conversations varies from three to five. In one artificial meeting, four speakers are involved, taking four pre-arranged roles (as industrial designer, interface designer, marketing and project manager). Other artificial meetings also appear in the AMI corpus, such as a film club scenario. Generally, the speakers are mostly static or with small movements. In addition, calibration information is not available which is required for 3D tracking as it is needed to project the coordinates from the two-dimensional (2D) image into 3D space.

CLEAR (CLassification of Events, Activities and Relationships) is the next dataset created for people identification, activities, human-human interaction and relevant scenarios [112]. Recordings are captured with multiple users in realistic meeting rooms equipped with a multitude of audio-visual sensors. The rooms have five calibrated cameras, and four of them are mounted to the corners of the room while the last panoramic camera is mounted to the ceiling of the room. All cameras are synchronized with the audio streams collected by the linear microphone array placed on the walls. In most scenarios, the speakers are generally still and seated around the table. They speak one by one.

Another dataset is SPEVI (Surveillance performance evaluation initiative) [113] created for single- and multi-modal people detection and tracking. Sequences are captured by a video camera and two linear microphone arrays. The SPEVI dataset has three sequences. The sequences motinas_Room160 and motinas_Room105 are captured in rooms with reverberation. The sequence motinas_Chamber is captured in a reduced reverberation room. In this dataset, audio signals were recorded with linear microphone arrays and the calibration information is not available.

One of the most challenging datasets that can be used for the evaluation of audio-visual tracking algorithm is AV16.3 corpus which is developed by the IDIAP research institute [114]. The corpus AV16.3 involves various scenarios where subjects are moving and speaking at the same time whilst being recorded by three calibrated video cameras and two circular eight-element microphone arrays.

Recordings in the AV16.3 involve challenging scenarios such as object initialization, partial and total occlusion, overlapped speech, illumination change, close and far locations, variable number of objects, and small and large angular separations. Circular microphone arrays were used to record the audio signals at 16 kHz and video sequences were captured at 25 Hz. The recordings of audio and video were performed independently from each other. Each video frame is a colour image of 288 × 360 pixels and some sequences are annotated to get the ground truth (GT) speaker position which allows one to measure the accuracy of each tracker and to compare the performance of the algorithms. In addition, it provides calibration information of the cameras and challenging scenarios like occlusions and moving speakers.

The most recently released dataset is 'S3A speaker tracking with Kinect2' [115, 116] which uses a Kinect for Windows V2.0 for recording the visual data and dummy head for recording the audio data. It contains four sequences in a studio where people are talking and walking slowly around a dummy head which is located at the centre of the room. Different from other cameras, Kinect sensor provides in-depth information besides the colour which helps to extract the 3D position of the speaker without using additional view of the scene. In addition, annotated data are provided which can be used as ground truth data to estimate the performance of the tracker.

6. Performance metrics

Several metrics have been proposed to evaluate the performance of tracking methods in the literature. In this section, four metrics are introduced.

The first one is the mean absolute error (MAE), which is computed as the Euclidean distance in pixels between the estimated and the ground truth positions, and then divided by the number of frames. This metric offers simplicity and explicit output for the performance comparison.

The multiple object tracking (MOT) metric is the next metric which was proposed in Ref. [117]. It is defined with MOT precision (MOTP) and MOT accuracy (MOTA) quantities. The precision is measured with the MOTP using a pre-defined threshold value

$$MOTP = \frac{\sum_{i,k} d_k^i}{\sum_k c_k} \tag{3}$$

where d_k^i is the distance between the ith object and its corresponding hypothesis and c_k is the number of matches between the objects and hypotheses for time frame k.

Tracking errors are measured with the MOTA which covers the false positives, false negatives and mismatches. If the error is greater than the threshold value, it is assumed that the false positive and false negative count if the speaker is not tracked with the accuracy measured by the threshold. Mismatches are the case where the speaker identity is switched [117]

$$MOTA = 1 - \frac{\sum_k (m_k + fp_k + mm_k)}{\sum_k g_k} \tag{4}$$

where m_k, fp_k, mm_k and g_k define the number of misses (false negatives), false positives, mismatches and objects present, respectively, for the time frame k.

The next metric is the trajectory-based measures (TBMs) proposed in Refs. [118, 119], where the performance is measured based on trajectory. It categorizes the trajectories as mostly

http://dx.doi.org/10.5772/intechopen.68146

tracked (MT), mostly lost (ML) and partially tracked (PT). MT is defined as if the tracker follows at least 80% of its ground truth (GT) trajectory. If the tracker follows less than 20% of its GT, it is called ML. If the followed trajectory is between 20 and 80% of the GT trajectory, it is called PT. Also, track fragmentation (Frag) is defined as the total number of times that GT is interrupted. Identity switches (IDs) are computed by calculating change in GT identity.

OSPA-T (Optimal Subpattern Assignment for Tracks) [120] is the last performance metric designed for the evaluation of multi-speaker tracking systems. It is an improved version of the OSPA metric [121] by extending it for tracking management evaluation. To transfer the cardinality error into the state error, a penalty value is used in the OSPA. So its performance evaluation includes both source number estimation and speaker position estimation:

$$e_{\mathrm{OSPA}}(\hat{\mathcal{X}}_k, \mathcal{X}_k) = \min_{\pi \in \Pi_{\hat{\Xi}_k, \Xi_k}} \sqrt[a]{\frac{1}{\Xi_k}\left(\sum_{i=1}^{\hat{\Xi}_k} \overline{d}^{(c)}(\hat{\mathbf{x}}_{i,k}, \mathbf{x}_{\pi_i,k})^a + c^a(\Xi_k - \hat{\Xi}_k)\right)} \tag{5}$$

where $\hat{\mathcal{X}}_k = \{\hat{\mathbf{x}}_{1,k}, \ldots, \hat{\mathbf{x}}_{\hat{\Xi}_k,k}\}$ is an estimation of the ground-truth state set $\mathcal{X}_k = \{\mathbf{x}_{1,k}, \ldots, \mathbf{x}_{\Xi_k,k}\}$ and $\Pi_{\hat{\Xi}_k,\Xi_k}$ is the set of maps $\pi : 1, \ldots, \hat{\Xi}_k \rightarrow 1, \ldots, \Xi_k$. The state cardinality estimation $\hat{\Xi}_k$ may not be the same as the ground truth Ξ_k. The OSPA error defined in Eq. (5) is for $\hat{\Xi}_k \leq \Xi_k$. If $\Xi_k < \hat{\Xi}_k$, then $e_{\mathrm{OSPA}}(\hat{\mathcal{X}}_k, \mathcal{X}_k) = e_{\mathrm{OSPA}}(\mathcal{X}_k, \hat{\mathcal{X}}_k)$. The function $\overline{d}^{(c)}$ is denoted as $\min(c, \overline{d}(\cdot))$. Here, c is defined as the cut-off value in order to weight the penalties for cardinality and localization errors. Additionally, the metric order is defined by a which determines the sensitivity to outliers. The OSPA-T metric differs from other metrics since it considers not only the position estimation of the speaker but also the estimation of the number of speakers in the evaluation of the tracking results. As OSPA-T measures the error based on these two terms, state (position estimation) and cardinality (number of speaker estimation), it causes ambiguities about how much error is contributed from each term to the final error. In addition to the x_1 and x_2 variables of the state vector, the scale variable, s, may be considered in the evaluation. However, this will cause more ambiguities in the contributions of the terms to the final error and deteriorate the reliability of the metric.

As a summary, four metrics are introduced which evaluate the methods from their own perspectives. To see how well the tracker follows its trajectory, the TBM can be used to measure its performance. If the tracking error needs to be estimated, the MAE or the more advanced option MOT can be used to see how accurately the tracker follows the target. If an unknown and variable number of targets need to be tracked, then the OSPA-T metric is more suitable than the others as it considers both position estimation and the estimated number of targets in the performance evaluation.

7. Experimental results and analysis

In this chapter, six trackers are included to cover the recent paradigms. The trackers are restricted to the ones either for which access to the source code has been permitted or tracker performance has been reported on commonly used datasets.

To deal with the tracking problem for unknown and time-varying number of speakers, Kılıç et al. [14] propose to use particle PHD (SMC-PHD) filter. DOA information is employed as an audio cue and it is integrated with video data under SMC-PHD filter framework. Audio data are used to determine when to propagate and re-allocate surviving, spawned and born particles based on their types. The particles are concentrated around the DOA line, which is drawn from the centre of the microphone array to the estimated speaker position by audio information.

As a baseline algorithm, the visual SMC-PHD (V-SMC-PHD) filter, which uses colour information as a visual cue, is compared with the audio-visual SMC-PHD (AV-SMC-PHD) to see the advantage of using multi-modal information in challenging tracking scenarios like occlusion. Sequence 24 from AV16.3 dataset is run for V-SMC-PHD and AV-SMC-PHD, and tracking results are given in **Figure 5**.

The first row shows the results of V-SMC-PHD filter which fails to track after occlusion. Also, it shows poor performance before the occlusion in terms of the detection of the speakers. It is reported in Ref. [14] that the AV-SMC-PHD filter tracks the speakers more accurately and shows better performance than the V-SMC-PHD filter in terms of accuracy and ability for re-detection of the speakers after lost.

The same experiments are repeated for three-speaker case using Sequence 45 camera #3 from the AV16.3 dataset and the results are given in **Figure 6**. It is reported in Ref. [14] that AV-SMC-

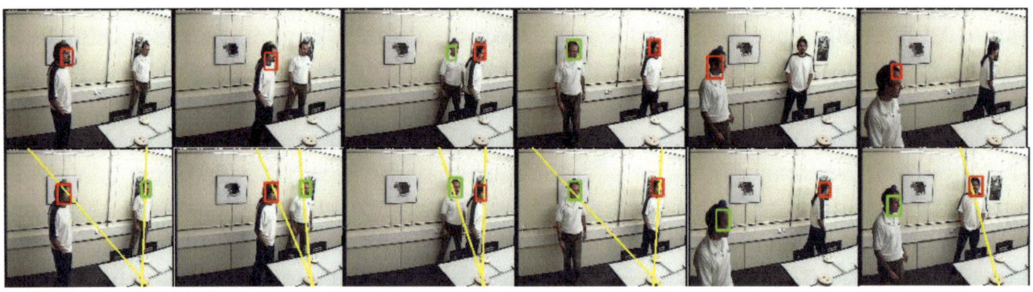

Figure 5. AV16.3, sequence 24 camera #1: occlusions with two speakers [14]. Performance of the V-SMC-PHD filter is shown in the first row. The second row is given for the AV-SMC-PHD filter.

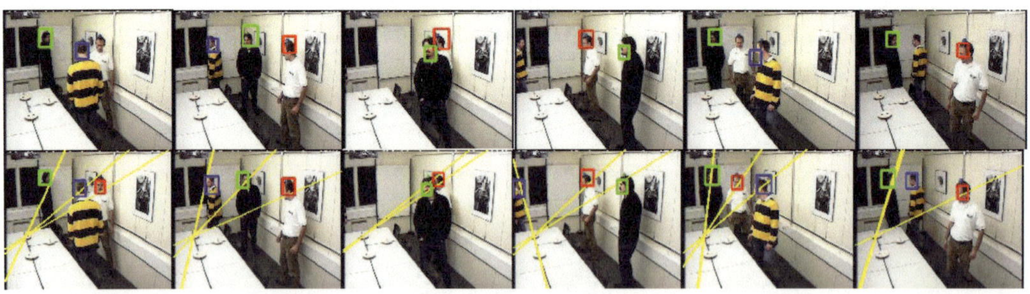

Figure 6. AV16.3, sequence 45 camera #3: occlusions with three speakers [14]. The tracking results of the V-SMC-PHD and the AV-SMC-PHD filters are shown in the first and second rows, respectively.

PHD filter has better capability in detecting and following all the speakers even after the occlusions.

To improve the estimation accuracy of the AV-SMC-PHD filter, [12] integrates the mean-shift method in order to shift the particles to a local maximum of the distribution function which drives particles closer the speaker position. The generic mean-shift algorithm is modified for multiple-speaker case and applied after the audio contribution to the particles, and this algorithm is named as AVMS-SMC-PHD filter.

Even though the integration of the mean-shift improves the estimation accuracy, applying the mean-shift process to all the particles introduces extra computational cost [12]. To address this problem, [12] proposes a sparse sampling scheme which chooses sparse particles and runs the mean-shift method only on those particles rather than all the particles which results in a significant reduction in computational cost. This method is named as sparse-AVMS-SMC-PHD filter. Another tracking algorithm is given in Ref. [122], which uses the merits of dictionary learning for multi-speaker tracking. It is tested using some sequences (seq24, seq25 and seq30) of the AV16.3 dataset.

The results of these five trackers on sequences of AV16.3 are given in **Table 1** and the OSPA-T metric is used for comparison. The tracker in Ref. [122] outperforms the V-SMC-PHD; however, the AVMS-SMC-PHD shows better performance than the others.

These tracking results are compared with those of [123] which uses the PHD filter for tracking and reports the results only for seq24 cam1 and cam2 in terms of Wasserstein distance. **Table 2** shows the results of six trackers.

		Tracking algorithm #1 [122]	V SMC-PHD [14]	AV SMC-PHD [14]	AVMS SMC-PHD [14]	Sparse AVMS SMC-PHD [14]
seq24	cam1	22.28	27.12	17.71	13.93	14.50
	cam2	17.60	25.91	19.83	14.97	15.35
	cam3	28.18	24.32	18.94	14.12	15.72
seq25	cam1	21.49	25.84	19.13	15.72	17.17
	cam2	19.17	25.66	18.47	13.93	15.39
	cam3	29.35	29.99	21.61	17.07	17.62
seq30	cam1	35.98	35.60	25.22	16.65	19.27
	cam2	28.40	24.97	19.37	14.86	16.16
	cam3	34.60	37.64	25.31	19.29	19.67
seq45	cam1	NA	48.68	29.46	22.95	23.40
	cam2	NA	39.24	29.47	21.47	23.16
	cam3	NA	39.09	28.43	22.43	23.80
Average		**26.34**	**32.01**	**22.75**	**17.28**	**18.43**

Table 1. Comparison results of the tracking algorithms for the AV16.3 dataset using the OSPA-T metric [14].

seq24	Tracking algorithm #1 [122]	Tracking algorithm #2 [123]	V SMC-PHD [14]	AV SMC-PHD [14]	AVMS SMC-PHD [14]	Sparse AVMS SMC-PHD [14]
cam1	9.02	7.20	16.96	7.94	6.67	7.45
cam2	6.40	4.80	19.17	7.59	5.24	5.73
Average	**7.71**	**6.00**	**18.06**	**7.76**	**5.96**	**6.59**

Table 2. Tracking algorithms are compared in terms of mean Wasserstein distance (in pixel) [14].

Among six trackers, the AVMS-SMC-PHD outperforms the other trackers in terms of the average accuracy.

The trackers of [14] are also tested in different datasets. One sequence from each AMI and CLEAR dataset is used to test the trackers. **Figure 7** shows the results of V-SMC-PHD and AV-SMC-PHD for a sequence of the AMI dataset. In this dataset, the speakers talk one by one. Hence, one DOA line is drawn per time instance. Since the speakers remain still, the visual trackers do not fail to track the speakers.

Other sequence is UKA_20060726 from the CLEAR dataset where the speakers talk one by one and mostly sit around the table. The performance of visual and audio-visual trackers is given in **Figure 8**.

The average error of the trackers for sequences IS1001a and UKA_20060726 is given in **Table 3** in terms of the OSPA-T metric. It is reported in Ref. [14] that there is no significant difference on the performance of the visual and audio-visual trackers since the speakers talk one by one. The audio-visual tracker runs as a visual tracker for the silent speakers, while it is more

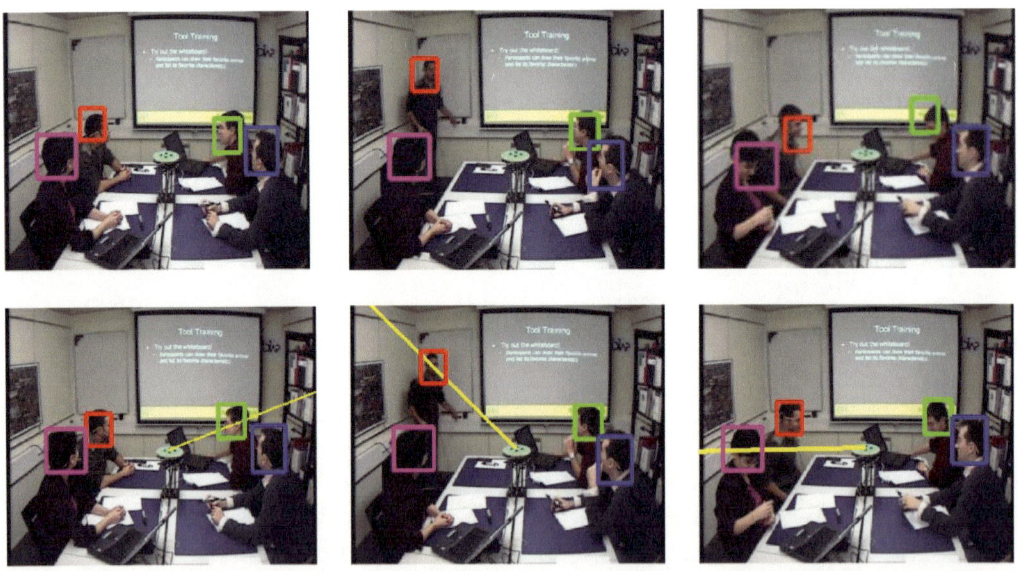

Figure 7. AMI dataset, sequence IS1001a. The first and second rows show the results of the V-SMC-PHD and the AV-SMC-PHD filter, respectively [14].

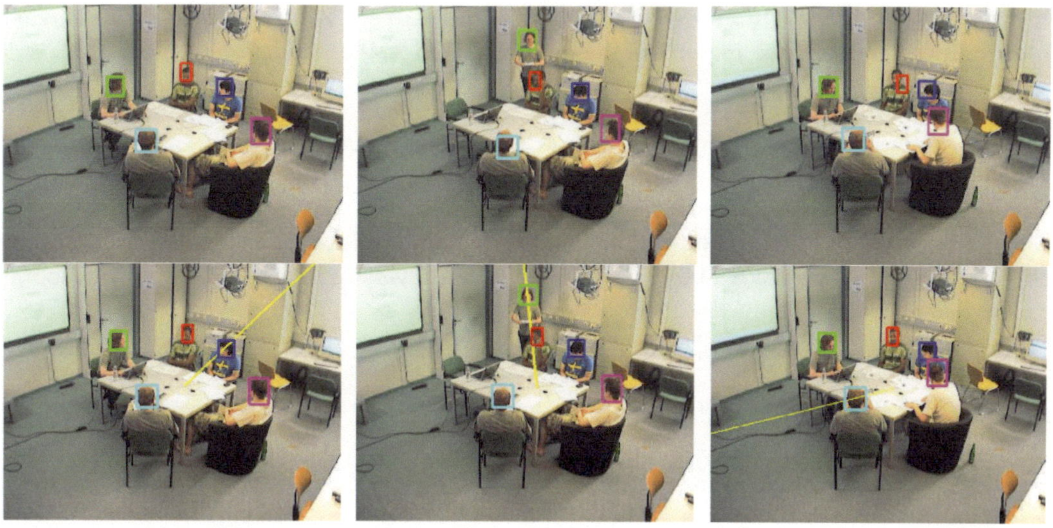

Figure 8. CLEAR dataset, sequence UKA_20060726. The first and second rows show the results of the V-SMC-PHD and the AV-SMC-PHD filters, respectively [14].

Sequences	V SMC-PHD [14]	AV SMC-PHD [14]	AVMS SMC-PHD [14]	Sparse AVMS SMC-PHD [14]
IS1001a	25.32	21.51	18.91	20.37
UKA_20060726	28.33	25.94	23.14	24.82

Table 3. Comparison results of the tracking algorithms for the AMI and CLEAR dataset.

effective for the talking speakers because of the additional information coming from audio modality.

8. Chapter summary

In this chapter, a review of multi-speaker tracking has been provided on modalities, existing tracking techniques, datasets and performance metrics that have been developed over the past few decades.

After a broad survey of the tracking methods, a technical background of the methods such as particle filtering, random finite set, PHD filter and mean-shift, which are commonly used as baseline methods in the literature, is introduced with their basic mathematical, statistical concepts and definitions, which are required for understanding the mathematics and techniques behind the proposed tracking algorithms.

In order to perform a quantitative evaluation of the proposed algorithms, both audio and video sequences are required. Publicly available datasets such as AV16.3, CLEAR, AMI, SPEVI and S3A were introduced with the fundamental differences including physical setup, scenarios and challenges.

Moreover, performance metrics were analysed in order to see which aspects are considered more in the evaluation and impacts of these perspectives on the evaluation results.

Acknowledgements

This work was supported in part by the Engineering and Physical Sciences Research Council (EPSRC) Grant number EP/K014307/2 and the MOD University Defence Research Collaboration in Signal Processing.

Author details

Volkan Kılıç[1]* and Wenwu Wang[2]

*Address all correspondence to: volkan.kilic@ikc.edu.tr

1 Izmir Katip Celebi University, Izmir, Turkey

2 University of Surrey, Guildford, UK

References

[1] Liu Q, et al. Automating camera management for lecture room environments. In: Proceedings of the SIGCHI Conference on Human Factors in Computing Systems. ACM; 2001

[2] Talantzis F, Pnevmatikakis A, Constantinides AG. Audio–visual active speaker tracking in cluttered indoors environments. IEEE Transactions on Systems, Man, and Cybernetics, Part B (Cybernetics). 2008;**38**(3):799–807

[3] Wölfel M, McDonough JW. Combining multi-source far distance speech recognition strategies: beamforming, blind channel and confusion network combination. In: INTERSPEECH; 2005

[4] Potamianos G, Neti C, Deligne S. Joint audio-visual speech processing for recognition and enhancement. In: AVSP 2003-International Conference on Audio-Visual Speech Processing; 2003

[5] Naphade MR, et al. Probabilistic multimedia objects (multijects): A novel approach to video indexing and retrieval in multimedia systems. In: ICIP 98. Proceedings of the 1998 International Conference on Image Processing. IEEE; 1998

[6] Shivappa ST, Rao BD, Trivedi MM. Audio-visual fusion and tracking with multilevel iterative decoding: Framework and experimental evaluation. IEEE Journal of Selected Topics in Signal Processing. 2010;**4(5)**:882–894

[7] Hampapur A, et al. Smart video surveillance: exploring the concept of multiscale spatiotemporal tracking. IEEE Signal Processing Magazine. 2005;**22(2)**:38–51

[8] Kılıç V, et al. Audio constrained particle filter based visual tracking. In: 2013 IEEE International Conference on Acoustics, Speech and Signal Processing. IEEE; 2013

[9] Kılıç V, et al. Audio assisted robust visual tracking with adaptive particle filtering. IEEE Transactions on Multimedia. 2015;**17**(2):186–200

[10] Katsaggelos AK, Bahaadini S, Molina R. Audiovisual fusion: Challenges and new approaches. Proceedings of the IEEE. 2015;**103(9)**:1635–1653

[11] Atrey PK, et al. Multimodal fusion for multimedia analysis: A survey. Multimedia Systems. 2010;**16(6)**:345–379

[12] Germa T, et al. Vision and RFID data fusion for tracking people in crowds by a mobile robot. Computer Vision and Image Understanding. 2010;**114(6)**:641–651

[13] Liu Q, et al. Identity association using PHD filters in multiple head tracking with depth sensors. In: 2016 IEEE International Conference on Acoustics, Speech and Signal Processing (ICASSP). IEEE; 2016

[14] Kılıç V, et al. Mean-shift and sparse sampling-based SMC-PHD filtering for audio informed visual speaker tracking. IEEE Transactions on Multimedia. 2016;**18**(12):2417–2431

[15] Kilic V. Audio-visual tracking of multiple moving speakers [PhD thesis]. University of Surrey; 2016

[16] Smeulders AW, et al. Visual tracking: An experimental survey. IEEE Transactions on Pattern Analysis and Machine Intelligence. 2014;**36(7)**:1442–1468

[17] Liu Q, Zhao X, Hou Z. Survey of single-target visual tracking methods based on online learning. IET Computer Vision. 2014;**8(5)**:419–428

[18] Walia GS, Kapoor R. Human detection in video and images—a state-of-the-art survey. International Journal of Pattern Recognition and Artificial Intelligence. 2014;**28 (03)**:1455004

[19] Fallon MF, Godsill SJ. Acoustic source localization and tracking of a time-varying number of speakers. IEEE Transactions on Audio, Speech, and Language Processing. 2012;**20 (4)**:1409–1415

[20] Potamitis I, Chen H, Tremoulis G. Tracking of multiple moving speakers with multiple microphone arrays. IEEE Transactions on Speech and Audio Processing. 2004;**12(5)**:520–529

[21] Barnard M, Wang W. Audio head pose estimation using the direct to reverberant speech ratio. Speech Communication. 2016;**85**:98–108

[22] Lanz O. Approximate Bayesian multibody tracking. IEEE Transactions on Pattern Analysis and Machine Intelligence. 2006;**28(9)**:1436–1449

[23] Beal MJ, Jojic N, Attias H. A graphical model for audiovisual object tracking. IEEE Transactions on Pattern Analysis and Machine Intelligence. 2003;**25(7)**: 828–836

[24] Walia GS, Kapoor R. Recent advances on multicue object tracking: A survey. Artificial Intelligence Review. 2016;**46(1)**:1–39

[25] Sullivan J, Rittscher J. Guiding random particles by deterministic search. In: ICCV 2001. Proceedings of the Eighth IEEE International Conference on Computer Vision. IEEE; 2001

[26] Zhou SK, Chellappa R, Moghaddam B. Visual tracking and recognition using appearance-adaptive models in particle filters. IEEE Transactions on Image Processing. 2004;**13 (11)**:1491–1506

[27] Comaniciu D, Meer P. Mean shift: A robust approach toward feature space analysis. IEEE Transactions on Pattern Analysis and Machine Intelligence. 2002;**24(5)**:603–619

[28] Comaniciu D, Ramesh V, Meer P. Kernel-based object tracking. IEEE Transactions on Pattern Analysis and Machine Intelligence. 2003;**25(5)**:564–577

[29] Gatica-Perez D, et al. Audio-visual speaker tracking with importance particle filters. In: ICIP 2003. Proceedings of the 2003 International Conference on Image Processing. IEEE; 2003

[30] Bar-Shalom Y. Tracking and Data Association. Academic Press Professional, Inc.; 1987

[31] Isard M, Blake A. Condensation—Conditional density propagation for visual tracking. International Journal of Computer Vision. 1998;**29(1)**:5–28

[32] Kılıç V, et al. Adaptive particle filtering approach to audio-visual tracking. In: Signal Processing Conference (EUSIPCO), 2013 Proceedings of the 21st European. IEEE; 2013

[33] Closas P, Fernández-Prades C. Particle filtering with adaptive number of particles. In: Aerospace Conference. IEEE; 2011

[34] Fox D. Adapting the sample size in particle filters through KLD-sampling. The International Journal of Robotics Research. 2003;**22(12)**:985–1003

[35] Soto A. Self Adaptive Particle Filter. In: IJCAI; 2005

[36] Mahler RP. Statistical Multisource-Multitarget Information Fusion. Boston, MA, USA: Artech House, Inc.; 2007

[37] Vo B.-N, Singh SS, Ma W-K. Tracking multiple speakers using random sets. In: ICASSP (2); 2004

[38] Kılıç V, et al. Audio-visual tracking of a variable number of speakers with a random finite set approach. In: 2014 17th International Conference on Information Fusion (FUSION). IEEE; 2014

[39] Tang X, et al. A multiple-detection probability hypothesis density filter. IEEE Transactions on Signal Processing. 2015;**63(8)**:2007–2019

[40] Mahler RP. Multitarget Bayes filtering via first-order multitarget moments. IEEE Transactions on Aerospace and Electronic Systems. 2003;**39(4)**:1152–1178

[41] Vo B-N, Ma W-K. A closed-form solution for the probability hypothesis density filter. In: 2005 7th International Conference on Information Fusion. IEEE; 2005

[42] Vo B-N, Ma W-K. The Gaussian mixture probability hypothesis density filter. IEEE Transactions on Signal Processing. 2006;**54(11)**:4091–4104

[43] Vo B-N, Singh S, Doucet A. Sequential Monte Carlo implementation of the PHD filter for multi-target tracking. In: Proceedings of the International Conference on Information Fusion; 2003

[44] Vo B-N, Singh S, Doucet A. Sequential Monte Carlo methods for multitarget filtering with random finite sets. IEEE Transactions on Aerospace and Electronic Systems. 2005;**41(4)**:1224–1245

[45] Kılıç V, et al. Audio informed visual speaker tracking with SMC-PHD filter. In: 2015 IEEE International Conference on Multimedia and Expo (ICME). IEEE; 2015

[46] Deguchi K, Kawanaka O, Okatani T. Object tracking by the mean-shift of regional color distribution combined with the particle-filter algorithms. In: ICPR 2004. Proceedings of the 17th International Conference on Pattern Recognition. IEEE; 2004

[47] Shan C, Tan T, Wei Y. Real-time hand tracking using a mean shift embedded particle filter. Pattern Recognition. 2007;**40(7)**:1958–1970

[48] Shan C, et al. Real time hand tracking by combining particle filtering and mean shift. In: Proceedings of the Sixth IEEE International Conference on Automatic Face and Gesture Recognition. IEEE; 2004

[49] Wang J, Yagi Y. Adaptive mean-shift tracking with auxiliary particles. IEEE Transactions on Systems, Man, and Cybernetics, Part B (Cybernetics). 2009;**39(6)**:1578–1589

[50] Zoidi O, Tefas A, Pitas I. Visual object tracking based on local steering kernels and color histograms. IEEE Transactions on Circuits and Systems for Video Technology. 2013;**23 (5)**:870–882

[51] Dardari D, Closas P, Djurić PM. Indoor tracking: Theory, methods, and technologies. IEEE Transactions on Vehicular Technology. 2015;**64(4)**:1263–1278

[52] Yang C, Duraiswami R, Davis L. Efficient mean-shift tracking via a new similarity measure. In: 2005 IEEE Computer Society Conference on Computer Vision and Pattern Recognition (CVPR'05). IEEE; 2005

[53] Raja Y, McKenna SJ, Gong S. Segmentation and tracking using colour mixture models. In: Asian Conference on Computer Vision. Springer; 1998

[54] Yilmaz A, Li X, Shah M. Contour-based object tracking with occlusion handling in video acquired using mobile cameras. IEEE Transactions on Pattern Analysis and Machine Intelligence. 2004;**26(11)**:1531–1536

[55] Wang Y, Lee O. Active mesh-a feature seeking and tracking image sequence representation scheme. IEEE Transactions on Image Processing. 1994;**3**(5):610–624

[56] Micilotta AS, Ong E-J, Bowden R. Real-time upper body detection and 3D pose estimation in monoscopic images. In: European Conference on Computer Vision. Springer; 2006

[57] Fergus R, Perona P, Zisserman A. Object class recognition by unsupervised scale-invariant learning. In: Proceedings of the 2003 IEEE Computer Society Conference on Computer Vision and Pattern Recognition. IEEE; 2003

[58] Shotton J, et al. Textonboost for image understanding: Multi-class object recognition and segmentation by jointly modeling texture, layout, and context. International Journal of Computer Vision. 2009;**81(1)**:2–23

[59] Winn J, Criminisi A, Minka T. Object categorization by learned universal visual dictionary. In: Tenth IEEE International Conference on Computer Vision (ICCV'05). Vol. 1. IEEE; 2005

[60] Manjunath BS, Ma W-Y. Texture features for browsing and retrieval of image data. IEEE Transactions on Pattern Analysis and Machine Intelligence. 1996;**18(8)**:837–842

[61] Yang H, et al. Recent advances and trends in visual tracking: A review. Neurocomputing. 2011;**74(18)**:3823–3831

[62] Ojala T, Pietikainen M, Maenpaa T. Multiresolution gray-scale and rotation invariant texture classification with local binary patterns. IEEE Transactions on Pattern Analysis and Machine Intelligence. 2002;**24(7)**:971–987

[63] Perez P, Vermaak J, Blake A. Data fusion for visual tracking with particles. Proceedings of the IEEE. 2004;**92(3)**:495–513

[64] Lowe DG. Distinctive image features from scale-invariant keypoints. International Journal of Computer Vision. 2004;**60(2)**:91–110

[65] Ke Y, Sukthankar R. PCA-SIFT: A more distinctive representation for local image descriptors. In: CVPR 2004. Proceedings of the 2004 IEEE Computer Society Conference on Computer Vision and Pattern Recognition. IEEE; 2004

[66] Sigal L, Sclaroff S, Athitsos V. Estimation and prediction of evolving color distributions for skin segmentation under varying illumination. In: Proceedings of the IEEE Conference on Computer Vision and Pattern Recognition. IEEE; 2000

[67] Brandstein MS, Silverman HF. A practical methodology for speech source localization with microphone arrays. Computer Speech & Language. 1997;**11(2)**:91–126

[68] DiBiase JH, Silverman HF, Brandstein MS. Robust localization in reverberant rooms. In: Microphone Arrays. Springer; 2001. pp. 157–180

[69] Brandstein MS. A framework for speech source localization using sensor arrays. 1995

[70] Schmidt R. Multiple emitter location and signal parameter estimation. IEEE Transactions on Antennas and Propagation. 1986;**34(3)**:276–280

[71] Wang H, Kaveh M. Coherent signal-subspace processing for the detection and estimation of angles of arrival of multiple wide-band sources. IEEE Transactions on Acoustics, Speech, and Signal Processing. 1985;**33(4)**:823–831

[72] Ma W-K, et al. Tracking an unknown time-varying number of speakers using TDOA measurements: a random finite set approach. IEEE Transactions on Signal Processing. 2006;**54(9)**:3291–3304

[73] Nguyen Q, Choi J. Localization and tracking for simultaneous speakers based on time-frequency method and probability hypothesis density filter. In: 2011 IEEE International Conference on Robotics and Biomimetics (ROBIO). IEEE; 2011

[74] Pham NT, Huang W, Ong S. Tracking multiple speakers using CPHD filter. In: Proceedings of the 15th ACM international conference on Multimedia. ACM; 2007

[75] Bernardin K, Gehrig T, Stiefelhagen R. Multi-level particle filter fusion of features and cues for audio-visual person tracking. In: Multimodal Technologies for Perception of Humans. Springer; 2008. pp. 70–81

[76] Checka N, et al. Multiple person and speaker activity tracking with a particle filter. In: Proceedings (ICASSP'04) of the IEEE International Conference on Acoustics, Speech, and Signal Processing. IEEE; 2004

[77] Gatica-Perez D, et al. Audiovisual probabilistic tracking of multiple speakers in meetings. IEEE Transactions on Audio, Speech, and Language Processing. 2007;**15(2)**:601–616

[78] Heuer M, et al. Multi-modal fusion with particle filter for speaker localization and tracking. In: 2011 International Conference on Multimedia Technology (ICMT). IEEE; 2011

[79] Hoseinnezhad R, et al. Bayesian integration of audio and visual information for multi-target tracking using a CB-MeMBer filter. In: 2011 IEEE International Conference on Acoustics, Speech and Signal Processing (ICASSP). IEEE; 2011

[80] Talantzis F, Pnevmatikakis A, Polymenakos LC. Real time audio-visual person tracking. In: 2006 IEEE Workshop on Multimedia Signal Processing. IEEE; 2006

[81] Vermaak J, et al. Sequential Monte Carlo fusion of sound and vision for speaker tracking. In: ICCV 2001. Proceedings of the Eighth IEEE International Conference on Computer Vision; 2001; IEEE

[82] Adams M, Vo B-N, Mahler R. Advances in probabilistic modeling: Applications of stochastic geometry [From the Guest Editors]. IEEE Robotics & Automation Magazine. 2014;**21(2)**:21–24

[83] Gehrig T, et al. Kalman filters for audio-video source localization. In: IEEE Workshop on Applications of Signal Processing to Audio and Acoustics. IEEE; 2005

[84] McGee LA, Schmidt SF. Discovery of the Kalman filter as a practical tool for aerospace and industry. NASA, Moffett Field, CA, USA, NASATM-86847, 1985

[85] Mahler RP. "Statistics 101" for multisensor, multitarget data fusion. IEEE Aerospace and Electronic Systems Magazine. 2004;**19(1)**:53–64

[86] Mahler R. PHD filters of higher order in target number. IEEE Transactions on Aerospace and Electronic Systems. 2007;**43(4)**:1523–1543

[87] Beyan C, Temizel A. Adaptive mean-shift for automated multi object tracking. IET Computer Vision. 2012;**6(1)**:1–12

[88] Leichter I, Lindenbaum M, Rivlin E. Mean shift tracking with multiple reference color histograms. Computer Vision and Image Understanding. 2010;**114(3)**:400–408

[89] Collins RT. Mean-shift blob tracking through scale space. In: Proceedings of the 2003 IEEE Computer Society Conference on Computer Vision and Pattern Recognition. IEEE; 2003

[90] Li P. An adaptive binning color model for mean shift tracking. IEEE Transactions on Circuits and Systems for Video Technology. 2008;**18(9)**:1293–1299

[91] Li Z, Tang Q, Sang, N. Improved mean shift algorithm for occlusion pedestrian tracking. Electronics Letters. 2008;**44(10)**:622–623

[92] Maggio E, Cavallaro A. Hybrid particle filter and mean shift tracker with adaptive transition model. In: ICASSP (2). Citeseer; 2005

[93] Chang C, Ansari R, Khokhar A. Multiple object tracking with kernel particle filter. In: 2005 IEEE Computer Society Conference on Computer Vision and Pattern Recognition (CVPR'05). IEEE; 2005

[94] Blackman S, Popoli R. Design and Analysis of Modern Tracking Systems (Book). Norwood, MA: Artech House, 1999

[95] Panta K, et al. Probability hypothesis density filter versus multiple hypothesis tracking. In: Defense and Security. International Society for Optics and Photonics; 2004

[96] Bar-Shalom Y, Li X-R. Multitarget-Multisensor Tracking: Principles and Techniques. Storrs, CT: University of Connecticut; 1995

[97] Chakravorty R, Challa S. Multitarget tracking algorithm-Joint IPDA and Gaussian mixture PHD filter. In: FUSION'09. 12th International Conference on Information Fusion. IEEE; 2009

[98] Jaward M, et al. Multiple object tracking using particle filters. In: 2006 IEEE Aerospace Conference. IEEE; 2006

[99] Kim K, Davis LS. Multi-camera tracking and segmentation of occluded people on ground plane using search-guided particle filtering. In: European Conference on Computer Vision. Springer; 2006

[100] Wang Y, Jing Z, Hu S. Data association for PHD filter based on MHT. In: 2008 11th International Conference on Information Fusion. IEEE; 2008

[101] Arulampalam MS, et al. A tutorial on particle filters for online nonlinear/non-Gaussian Bayesian tracking. IEEE Transactions on Signal Processing. 2002;**50(2)**:174–188

[102] Gordon N, Doucet A, Freitas J. Sequential Monte Carlo Methods in Practice. Springer-Verlag; 2001

[103] Clark D, Vo B-N. The random set filtering website. Internet: http://randomsets.eps.hw.ac.uk/tutorial.html [Dec. 01, 2015].

[104] Feng P, et al. Adaptive retrodiction particle PHD filter for multiple human tracking. IEEE Signal Processing Letters. 2016;**23(11)**:1592–1596

[105] Yu W, et al. Multi-scale mean shift tracking. IET Computer Vision. 2014;**9(1)**:110–123

[106] Anand S, et al. Semi-supervised kernel mean shift clustering. IEEE Transactions on Pattern Analysis and Machine Intelligence. 2014;**36(6)**:1201–1215

[107] Yuan X, Li SZ. Half quadratic analysis for mean shift: With extension to a sequential data mode-seeking method. In: 2007 IEEE 11th International Conference on Computer Vision. IEEE; 2007

[108] Tao W, Jin H, Zhang Y. Color image segmentation based on mean shift and normalized cuts. IEEE Transactions on Systems, Man, and Cybernetics, Part B (Cybernetics). 2007;**37 (5)**:1382–1389

[109] Comaniciu D, Ramesh V. Mean shift and optimal prediction for efficient object tracking. In: Proceedings of the 2000 International Conference on Image Processing. IEEE; 2000

[110] Ukrainitz Y, Sarel B. Mean shift theory and applications. Internet: http://www.wisdom.weizmann.ac.il/~vision/courses/2004_2/files/mean_shift/mean_shift.ppt [Oct. 24, 2014].

[111] Carletta J, et al. The AMI meeting corpus: A pre-announcement. In: International Workshop on Machine Learning for Multimodal Interaction. Springer; 2005

[112] Mostefa D, et al. The CHIL audiovisual corpus for lecture and meeting analysis inside smart rooms. Language Resources and Evaluation. 2007;**41(3–4)**:389–407

[113] M. Taj, School of Electron. Eng. and Comput. Sci., Queen Mary Univ. of London, London, U.K., Surveillance performance evaluation initiative (SPEVI) audiovisual people dataset, 2007 [Online]. Available: http://www.eecs.qmul.ac.uk/~andrea/spevi.html, accessed Aug. 24, 2014.

[114] Lathoud G, Odobez J-M, Gatica-Perez D. AV16. 3: an audio-visual corpus for speaker localization and tracking. In: International Workshop on Machine Learning for Multimodal Interaction. Springer; 2004

[115] *S3A*. 2017. Available from: http://cvssp.org/data/s3a/

[116] Campos T, Liu Q, Barnard M. S3A Speaker Tracking with Kinect2. 2017. Available from: http://epubs.surrey.ac.uk/807708/

[117] Bernardin K, Stiefelhagen R. Evaluating multiple object tracking performance: the CLEAR MOT metrics. EURASIP Journal on Image and Video Processing. 2008;**2008(1)**:1–10

[118] Li Y, Huang C, Nevatia R. Learning to associate: Hybridboosted multi-target tracker for crowded scene. In: CVPR 2009. IEEE Conference on Computer Vision and Pattern Recognition. IEEE; 2009

[119] Wu B, Nevatia R. Tracking of multiple, partially occluded humans based on static body part detection. In: 2006 IEEE Computer Society Conference on Computer Vision and Pattern Recognition (CVPR'06). IEEE; 2006

[120] Ristic B, et al. A metric for performance evaluation of multi-target tracking algorithms. IEEE Transactions on Signal Processing. 2011;**59(7)**:3452–3457

[121] Schuhmacher D, Vo B-T, Vo B-N. A consistent metric for performance evaluation of multi-object filters. IEEE Transactions on Signal Processing. 2008;**56(8)**:3447–3457

[122] Barnard M, et al. Robust multi-speaker tracking via dictionary learning and identity modeling. IEEE Transactions on Multimedia. 2014;**16(3)**:864–880

[123] Pham NT, Huang W, Ong SH. Tracking multiple objects using probability hypothesis density filter and color measurements. In: IEEE International Conference on Multimedia and Expo. IEEE; 2007

Chapter 4

Motion Tracking and Potentially Dangerous Situations Recognition in Complex Environment

Houssam Salmane, Yassine Ruichek and
Louahdi Khoudour

Additional information is available at the end of the chapter

http://dx.doi.org/10.5772/68141

Abstract

In recent years, video surveillance systems have been playing a significantly important role in the human safety and security field by monitoring public or private areas. In this chapter, we have discussed the development of an intelligent surveillance system to detect, track and identify potentially hazardous events that may occur at level crossings (LC). This system starts by detecting and tracking objects on the level crossing. Then, a danger evaluation method is built using hidden Markov model in order to predict trajectories of the detected objects. The trajectories are analyzed with a credibility model to evaluate dangerous situations at level crossings. Synthetics and real data are used to test the effectiveness and the robustness of the proposed algorithms and the whole approach by considering various scenarios within several situations.

Keywords: video surveillance system, tracking and recognition, level crossing, hidden Markov model (HMM)

1. Introduction

Improving safety at level crossing (LC) became an important academic research topic in the transportation field and took increasingly railway undertaking concerns. European countries and European projects try to upgarde level crossing safety which is quite weak today. These projects, like SELCAT "Safer European Level Crossing Appraisal and Technology" [1], has set up some databases of accidents at European level. United States presents very well equipped level crossing with advanced means for sensing and telecommunication [2]. Selectra Vision Company in Italy [3] has developed a surveillance system for detecting obstacles in the monitored area of a level crossing using a 3D laser scanner. Nevertheless, developing a new LC safety system which allows quantifying the risk within the LC environment and transmitting it to road users, rail managers and even train drivers still is the main focus for technical solutions.

One of the objectives of the proposed work is to perform a video analysis-based system in order to evaluate the degree of danger of each detected and tracked moving object at level crossing.

The first step of our proposed video surveillance system starts by robustly detecting and separating moving objects crossing the LC. Many approaches are used in the literature to detect objects in real time; examples are Independent Components Analysis [4], Histogram of Oriented Gradients [5], Wavelet [6], Eigen backgrounds [7], kernel and contour tracking [8, 9] or Kalman and particle filters [10, 11]. However, these techniques require further development to distinguish between detected objects.

That is why our approach consists of detecting all moving pixels based on a background subtraction approach. To obtain separated objects, we propose a model based on clustering the detected pixels, affected by motion, by comparing a specific energy vector associated to each target. Finally, the tracking of each pixel detected within a moving object is achieved by using a Harris corners-based optical flow propagation technique, followed by a Kalman filtering-based rectification.

The second step is focused on predicting trajectories of the detected moving objects such as to avoid potentially dangerous level crossing accident scenarios (vehicle stopped at LC for example). Gaussian mixture model (GMM) [12], hidden Markov model (HMM) [13], Hierarchical and Couple Hidden Markov Model [14, 15] are usually used for representing and recognizing objects' trajectories. However, these methods need a high number of statistical measures to be accurate. Using a real-time hidden Markov model, the degree of dangerousness related to each object is instantly estimated by analyzing each object's trajectory considering different sources of danger (position, velocity, acceleration…). All the information obtained from the sources of danger is fused using Dempster-Shafer technique [16]. **Figure 1** illustrates the synopsis of the proposed video surveillance security system.

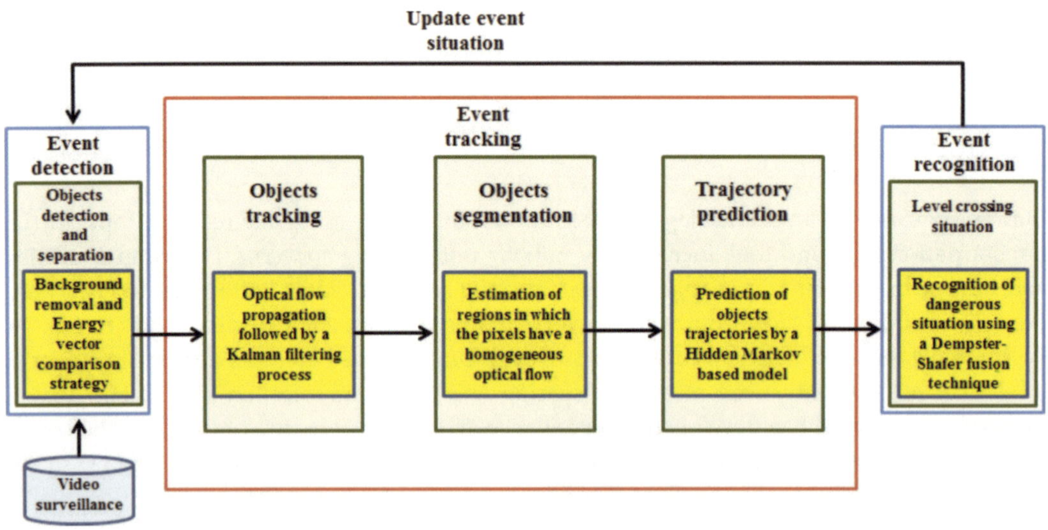

Figure 1. Synoptic of the video surveillance security system installed at Level crossing.

http://dx.doi.org/10.5772/68141

The remaining of the chapter is organized as follows. Section2 is dealing with object detection and separation. In Section3, the tracking process is developed. Section4 describes the proposed method for evaluating and recognizing dangerous situations in a level crossing environment. In Section5, some evaluation results are provided based on typical accident scenarios played in a real level crossing environment. Finally, in Section6, some conclusions and short-term perspectives are provided.

2. Object detection and separation

In this section, a method has been developed to detect and separate moving objects in the level crossing surveillance zone. This method starts by detecting pixels affected by motion, by using background subtraction technique as a preprocessing phase; each image processed at each step, a subtraction from the background image is carried out. The main aim of this procedure is to extract the moving pixels in the current image (**Figure 2b**). Furthermore, a subtraction from the previous image is also carried out in order to obtain the moving pixels situated on the edges of the object. (**Figure 2c**). The procedure continues by determining in the current image the required targets. A target in the image is defined by a set of connected pixels affected by motion. A bounding box is then associated for each group of connected pixels (**Figure 3**).

Each created bounding box may belong to an existing target extracted from the previous frame, or representing a new target extracted from the current frame (**Figure 3**). The intersection between all created bounding boxes in the current frame and those representing the targets extracted from the previous frame is analyzed in order to determine the number and the shape of all moving objects (targets) in the current frame; a bounding box created from the current frame is considered as a new target if and only if it does not intersect any existing bounding box representing a target extracted from the previous frame. On the other case, if a bounding box created from the current frame intersects existing targets, an iterative separation method is applied. During each iteration, a pixel in the current bounding box should be assigned to one of the existing targets.

The pixels clustering process starts by defined two energy vectors. The first energy vector E^i_{target}, initialized to zero, is concerned with each existing target number *i*. This energy is then updated iteratively. The second energy vector E^i_{pixel} is defined for each pixel located at the position (x, y) with respect to the target number *i*. This energy is expressed as follows:

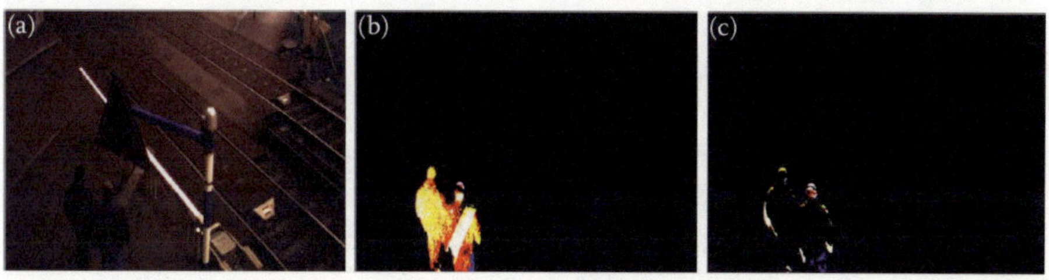

Figure 2. Detection of moving pixels. (a) Current image. (b) Detected moving pixels. (c) Moving pixels situated in the contour of the objects.

$$E^i_{pixel} = \left[E^i_D, E^i_F, E^i_I, E^i_G\right]^T \quad (1)$$

where E^i_G, E^i_I, E^i_F, E^i_D are, respectively, the distance, optical flow, intensity and gradient energies.

For each iteration, the pixel (x, y) is assigned to the target that provides the maximum number of closest components between the energy vectors E^i_{pixel} and E^i_{target}, if the pixel (x, y) is assigned to the target number p. The energy vector E^p_{target} is then updated as follows:

$$E^p_{target} = \left(\frac{N*E^p_{target} + E^i_{pixel}}{N+1}\right) \quad (2)$$

where N is the number of pixels in the target number p, before adding the pixel (x, y). **Figure 4** shows the results of the multiobjects separation method.

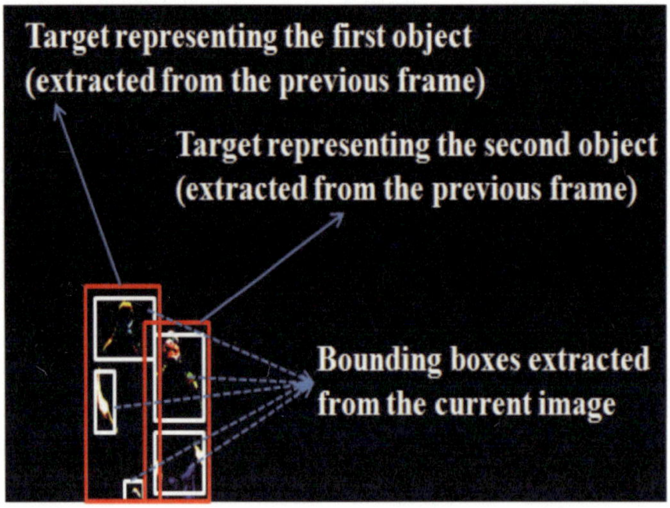

Figure 3. Bounding boxes extraction.

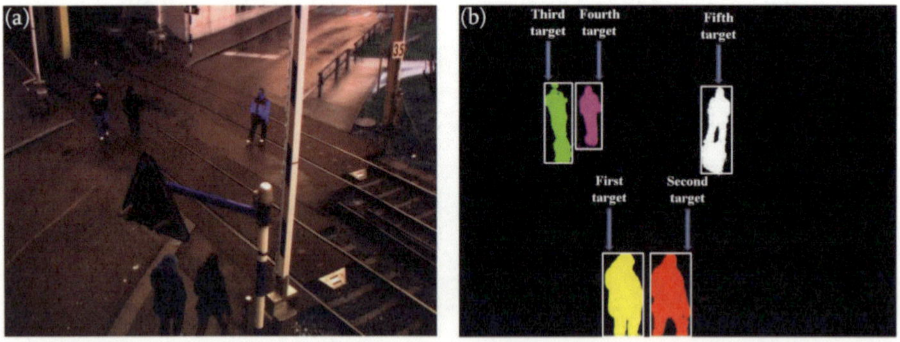

Figure 4. Multiobjects separation result. (a) Original frame with five moving objects. (b) Objects separation result.

http://dx.doi.org/10.5772/68141

3. Event tracking

3.1. Objects tracking

Once the targets are extracted from the current frame, the objective is to develop a dense optical flow computation algorithm to track them. We firstly estimate the optical flow of Harris points using an iterative Lucas-Kanade algorithm [17]. We consider that these particular points have a stable optical flow. The optical flow for every pixel of the detected objects is then estimated by propagating the optical flow of Harris points using a Gaussian distribution. The mean and standard deviation of the distribution are taken as the mean and standard deviation of the Harris points' optical flow [19]. The results of the optical flow propagation process are then processed by Kalman filtering to correct the optical flow of all the pixels of the detected objects [18, 19].

The tracking process is tested and evaluated in [18, 19]. **Figure 5** shows an example of multiobjects tracking by combining the objects detection and separation method, and the tracking process.

Figure 5. Tracking process: from right to left.

3.2. Optical flow–based object segmentation

Given a target, the objective is to partition it into multiple rectangular boxes representing different regions based on optical flow of its pixels. To achieve that, we use a recursive algorithm, which compares neighboring pixels to extract regions in which the pixels have a homogeneous optical flow. Only regions with a significant size are conserved (determined experimentally in dependence of the camera's view around the level crossing area and the resolution of the camera). **Figure 6** presents optical flow–based segmentation results for a moving object tracked in an image sequence. In order to predict the normal (supposed) trajectories, the extracted regions are represented by the gravity centers of the boxes surrounding them. Then, each specific trajectory should be linked to the gravity center of its extracted region.

3.3. Ideal trajectory prediction

Let us consider, thanks to optical flow, an extracted region. When we consider the center of the region, two trajectories could be defined: current ideal trajectory and predicted ideal trajectory. The current ideal trajectory corresponds to the trajectory that the center of the region should follow to avoid potential dangerous situations (**Figure 9**). The predicted ideal trajectory corresponds to the trajectory that should be followed to come back toward the current ideal trajectory (**Figure 7**). A statistical approach based on a hidden Markov model (HMM) is

Figure 6. Segmentation of an object using optical flow procedure.

proposed to predict the new ideal trajectory: the predicted ideal trajectory of the considered region center at time instant t (state q_t: initial state of the HMM) is constructed from the states $(q_{t+1}, \ldots, q_{t+t_f})$ generated by the HMM using Forward-Backward, Viterbi and Baum-Welch algorithms [20, 21]. We also associate to the considered region center the four following parameters: velocity $(V_{t+1}, \ldots, V_{t+t_f})$, acceleration $(a_{t+1}, \ldots, a_{t+t_f})$, orientation $(o_{t+1}, \ldots, o_{t+t_f})$, position $(p_{t+1}, \ldots, p_{t+t_f})$ and the distance $(D_{t+1}, \ldots, D_{t+t_f})$ from the region center to the current ideal trajectory.

Figure 8 shows the general architecture of the proposed HMM and how the predicted ideal trajectory is performed from the considered region center.

As shown in **Figure 8a**, the random hidden state variable q_t corresponds to the position of the considered region center at time t. The random observation variable u_t represents simultaneously the acceleration, orientation, velocity and position of the considered region center at time t. a_{t+1}^{t} represents the transition probability from state q_t to state q_{t+1}, and b_t represents the distribution of the observation at time t.

As illustrated in **Figure 8b**, given the velocity vector $\overrightarrow{V_t}$ at time t, calculated from optical flow, the state q_{t+1} in the HMM is reached from the state q_t with a probability of 1. Given the acceleration, orientation and velocity at time t, the velocity $\overrightarrow{V_{t+1}}$ at time $t+1$ is then predicted.

http://dx.doi.org/10.5772/68141

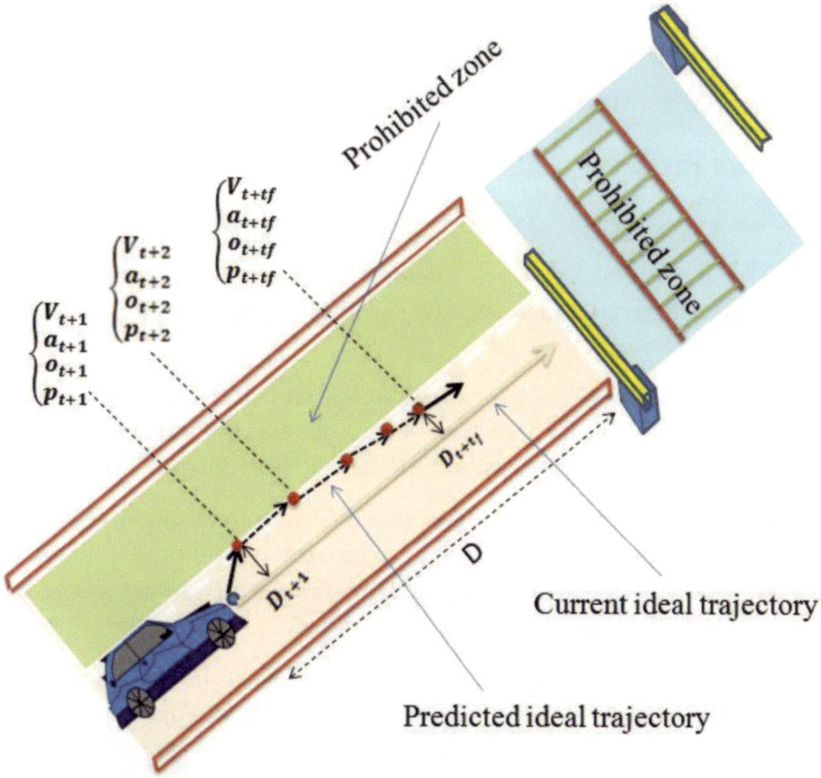

Figure 7. Ideal trajectory prediction by using HMM.

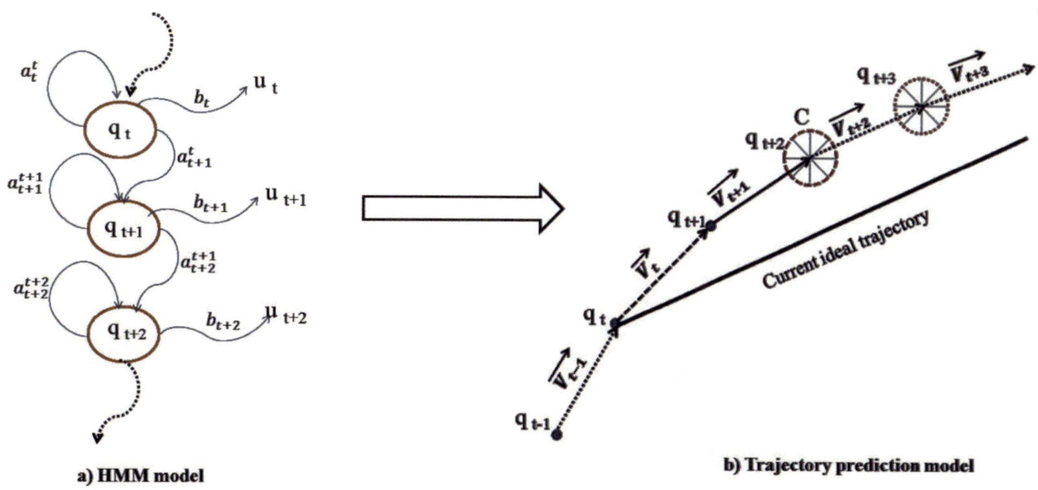

Figure 8. Schematic representation of the HMM for ideal trajectory prediction. (a) HMM model. (b) Trajectory prediction model.

As illustrated in **Figure 8b**, we next define a circle C. The center of the circle C is the end point of the velocity vector $\overrightarrow{V_{t+1}}$ and the radius of this circle is the maximum absolute acceleration.

4. Evaluation of the level of dangerousness (recognition of dangerous situations)

On the basis of the previous steps, we present in this section a method to evaluate and recognize potential dangerous situations when a moving object is detected within the monitored area of a level crossing.

To analyze the predicted ideal trajectory, various sources of dangerousness are considered based on Dempster-Shafer theory [16]. This theory combines the dangers produced by the different sources in order to obtain a measure of the degree of danger.

For each region center, five sources of danger are considered: acceleration, orientation, velocity, position and distance between the predicted and the current ideal trajectories. A mass assignment is then defined for each source of danger. Let m^i be the belief mass related to the danger source number i. The belief masses are defined as follows:

The mass assignment m^1 (position) is computed from the distance between the predicted position p_{t+t_f} at time instant $t + t_f$ and the barrier of the level crossing:

$$m^1 = \frac{|P_d - 0.5|}{0.5} \tag{3}$$

$$P_d = \int_{-\infty}^{d_c^{t_f}} G_{d_N,\sigma_d}(x)dx \quad \sigma_d = \sqrt{D_{max}} \quad d_N = 0 \tag{4}$$

where $G_{d_N,\sigma_d}(x)$ is a Gaussian distribution of the variable x. $d_N = 0$ and σ_d are, respectively, its mean and standard deviation. D_{max} is the maximum distance that an object can traverse in the image. $d_c^{t_f}$ is a function given as follows:

$$d_c^{t_f} = \begin{cases} W & \text{if } \vec{D_p} \,.\, \vec{V_c^{t_f}} \leq 0 \\ W + \vec{D_p^*} \,.\, \vec{V_c^{t_f}} & \text{if } \vec{D_p} \,.\, \vec{V_c^{t_f}} > 0 \end{cases} \tag{5}$$

$$W = coef * sqrt(D_s) \quad D_s = \frac{D_{max}}{5} \tag{6}$$

$$coef = \frac{D_s}{D_p + D_i} \quad D_i = \begin{cases} 0 & \textit{if inside prohibited zone} \\ D_{max} & \textit{if outside prohibited zone} \end{cases} \tag{7}$$

$$\overrightarrow{D_p^*} = \left[\frac{1}{D_{p_x}} \ \frac{1}{D_{p_y}}\right]^T \tag{8}$$

http://dx.doi.org/10.5772/68141

where $\vec{D_p} = [D_{p_x} \quad D_{p_y}]^T$ is the distance from the region center to the barrier of the level crossing. $\vec{V_c^{t_f}}$ is the velocity of the considered region center at time t_f. The parameter W depends on the position of the region center in the level crossing zone (inside or outside a prohibited LC zone). More the value of $d_c^{t_f}$ is greater than zero more the belief mass m^1 will increase (degree of dangerousness increments).

The mass assignment m^2 (velocity) is computed from the difference between the predicted velocity $V_c^{t_f}$ at time instant t_f and a prefixed nominal velocity V_N.

$$m^2 = \begin{cases} 0.01 & if\ (V_c^{t_f} - V_N) \leq 0 \\ \dfrac{P_v - 0.5}{0.5} & if\ (V_c^{t_f} - V_N) > 0 \end{cases} \tag{9}$$

$$P_v = \int_{-\infty}^{V_c^{t_f}} G_{V_n, \sigma_v}(x) dx \ \sigma_v = \frac{V_N}{4} \tag{10}$$

where $V_c^{t_f}$ is the velocity of the considered region center at time t_f. V_N represents the maximal velocity that a target can reach in the image. $G_{V_n, \sigma_v}(x)$ is a Gaussian distribution, with a mean equal to V_N and a standard deviation equal to σ_v.

The mass assignment m^3 (orientation) is computed by comparing the angle of the predicted velocity V_t at time instant t and the angle of the current ideal trajectory.

$$m^3 = \frac{|P_o - 0.5|}{0.5} \tag{11}$$

$$P_o = \int_{-\infty}^{o_c^{t_f}} G_{O_N, \sigma_o}(x)\ dx\ \sigma_o = \frac{2 * \pi}{7} \tag{12}$$

where $o_c^{t_f}$ is the velocity orientation of the considered region center at time t_f. O_N is the orientation of the current ideal trajectory. $G_{O_N, \sigma_o}(x)$ is a Gaussian distribution, with a mean equal to O_N and a standard deviation equal to σ_o.

The mass assignment m^4 (acceleration) is computed from the difference between the predicted accelerations a_t and a_{t+t_f} at time instants t and $t + t_f$ respectively.

$$m^4 = \begin{cases} 0.01 & if\ (a_c^{t_f} - a_N) \leq 0 \\ \dfrac{P_a - 0.5}{0.5} & if\ (a_c^{t_f} - a_N) > 0 \end{cases} \tag{13}$$

$$P_a = \int_{-\infty}^{a_c^{t_f}} G_{a_N, \sigma_a}(x)\ dx\ \sigma_a = \frac{a_N}{4} \tag{14}$$

$$a_c^{t_f} = \frac{V_c^{t_f} - V_c^{t_i}}{n*T_{misejour}} \quad (15)$$

where $a_c^{t_f}$ is the acceleration of the considered region center at time t_f. a_N represents the maximal acceleration that a target can reach in the image. $G_{a_N,\sigma_a}(x)$ is a Gaussian distribution, with a mean equal to a_N and a standard deviation equal to σ_a.

Finally, the mass assignment m^5 (distance) is computed from the distance between the predicted position p_{t_f} at time instant t_f and the current ideal trajectory:

$$m^5 = \frac{|P_D - 0.5|}{0.5} \quad (16)$$

$$P_D = \int_{-\infty}^{D^{t_f}} G_{D_N,\sigma_D}(x)\, dx \quad \sigma_D = 2*V_n \quad D_N = 0 \quad (17)$$

where D^{t_f} is the the distance between the predicted position p_{t_f} of the considered region center at time t_f and the current ideal trajectory. $G_{D_N,\sigma_D}(x)$ is a Gaussian distribution, with a mean equal to $D_N = 0$ and a standard deviation equal to σ_D.

Once the degrees of dangerousness are computed for the five sources, Dempster-Shafer [16] combination is used to determine the degree of danger related to the considered region center:

$$Danger = Dempster - Shafer(m^1,\ m^2,\ m^3, m^4,\ m^5) \quad (18)$$

To determine the degree of danger of the target, we take simply the maximum value among the degrees of danger of all regions composing the target.

5. Video surveillance experimental results

To validate our work, we apply the proposed dangerous situation method on four typical accidental scenarios. These scenarios, registered at a level crossing in the north of France (Mouzon), correspond to real situations occurred in LC accidents (dangerous situations: vehicle zigzagging between the closed half barriers, presence of obstacle in the level crossing and pedestrian crossing level crossing area). Each analyzed scenario includes a sequence with more than 500 frames. **Table 1** presents the datasets and materials used in the analysis of our method.

5.1. Experimental methodology

In the framework of this chapter, we determine a pure quantitative degree of dangerousness from different scenarios identified at level crossing (see Eq. (18)). This system is able to detect potentially dangerous situations occurring at the LC both in the two cases (states of the barriers): barriers opened or barriers closed.

http://dx.doi.org/10.5772/68141

	Number of images analyzed	Processing power	Number of images analyzed per second	States of the barriers	Test site
Sequence 1 (Vehicle zigzagging LC)	520	Intel Core i5 – 2.67 GHz/3.7GB	7–10	Barriers closed	Mouzon-France
Sequence 2 (Presence of obstacle on LC)	1015	Intel Core i5 – 2.67 GHz/3.7GB	7–10	Barriers opened	Mouzon-France
Sequence 3 (Vehicles stopped on LC)	1380	Intel Core i5 – 2.67 GHz/3.7GB	7–10	Barriers opened	Mouzon-France
Sequence 4 (Pedestrians crossing LC)	1325	Intel Core i5 – 2.67 GHz/3.7GB	7–10	Barriers closed	Mouzon-France

Table 1. Dataset and materials.

In the case of closed barriers, when train approaching, we provide a level of dangerousness (see Eq. (18)), between 0 and 100%, which could be transmitted all the time to the drivers approaching the level crossing (LC). We could also send additional security advices when the level is greater than a threshold (for instance 75%). In any situation, the presence of any kind of moving objects between the barriers is not allowed. So, the velocity of cars or moving objects should decrease to zero when approaching the LC.

In the case of opened barriers, the surveillance system is working as well. Vehicles or moving objects could traverse the level crossing zone but they couldn't stop on the LC. In case of detection of dangerous situations, we can send information like: barriers open with a pedestrian, a vehicle or an object stopped on the rails.

Table 2 shows different situations that are taken into account by the system to measure the level of dangerousness. In both cases, it all depends on the way of the rail transport operator wants to monitor the LC. For the moment, the final system was not integrated in the daily management of a level crossing. So, when the system will be integrated in a rail network, we

	Closed barriers	Opened barriers
Position of objects inside the LC zone (between the barriers)	Not allowed	Allowed
Velocity of objects inside the LC zone (between the barriers)	Presence of objects not allowed	Different from zero
Acceleration of objects inside the LC zone (between the barriers)	Presence of objects not allowed	Different from zero and positive
Position of objects outside the LC zone (near the barriers)	Allowed only on the right side of the road	Allowed only on the right side of the road
Velocity of objects outside the LC zone (near the barriers)	Close to zero	Different or equal to zero
Acceleration of objects outside the LC zone (near the barriers)	Close to zero or negative (deceleration)	Different or equal to zero

Table 2. Situations allowed for open and closed barriers.

could imagine that the measure of the level of dangerousness will be validated qualitatively by the rail safety experts.

5.2. Scenarios of accident analyzed by the system

Vehicle zigzagging between two closed barriers of LC (**Figure 9**): In this scenario, a vehicle is approaching the LC, while the barriers are closed. The vehicle crosses the LC, zigzagging between the closed barriers (**Figure 9**). The purple lines in **Figure 9** represent the current ideal trajectory of the center of each extracted region from the object. The white points in the figure represent the instantly predicted displacement of the center of the extracted regions. As shown in **Figure 9**, if a detected vehicle is approaching the LC and using an abnormal trajectory, the degree of danger is going to increase gradually to reach 70%. Then, when the vehicle enters the LC, this degree continues to grow until reaching 100%. The level of danger begins to decrease when the vehicle is moving away from the LC (Degree of danger DV1 = 40%).

Vehicle stopped (**Figure 10**): In this scenario, a vehicle crosses the level crossing while the barriers are open (**Figure 10**). Suddenly, the vehicle stops inside the dangerous zone and becomes a fixed obstacle. After a while, the vehicle moves and leaves the LC. Concerning danger evaluation, the degree of dangerousness related to the detected vehicle increases when it moves toward the level crossing. It reaches 46% during the crossing of the zone of danger. When the vehicle stops in the zone of danger, the stationary is detected and the degree of dangerousness takes a value of 100%. When the vehicle begins to leave the LC, the level of danger decreases progressively.

Queuing across the rail level crossing (**Figure 11**)*:* In this scenario, a first vehicle stops just after the dangerous zone. Sometime later, two other vehicles find themselves blocked behind the first vehicle, which is motionless. This situation leads to a queue of cars inside the LC (**Figure 11**). When the two vehicles detected inside the LC are stopped inside the zone of danger, their degree of dangerousness increases progressively and reach their maximum (100%). When the two vehicles restart moving, the degree of dangerousness drops to 46% and decreases gradually, as the vehicles leave away the level crossing.

Pedestrians' scenario (**Figure 12**): In this scenario, three pedestrians (P1, P2 and P3) are walking around the level crossing zone as the barriers are closed. Pedestrian P1 is moving toward the zone of danger (Degree of danger DP1 = 26%), while pedestrian P2 is crossing is crossing the level crossing area (DP2 = 100%), and Pedestrian P3 is stopped on the middle part of the level crossing near from the rails (DP3 = 100%). After a moment, pedestrian P1 arrives near pedestrian P2, and they are stopped on the rails of the LC, taking into account that the stationary inside the level crossing is always detected by the system. So, the degree of dangerousness related to the pedestrian P1 increases progressively from DP1 = 26% and reaches their maximum DP1 = 100% on the rails. At the end of the scenario, pedestrian P2 is leaving the level crossing zone (Degree of danger DP2 decreases to 11%), when pedestrian P1 is moving toward the stopped pedestrian P3. A vehicle passing near from the LC is also detected in this scenario (DV = 13%).

As a conclusion of these tests, the measure of the prediction system that calculates the level of dangerousness for each moving or stopped object around the LC is able to detect different kind of dangerous scenarios in the case of closed or opened barriers (vehicle zigzagging, stopped

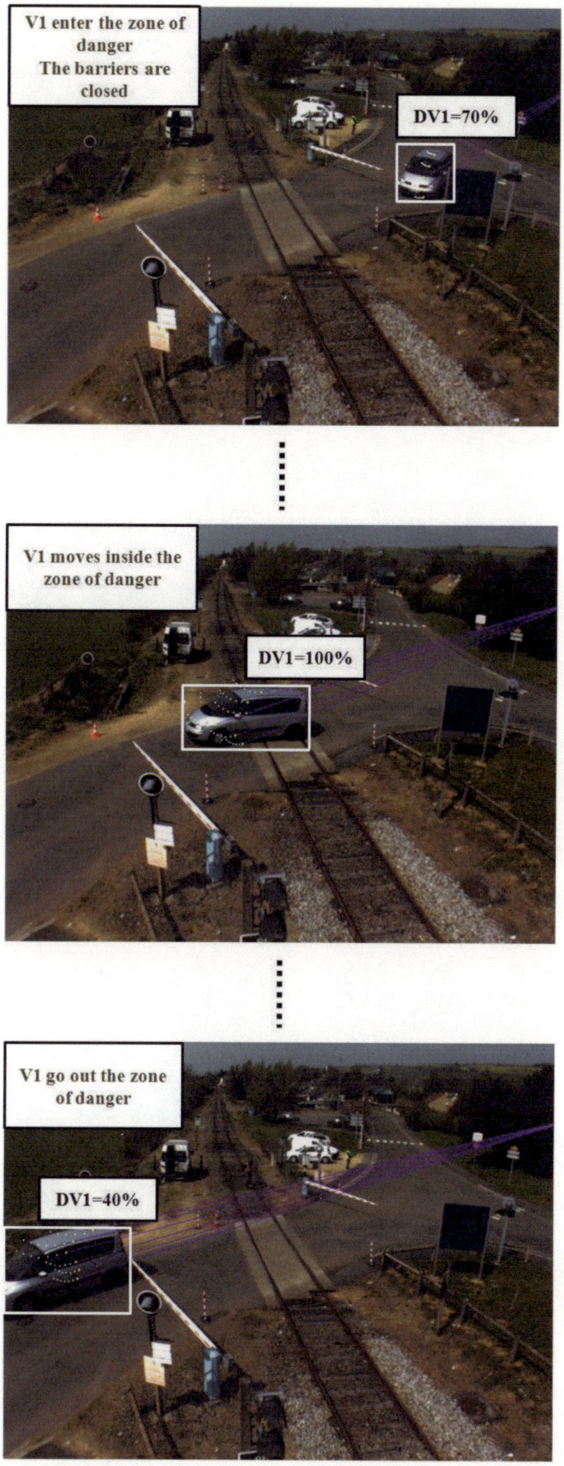

Figure 9. Vehicle zigzagging. DV1 represents the degree of danger associated with the vehicle.

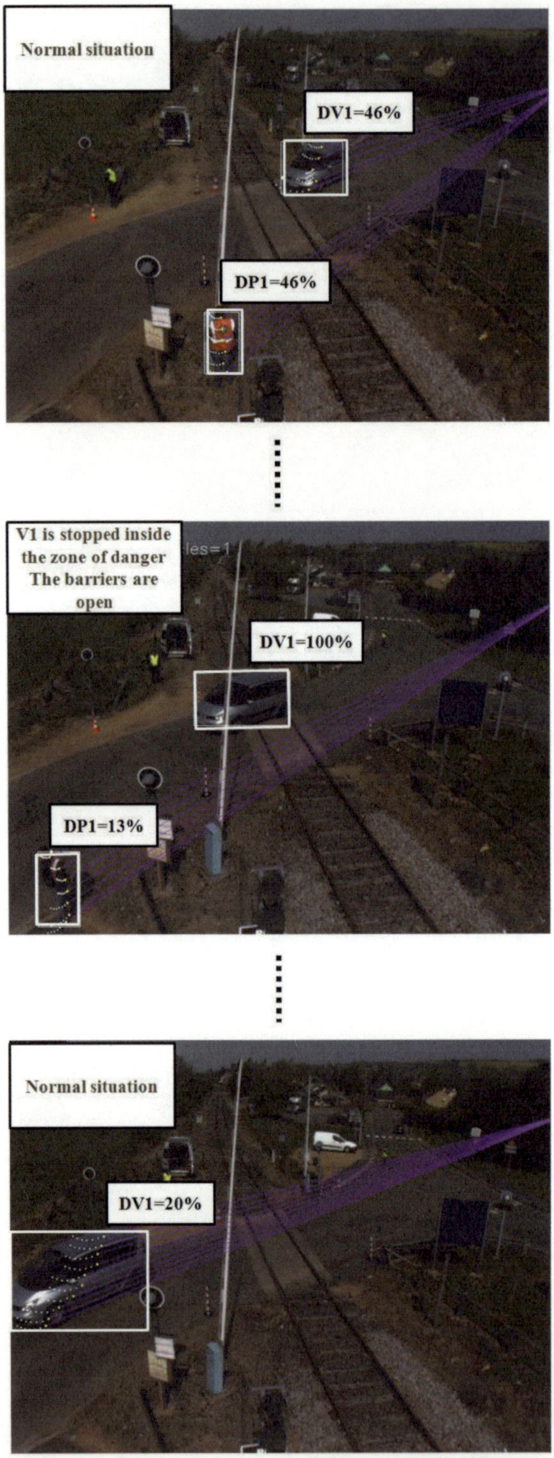

Figure 10. The presence of obstacle (vehicle) in the level crossing. DV1 represents the degree of danger associated with the vehicle.

http://dx.doi.org/10.5772/68141

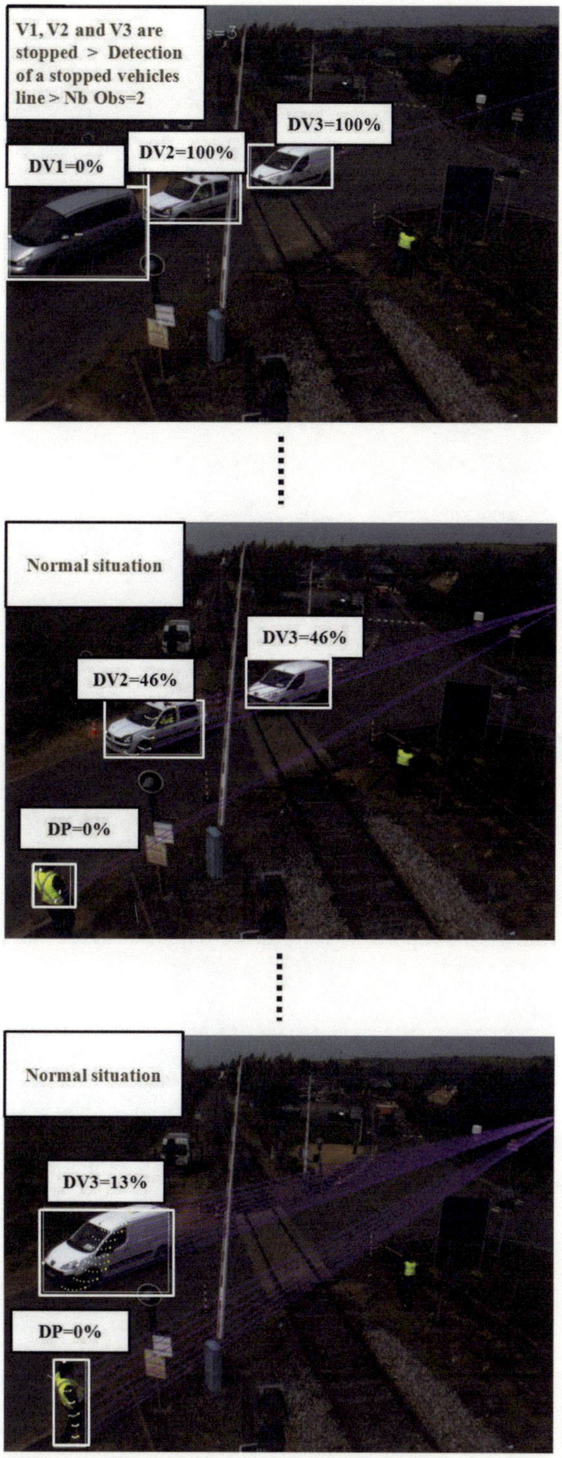

Figure 11. The presence of stopped vehicles line on the LC. DV*i* represents the degree of danger associated with the vehicle number *i*. DP represents the degree of danger associated with a pedestrian outside the LC zone.

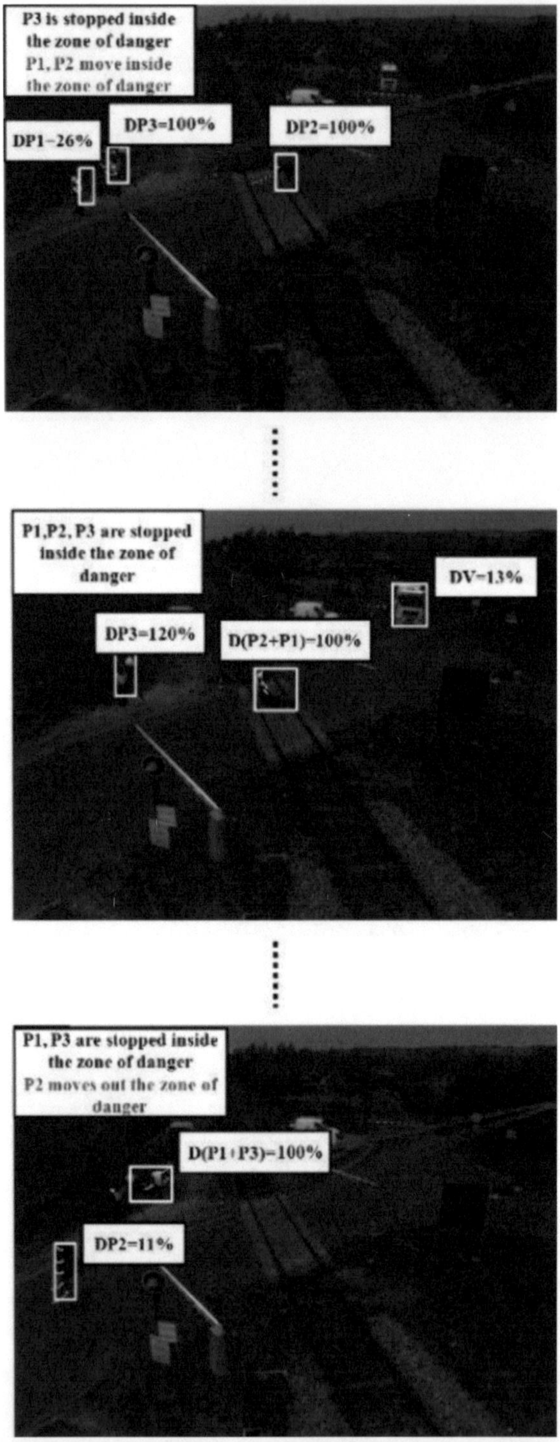

Figure 12. Three pedestrians walking around the level crossing area.

http://dx.doi.org/10.5772/68141

vehicles, pedestrians around the LC). Then, this system proves his effectiveness as a measure of the level of dangerousness but it also requires to be validated qualitatively after installing this system definitely on a rail transport.

6. Conclusion

Detection of moving objects is an important and basic task for video surveillance systems, for which you can define the initial position of the moving objects in a surveillance scene. However, the detection and separation of the moving objects process become difficult when the objects are close to each other in the scene. In our approach, we propose a method to completely separate the corresponding pixels of each defined target. One of the other objectives of this project is to develop a video surveillance system that will be able to detect and recognize potential dangerous situation around level crossings. Different typical LC accident scenarios (e.g., presence of obstacles, zigzagging between the barriers, stopped cars line) acquired in real conditions are experimentally evaluated by applying the proposed dangerous situation recognition system.

Acknowledgements

This work is developed within the framework of PANsafer project (Towards a safer level crossing), supported by the ANR French work program.

Author details

Houssam Salmane[1]*, Yassine Ruichek[2] and Louahdi Khoudour[3]

*Address all correspondence to: salmanehoussam@gmail.com

1 Observatory of Paris, LESIA-CNRS, Meudon, France

2 Le2i FRE2005, CNRS, Arts et Métiers, University of Bourgogne Franche-Comté, UTBM, Belfort, France

3 CEREMA, Centre for Studies and Expertise on Risks, Environment, Mobility, and, Urban and Country Planning, Toulouse, France

References

[1] Schnieder E, Slovak R, El Koursi EM, Tordai L, Woods M. A European contribution to level crossing safety. Proceedings of FOVUS, Stuttgart, Germany. September 2008:222–228

[2] US DOT FRA web site. Intelligent Grade Crossings: IGC. Available from: https://www.fra.dot.gov/Page/P0309

[3] Selectra Vision Company. Level Crossing Surveillance [Internet]. Available from: http://www.selectravision.com/obstacle-lxs.php

[4] Fakhfakh N, Khoudour L, et al. Background Subtraction and 3D Localization of Moving and Stationary Obstacles at Level Crossings. International Conference on Image Processing Theory, Tools and Applications. 2010:72–78

[5] Oreifej O, Liu Z. Histogram of oriented 4d normals for activity recognition from depth sequences. Proceedings of the IEEE Conference on Computer Vision and Pattern Recognition. 2013:716–723

[6] Prakash O, Khare M, Binh NT, Khare A. Human object detection in images using shift-invariant stationary wavelet transform. Proceedings of the International Conference on Recent Cognizance in Wireless Communication & Image Processing. 2016;481–487

[7] Vosters L, Shan C, Gritti T. Real-time robust background subtraction under rapidly changing illumination conditions. Image and Vision Computing, Elseiver. 2012;**30**:1004–1015

[8] Hare S, Golodetz S, Saffari A, Vineet V. Cheng MM, Hicks SL, Torr PH. Structured output tracking with kernels. IEEE Transactions on Pattern Analysis and Machine Intelligence. 2016;**38**:2096–2109

[9] Blake A, and Isard M. Active Contours: The Application of Techniques from Graphics, Vision,Control Theory and Statistics to Visual Tracking of Shapes in Motion. 1998, 1st edn. Springer-Verlag New York, Inc. Secaucus, NJ, USA, ISBN:3540762175

[10] Arvind BC, Nagaraj SK, Seelamantula CS, Gorthi SS. Active-disc-based Kalman filter technique for tracking of blood cells in microfluidic channels. Phoenix, Arizona, USA: IEEE International Conference on Image Processing (ICIP). 2016;3394–3398

[11] Fukui S, Hayakawa S, Iwahori Y, Nakamura T, Bhuyan MK. Particle Filter Based Tracking with Image-based Localization. Procedia Computer Science. 2016;**96**:977–986

[12] Klitzke L, Koch C. Robust object detection for video surveillance using stereo vision and Gaussian mixture model. Journal of WSCG (World Society for Computer Graphics). Václav Skala-UNION Agency. 2016;**24**(1):9–17

[13] Vojir T, Matas J, Noskova J. Online adaptive hidden markov model for multi-tracker fusion. Computer Vision and Image Understanding. 2016;**153**:109–119

[14] Karaman S, Benois-Pineau J, Dovgalecs V, Mégret R, Pinquier J, André-Obrecht R, Gaëstel Y, Dartigues JF. Hierarchical Hidden Markov Model in detecting activities of daily living in wearable videos for studies of dementia. Multimedia Tools and Applications. 2014;**69**:743–771

[15] Natarajan P, Nevatia R. Coupled Hidden Semi Markov Models for Activity Recognition, Proceedings of IEEE Workshop on Motion and Video Computing. 2007. WMVC '07. IEEE Workshop on p. 10−10. doi: 10.1109/WMVC.2007.12

http://dx.doi.org/10.5772/68141

[16] Hong X, Huang Y, Ma W, Miller P, Liu W, Zhou H. Video event recognition by Dempster-Shafer theory. Proceedings of the Twenty-first European Conference on Artificial Intelligence. ECAI'14. Prague, Czech Republic: IOS Press, 2014, pp. 1031–1032. ISBN: 978-1-61499-418-3

[17] Tamgade SN, Bora VR. Motion vector estimation of video image by pyramidal implementation of Lucas Kanade optical flow, Second International Conference on Emerging KES Center, Australia & MIR Labs: Trends in Engineering & Technology. 2009:914–917

[18] Salmane H, Ruichek Y, Khoudour L. Gaussian propagation model based dense optical flow for objects tracking, International Conference on Image Analysis and Recognition ICIAR. 2012:234–244

[19] Salmane H, Ruichek Y, Khoudour L. Object tracking using Harris corner points based optical flow propagation and Kalman filter, IEEE Intelligent Transportation Systems Conference ITSC. The George Washington University Washington, DC, USA, 2011:67–73

[20] Raguet H, Fadili J, Peyré G. A generalized forward-backward splitting. SIAM Journal on Imaging Sciences. 2013;**6**:1199–1226

[21] Wang D, Huang L. HMM based distributed arithmetic coding and its application in image coding. Fifth International Conference on Machine Vision (ICMV 12). Wuhan, China, 2013

Section 2

Gesture Recognition

Chapter 5

Human Action Recognition with RGB-D Sensors

Enea Cippitelli, Ennio Gambi and Susanna Spinsante

Additional information is available at the end of the chapter

http://dx.doi.org/10.5772/68121

Abstract

Human action recognition, also known as HAR, is at the foundation of many different applications related to behavioral analysis, surveillance, and safety, thus it has been a very active research area in the last years. The release of inexpensive RGB-D sensors fostered researchers working in this field because depth data simplify the processing of visual data that could be otherwise difficult using classic RGB devices. Furthermore, the availability of depth data allows to implement solutions that are unobtrusive and privacy preserving with respect to classic video-based analysis. In this scenario, the aim of this chapter is to review the most salient techniques for HAR based on depth signal processing, providing some details on a specific method based on temporal pyramid of key poses, evaluated on the well-known MSR Action3D dataset.

Keywords: kinect, human action recognition, bag of key poses, RGB-D sensors

1. Introduction

The topic known as human action recognition (HAR) has become of interest in the last years mainly because different applications can be developed from the understanding of human behaviors. The technologies used to recognize activities can be varied and based on different approaches [1]. The use of environmental and acoustic sensors allows to infer the activity from the interaction of the user with the environment and the objects located in it, but vision-based solutions [2] and wearable devices [3] are usually the most used technologies to detect human body movements. RGB-D sensors, i.e., Red-Green-Blue and depth sensors, can be considered as enhanced vision-based devices since they can additionally provide depth data that can facilitate the detection of human movements. In fact, depth information may help to improve the performance of HAR algorithms because it is easier to implement a crucial process such as the extraction of human silhouette, reducing its dependence from shadows, light reflections, and color similarity [4]. Skeleton joints, which can be even exploited to calculate features for action recognition, are extracted from depth data [5].

The aim of this chapter is to discuss HAR algorithms exploiting RGB-D sensors, providing a review of the most salient methods proposed in literature and an overview of nonvision-based devices. A method for HAR exploiting skeleton joints and known as temporal pyramid of key poses is described and experimental results on a well-known RGB-D dataset are provided.

Section 2 of this chapter aims to review methods for human action recognition based on different technologies, with a particular focus on RGB-D data. An algorithm based on histograms of key poses exploiting skeleton joints extracted by Kinect is presented in Section 3. Finally, the last section of the chapter highlights the main conclusion on the proposed topic.

2. Methods and technologies for HAR

HAR methods can be implemented on data gathered from different technologies, which can infer the action from the movements made by the person, or from the interaction with objects or the environment. A review of sensors and technologies for detection of different human activities in smart homes can be found in Ref. [6], where the aim is to face the phenomenon of aging population. Following the same unobtrusive approach, researchers are working also on radio-based techniques [7], where they take advantage of signal attenuation due to the body, and channel fading of wireless radio. Other works have been also published considering wearable devices, such as smartphones, that can be used to collect data and to classify actions [8]. A more general architecture implemented with wearable devices requires the usage of small sensors with sensing and communication capabilities that can acquire data (usually related to acceleration) and send them to a central unit [9].

2.1. Related works on not vision-based devices

HAR based on data generated by environmental devices in home environment may exploit unobtrusive sensors equipping objects with which people usually interact, or other sensors that are installed in the rooms. State-changes sensors, which activate and deactivate if they detect a change, can provide powerful clues about movements in the apartment if placed on windows or doors. If attached to ovens and fridges, or toilet and washing machines, they can reveal kitchen-related activities or activities associated to toileting and doing laundry [10]. Passive infrared sensors (PIRs) detect the presence of a person in a room and a set of activities can be inferred if they are jointly used with other sensors, such as state-changes sensors and flush sensors, to detect the use of the toilet [11]. Multiple binary sensors such as motion detectors, contact switches, break-beam sensors, and pressure mats have been used in Ref. [12]. Using an approach based on particle filter and an ID sensor (RFID) to detect people's identity, the system can reveal information about the occupied rooms and the number of occupants, and recognize if they are moving or not and track their movement. An integrated platform including PIRs, magnetic sensors, force sensors, gas and smoke detection sensors, water and gas flux meters, power meters connected to some objects has been implemented in a laboratory environment [13]. Some simple activities, such as cooking, sitting, watching TV, can be easily inferred by processing the output data of sensors. Environmental sensors can be installed also in nursing homes, to support and help assistance of Alzheimer's disease patients [14]. In this scenario, even the detection of simple events such as "presence in bed" or "door opening" may be relevant to ensure comfort and safety of patients. Environmental sensors are completely unobtrusive and privacy preserving but they usually require some time for the installation. Furthermore, the amount of information that can be obtained from the sensors is limited, and does not include the extraction of human movements.

Other unobtrusive sensors revealing the interaction with the environment can be audio sensors. In fact, some activities generate sounds that can be captured using one or multiple microphones. Characteristic sounds are generated for example by chatting or reading newspapers activities, as well as drink and food intake events, that can be classified considering their features [15]. Tremblay et al. [16] proposed an algorithm to recognize a limited set of activities from six microphones installed at different positions in a test apartment. Two activities of daily living (ADLs), i.e., breakfast and household, constituted by multiple steps have been recognized with a promising accuracy. Multiple audio sensors in the same apartment could constitute a wireless sensor network (WSN), addressing the challenges of limited amount of memory and processing power of the nodes. However, it has been proven that low complexity features extraction algorithms can be adopted with good performance considering the indoor scenario [17]. Vuegen et al. [18] proposed a WSN constituted by seven nodes placed in different rooms: living room/kitchen, bedroom, bathroom and toilet, covering the entire apartment. A set of 10 ADLs has been recorded considering two test users and an artificial dataset to examine the influence of background noise. Acoustic sensors can be adopted in assistive environments to detect dangerous events such as falls [19, 20].

Radio-based techniques do not require any physical sensing module and they may work without the need of wearing any device, but only exploiting the existing WiFi links between the access point and connected devices. With one access point and three devices, a set of nine in-place activities (such as cooking, eating, washing dishes, etc.) and eight walking activities (distinguishing the direction of movement within the apartment) can be recognized [21]. Another radio-based technique is represented by micro-Doppler signatures (MDS). Commercial radar motes can be used to discern among a small set of activities, such as walking, running, and crawling, with high accuracy values [22]. A larger set of MDS captured from humans performing 18 movements has been collected and presented in Ref. [23]. Activities have been grouped in three categories: stationary, forward-moving and multitarget, and characterized both in free-space and through-wall environments, associating the general properties of the signatures to their phenomenological characteristics. Björklund et al. [24] included a set of five activities (crawling, creeping on their hands and knees, walking, jogging, and running) in their study. They evaluated the performance of an activity recognition algorithm based on a support vector machine (SVM) with features in the time-velocity domain and in the cadence-velocity domain, obtaining comparable results of about 90% of accuracy.

Wearable sensors can be used to extract the human movements since they usually provide acceleration data. Considering inertial data, many different features for human action recognition have been proposed, with the aim to reduce the complexity of the features extraction process and to enhance the separation among the classes [25]. Wearable inertial sensors are quite cheap and generate a limited amount of data that can be processed easily with respect to video data, even if they do not provide information about the context. The placement of wearable sensors can be an issue and this step has to be carefully addressed [26]. This choice mainly depends on the movements constituting the set of activities that have to be recognized. The placement on the waist of the subject is close to the center of mass, and can be used to represent activities involving the whole body. With this configuration, sitting, standing, and lying postures can be detected with a high degree of accuracy considering a dataset acquired in a laboratory environment [27]. The placement on the subject's waist, as well as the one on the subject's chest or knee, gives good results with transitional activities also in Ref. [28]. On the other hand, high level activities such as running (in a corridor or on a treadmill) and cycling are revealed mostly by an ear worn sensor, since it measures the change in body posture. The placement of wearable unit on the dominant wrist may help the discrimination of upper body movements constituting for example the activities of brushing teeth, vacuuming, and working at computer [29]. On the other hand, the recognition of gait-related activities, such as normal walking, stair descending, stair ascending, and so on, requires the positioning of the devices on the lower limbs. In particular, even if the shank's sensor could be enough to predict the activities, the usage of other IMUs, placed on tight, foot and waist, can enhance the final accuracy [30]. A multisensor system for activity recognition usually allows to increase the accuracy with respect to a single-sensor system, even if the latter employs a higher sampling rate, more complex features and a more sophisticated classifier [31]. The main drawback is the increasing level of obtrusiveness for the subject being monitored. Furthermore, if it may be acceptable to ask people to wear a device for a limited amount of time, for example to extract some parameters during movement assessment tests [32], it may be unacceptable to request wearing several IMUs to continuously track ADLs.

2.2. Related works on RGB-D sensors

Video-based devices (and especially RGB-D sensors) allow to extract activities from body movements but they are not obtrusive and they do not pose many issues about installation as environmental sensors do. Furthermore, RGB-D sensors do not raise problems related to radiation impact, differently from radar-based techniques, which can limit their acceptability. On the other hand, video-based sensors may be deemed not acceptable for privacy concerns but RGB-D sensors provide not negligible advantages from this point of view. In fact, when the data processing algorithms exploit only depth information, the privacy of the subject is preserved because no plain images are collected, and many details cannot be extracted from depth signal only. Different levels of privacy can be considered according to the user's preferences, thanks to the possibility to extract the human silhouette, or even to represent the human subject only by means of the skeleton [33].

Many different reviews on HAR based on vision sensors have been published in the past, each of which proposing its own taxonomy to classify different approaches [34–36]. Aggarwal and Xia [37], in their review, considered only methods based on 3D data that can be obtained from three different technologies: marker-based systems, stereo images or range sensors, and organizing the papers in five categories based on the features considered.

The review of action recognition algorithms based on RGB-D sensors is organized considering the data processed by the algorithms, separating methods based on depth data from others exploiting skeleton information. Due to the simple extraction process of the silhouette from depth data, approaches based on this information may exploit features extracted from silhouettes. Li et al. [38] calculate a bag of 3D points from human silhouette, sampling the points on the contours of the planar projections of the 3D depth map. An action graph, where each node is associated to a salient posture, is adopted to explicitly model the dynamics of the actions. Features from 2D silhouettes have been considered in Ref. [39], where an action is modeled as a sequence of key poses, extracted by means of a clustering algorithm, from a training dataset. Dynamic time warping (DTW) is suitable in this case because sequences can be inconsistent in terms of time scale, but they preserve the time order, and DTW can associate an unknown sequence of key poses to the closest sequence in the training set, thus performing the recognition process. Other approaches exploiting depth data considered the extraction of local or holistic descriptors. Local spatio-temporal interest points (STIPs), which have been used with RGB data, can be adapted to depth including additional strategies to reduce the noise typical of depth data, such as the inaccurate identification of objects' borders, or the presence of holes in the frame [40]. A spatio-temporal subdivision of the space in multiple segments has been proposed in Ref. [41], where the occupancy patterns are extracted from a 4D grid. Holistic descriptors, namely histogram of oriented 4D normals (HON4D) and histogram of oriented principal components (HOPC) have been exploited respectively in Refs. [42, 43]. HON4D is based on the orientation of normal surfaces in 4D while HOPC can represent the geometric characteristics of a sequence of 3D points.

Skeleton joints represent a compact and effective description of the human body, for this reason they are assumed and exploited as input data by many action recognition algorithms. Kinect sensor provides 3D coordinates of 20 skeleton joints, thus motion trajectories in a 60-dimensional space can be associated to human motion [44]. A trajectory is the evolution of the positions of joint coordinates along a sequence of frames related to an action. A kNN classifier learns the trajectories of different actions and performs classification. Gaglio et al. [45] proposed an algorithm constituted by three steps: features detection, where the skeleton coordinates are elaborated to extract features; posture analysis, that consists in the detection of salient postures through a clustering algorithm and their classification with a support vector machine (SVM); and activity recognition, where a sequence of postures is modeled by an hidden Markov model (HMM). In Ref. [46], the coordinates of human skeleton models generate body poses and an action can be seen as a sequence of body poses over time. According to this approach, a feature vector is obtained representing each pose in a multidimensional feature space. A movement can be now represented as a trajectory in the feature space, which may constitute a signature of the associated action, if the transformation and features are carefully chosen. An effective representation based on skeleton joints is called APJ3D [47], which is built from 3D joint locations and angles. The key postures are extracted by a *k*-means clustering algorithm and, following a representation through an improved Fourier temporal pyramid, the recognition task is carried out with random forests. Xia et al. [48] proposed a method to compactly represent human postures with histograms of 3D joints (HOJ3D). The positions of the joints are translated into a spherical coordinate system and, after a reprojection of the HOJ3D vectors using linear discriminant analysis (LDA), a number of key postures are extracted from training sequences. The temporal evolution of postures is modeled through HMM.

Research on HAR using RGB-D sensors has been fostered by the release of many datasets. An extensive review of the datasets collected for different purposes, going for example from camera tracking and scene reconstruction to pose estimation or semantic reasoning, can be found in Ref. [49]. Another review, which is focused on RGB-D datasets for HAR, has been published in Ref. [50]. In the latter work, the datasets have been organized considering the methods applied for data collection, which can include a single view setup, with one capturing device, a multiview setup with more devices, or a multiperson setup where some interactions among different people are included in the set of classes.

A list of the most used datasets for HAR is provided in **Table 1**, where different features of each dataset are highlighted. Many datasets provide the most important data streams available with a RGB-D device, i.e., the color and depth frames along with skeleton coordinates. They are usually featured by a number of actions between 10 and 20, performed by different subjects (around 10), and repeated 2 or 3 times. Considering the set of actions included in the datasets, they can be used for two main applications that are the detection of daily activities (DA) and the human

Name	Data	Application	Actions	Actors	Times	Samples	Citations	Year
MSR DailyActivity3D [51]	C, D, S	DA	16	10	2	320	614	2012
MSR Action3D [38]	D, S	HCI	20	10	2 or 3	567	603	2010
UTKinect Action [48]	C, D, S	HCI/DA	10	10	2	200	444	2012
MSR ActionPairs [42]	D	DA	6	10	3	180	338	2013
CAD-60 [52]	C, D, S	DA	12	2 + 2	–	60	281	2012
CAD-120 [53]	C, D, S	DA	10	2 + 2	–	120	219	2013
RGBD-HuDaAct [54]	C, D	DA	12	30	2 or 4	1189	211	2011
MSRC-12 KinectGesture [55]	S	HCI	12	30	–	594	197	2012
MSR Gesture3D [56]	D	HCI	12	10	2 or 3	336	159	2012
Berkeley MHAD [57]	C, D, M, Au, Ac	HCI	11	7 + 5	5	~660	110	2013
G3D [58]	C, D, S	HCI	20	10	3	–	61	2012
Florence 3D Action [59]	C, S	DA	9	10	2 or 3	215	54	2012
ACT4 Dataset [60]	C, D	DA	14	24	>1	6844	53	2012
LIRIS Human Activities [61]	C, D	DA	10	21	–	–	49	2012
3D Online Action [62]	C, D, S	DA	7	24	–	–	41	2014
UPCV Action [46]	S	DA	10	20	–	–	39	2014
WorkoutSu-10 Gesture [63]	D, S	DA	10	15	10	1500	32	2013

Name	Data	Application	Actions	Actors	Times	Samples	Citations	Year
KARD [45]	C, D, S	HCI/DA	18	10	3	540	23	2014
UTD-MHAD [64]	C, D, S	HCI	27	8	4	861	22	2015
IAS-Lab Action [65]	C, D, S	DA	15	12	3	540	21	2013
NTU RGB+D [66]	C, D, S, IR	HCI/DA	60	40	–	56880	14	2016

Note: In the column related to data, each label represents the availability of a different type of data: RGB (C), Depth (D), Skeleton (S), Acceleration (Ac), Audio (Au), Mocap (M). The datasets can be oriented to two main applications: Daily Activities (DA) and Human Computer Interaction (HCI).

Table 1. List of the most important RGB-D datasets for Human Action Recognition, listed considering the number of citations according to Google Scholar on January 3rd 2017.

computer interaction (HCI). Datasets belonging to the first group usually include actions like *walking, eating, drinking,* and sometimes they are recorded in a real scenario, which introduces partial occlusions and a complex background [51, 52]. Datasets focused on HCI applications may contain actions like *draw x, draw circle, side kick,* and they are usually captured with a simpler background, even if they can be challenging, due to the similarity of many gestures and to the differences in speeds and way to perform the movement, considering different actors.

The oldest and the newest datasets included in the list are deeply discussed because of their characteristics. MSR Action3D [38] was the first relevant dataset for HAR, it has been released in 2010 and it includes 20 actions that are suitable for HCI. The following activities are included in the dataset: *high arm wave, horizontal arm wave, hammer, hand catch, forward punch, high throw, draw x, draw tick, draw circle, hand clap, two hand wave, side boxing, bend, forward kick, side kick, jogging, tennis swing, tennis serve, golf swing, pick-up, and throw*. As described in Ref. [38], the dataset has been often evaluated considering three subsets of 8 actions each, namely AS1, AS2, and AS3. As can be noticed from **Table 2**, AS1 and AS2 are built by grouping actions with similar movements, and AS3 includes actions that require more complex movements. From **Figure 1** it is possible to observe sequences of frames constituting two similar actions in AS1: *hammer* and *forward punch*. Sequences of frames from

AS1	AS2	AS3
(a02) *Horizontal arm wave*	(a01) *High arm wave*	(a06) *High throw*
(a03) *Hammer*	(a04) *Hand catch*	(a14) *Forward kick*
(a05) *Forward punch*	(a07) *Draw x*	(a15) *Side kick*
(a06) *High throw*	(a08) *Draw tick*	(a16) *Jogging*
(a10) *Hand clap*	(a09) *Draw circle*	(a17) *Tennis swing*
(a13) *Bend*	(a11) *Two-hand wave*	(a18) *Tennis serve*
(a18) *Tennis serve*	(a12) *Side boxing*	(a19) *Golf swing*
(a20) *Pick-up and throw*	(a14) *Forward kick*	(a20) *Pick-up and throw*

Table 2. Actions constituting the three subsets of MSR Action3D: AS1, AS2, AS3.

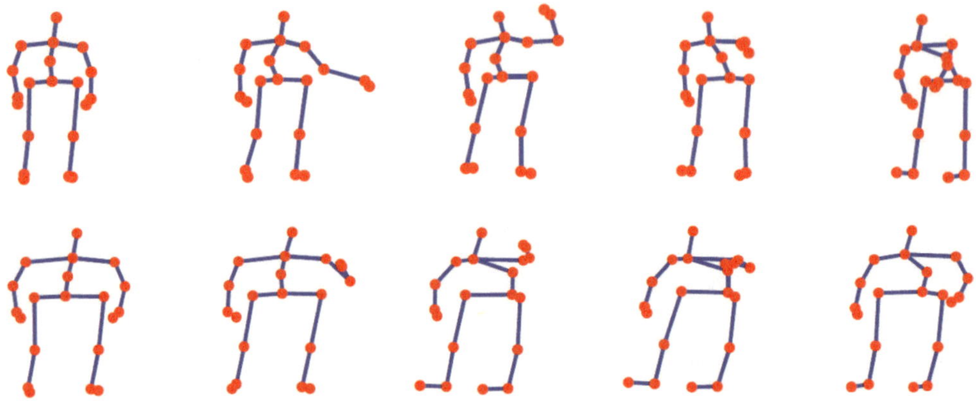

Figure 1. Sequences of frames constituting similar actions in AS1 subset of MSR Action3D: *hammer* (top) and *forward punch* (bottom).

Draw x and *Draw tick*, two similar actions in AS2, are shown in **Figure 2**. The dataset has been collected using a structured light depth sensor and the provided data are represented by depth frames, at a resolution of 320 × 240, and skeleton coordinates. The entire dataset includes 567 sequences but, considering that 10 of them are affected by wrong or missing skeletons, only 557 sequences of skeleton joint coordinates are available. The evaluation method usually adopted on this dataset is called cross-subject test [38] and takes into account samples from actors 1-3-5-7-9 for training, and the remaining data for testing. NTU RGB+D [66] is one of the most recent datasets for HAR and, to the authors' best knowledge, the largest. In fact, it includes 60 different actions that can be grouped in 40 daily actions (*reading, writing, wear jacket, take off jacket*), 9 health-related actions (*falling down, touch head, touch neck*), and 11 interactions (*walking toward each other, walking apart from each other, handshaking*). A number of 40 actors have been recruited to perform the actions multiple times, involving also 17 different setups of the Kinect v2 sensors adopted for data collection. Each

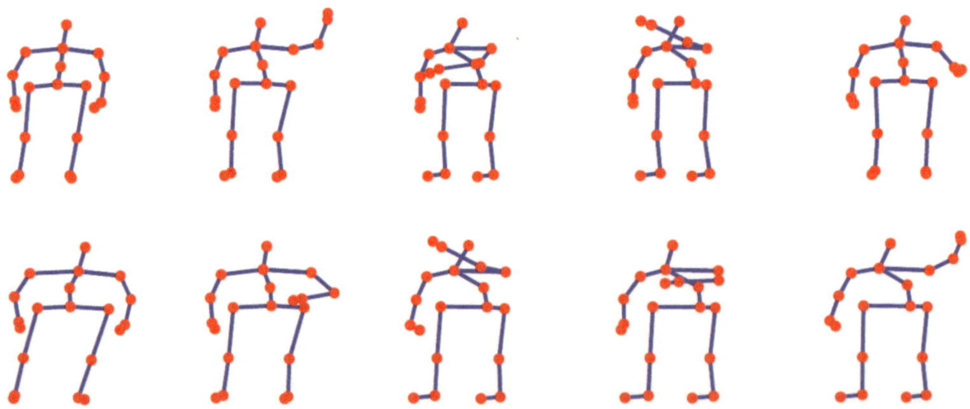

Figure 2. Sequences of frames constituting similar actions in AS2 subset of MSR Action3D: *draw x* (top) and *draw tick* (bottom).

action has been captured from three sensors simultaneously, having three different views of the same scene (0°, +45°, −45° directions). All the data provided by Kinect v2 (RGB, depth, infrared frames and skeleton coordinates) are collected and included in the released dataset. Two evaluation methods have been proposed in Ref. [66], aiming to test the goodness of HAR methods with unseen subjects and new views. In the cross-subject test, a specific list of subjects is used for training and the remaining represent the test data, while in the cross-view test the sequences from devices 2 and 3 are used for training and the ones from camera 1 are adopted for testing.

3. Human action recognition based on temporal pyramid of key poses

A HAR method that allows to achieve state-of-the-art results has been proposed in Ref. [67] and can be defined as temporal pyramid of key poses. It exploits the bag of key poses model [68] and it adopts a temporal pyramid to model the temporal structure of the key poses constituting an action sequence.

3.1. Algorithm overview

The algorithm based on temporal pyramid of key poses can be represented by the scheme shown in **Figure 3**. It performs four main steps that include the extraction of posture features, the adoption of the bag of key poses model, and the representation of the action sequence through a temporal pyramid of key poses; finally, the classification by a multiclass SVM takes place.

The algorithm takes as an input the coordinates of skeleton joints, that can be seen as a 3-dimensional vector $\mathbf{J}_i$ for the i-th joint of a body with P joints. The aim of the first step is to obtain view- and position-invariant features from the raw coordinates. The feature computation scheme derives from the one proposed in Ref. [69], but here a virtual joint called center-of-mass is introduced. Considering all the skeleton joints stored in the vector $\mathbf{P}_n$ related to the n-th frame of a sequence, the center-of-mass $\mathbf{J}_{cm}$ is calculated by averaging the coordinates of all the P joints. In order to normalize coordinates with respect to the size of the body, the normalization factor s is computed by averaging the L-2 norm between the skeleton joints and $\mathbf{J}_{cm}$, as follows:

$$s = \frac{1}{P} \sum_{i=0}^{P-1} \|\mathbf{J}_i - \mathbf{J}_{cm}\|_2 \tag{1}$$

The normalization with respect to the position of the skeleton is implemented considering the displacement between each joint position and the center-of-mass, normalized by the factor s. Each joint is thus represented by a 3 dimensional vector $\mathbf{d}_i$:

$$\mathbf{d}_i = \frac{\mathbf{J}_i - \mathbf{J}_{cm}}{s} \tag{2}$$

Finally, as can be noticed in the first part of **Figure 3**, each vector $\mathbf{p}_n$ corresponding to the coordinates of the skeleton in the n-th frame, is translated into a vector $\mathbf{f}_n$ which includes the features related to that skeleton.

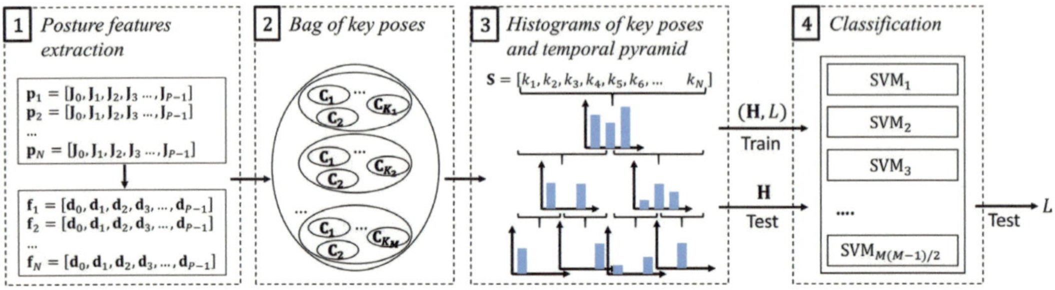

Figure 3. Global scheme of the algorithm based on temporal pyramid of key poses. Step 1 extracts the feature vectors related to posture while step 2 is represented by the bag of key poses model. The third phase exploits the temporal pyramid to model the temporal structure of the sequences and the last step is the classification phase.

Once the features related to the skeleton have been obtained, the bag of key poses method is adopted to extract the most significant postures and the action is then represented as a sequence of key poses. In more detail, the clustering algorithm *k*-means is applied considering separately the training sequences of each class, setting a different number of key poses for each action of the dataset, i.e., K_1 for class 1, K_2 for class 2, up to K_M if the dataset is constituted by M classes. Following the clustering process performed separately for each class, the key poses, which are the centres of the clusters, have to be merged to obtain a unique codebook. Finally, each posture feature vector is associated to the closest key pose in terms of Euclidean distance, and a sequence of key poses $\mathbf{S} = [k_{1,} k_{2,} k_{3,\ldots,} k_N]$ represents an action of N frames.

The temporal structure of an action can be represented with the adoption of a temporal pyramid. The idea is to provide different representations of the action: the most general one is provided at the first level of the pyramid, whereas the most detailed one is given at the last level. For each level, the computation of the histograms of key poses is implemented, having at the end of the process a histogram for each segment at each level. Starting from the consideration of the entire sequence at the first level of the pyramid, two segments are considered in the second level and they are split again in two at the third level, giving a number of seven histograms when three levels are considered. These histograms **H** represent the input data to the final step, which is the classifier.

The classification step aims to associate the data extracted from an unknown data sequence to the correct action label, knowing the training set. In particular, the classifier has to be trained with a set of histograms **H** for which the action labels L are known. Then, in the testing phase, an unknown **H** has to be associated to the corresponding L. A multiclass SVM has been chosen for classification purpose. The approach considered for the implementation of the multiclass scheme is defined as "one-versus-one," where a set of $M(M - 1)/2$ binary SVMs are required for a dataset of M classes, each of which has to distinguish two classes. The output class is elected with a voting strategy considering the result of each binary SVM.

3.2. Experimental results and discussion

This method has been evaluated on one of the most used RGB-D dataset for HAR: MSR Action3D [38]. The test scheme adopted is the cross-subject test, described in the previous section.

http://dx.doi.org/10.5772/68121

The algorithm requires to set different parameters in order to be executed, which are the number of key poses per class (clusters), the set of skeleton joints (features) and the set of training sequences (instances). These parameters can be chosen randomly or using some optimization strategies in order to maximize the performance. In this chapter, results are shown using both the options, adopting the optimization process, based on evolutionary [70] and coevolutionary [71] algorithms. These optimization strategies are applied as wrapper methods, associating the fitness of each individual in the population to the accuracy of the action recognition algorithm.

Since the idea is to optimize three parameters, the structure of each individual is constituted by three parts [72]. The first one is related to features, and it is a binary vector of length P, which is the number of joints in a skeleton. A bin is featured by a 1 value if the associated joint has to be considered by the action recognition algorithm; otherwise it is featured by a 0 value. The same approach is used for the part related to training instances, which is therefore represented by a binary vector of length I. Regarding the optimization of the number of key poses, it is necessary to adopt a vector of integer values with a length of M, where each bin is associated to a class of the dataset, and contains the number of its clusters. Crossover and mutation operators have to be used to evolve the population's individuals, and a standard 1-point crossover operator is applied for the subindividuals related to instances and clusters. A specific crossover operator which takes into account the structure of the skeleton joints is applied to the features part. Finally, three different mutation probabilities are considered, for the three parts of the individual.

In addition to the evolutionary algorithm, a cooperative coevolutionary optimization method can be also implemented. The main difference between evolutionary and coevolutionary approaches is in the organization of the population of individuals. In particular, in the latter case, each subindividual is part of a different population, thus generating a set of three populations. The selection of one element from each population is necessary to execute the action recognition algorithm and to extract the fitness value, which is associated to each subindividual. Crossover and mutation operators can be applied according to the same considerations made for the evolutionary computation. In order to improve the performance of the optimization process, different priorities are given to the individuals of the populations. In particular, in the populations related to features and instances, the individuals with a lower number of ones are preferred, while in the populations related to clusters, the individuals featuring a lower number of key poses are favored.

The three parameter selection methods can be described as follows:

- Random selection: the number of clusters required by the bag of key poses method is selected randomly within the interval [4, 26] for the subsets AS1 and AS2 and the interval [44, 76] for AS3. All the skeleton joints and training instances are included in the processing.
- Evolutionary optimization: the evolutionary algorithm selects the best combination of skeleton joints and *clusters*, considering all the training sequences. The same intervals adopted in the random selection are used for the optimization of the number of key poses.
- Coevolutionary optimization: the optimization method selects all the parameters required by the HAR algorithm: *features, clusters,* and *instances*. In this case, the intervals for *clusters* optimization are [4, 16] for AS1 and AS2, and [4, 64] for AS3.

The results are summarized in **Table 3**, where it can be noticed that, for all the parameters selection methods, the best results are obtained for AS3, AS1, and finally AS2. In fact, as already stated, subsets AS1 and AS2 group have similar gestures (**Figures 1** and **2**). More in detail, from **Figure 2** it is quite evident that *Draw x* and *Draw tick* involve the same poses, and the main cue to differentiate them is their order.

	AS1	AS2	AS3	Avg
Random selection	95.24	86.61	95.5	92.45
Evolutionary optimization	95.24	90.18	100	95.14
Coevolutionary optimization	95.24	91.96	98.2	95.13

Table 3. Results in terms of accuracy (%) obtained on MSR Action3D by the method based on temporal pyramid of key poses.

An average accuracy of 92.45% can be achieved considering the random selection of number of key poses. The subset AS2 is the most critical one, with an accuracy of 86.61% due to the aforementioned reasons. Considering evolutionary optimization, where the evaluated parameters are the number of key poses and the set of skeleton joints, there is a noticeable improvement in AS2 and AS3, and the HAR algorithm shows an average accuracy of 95.14%. Similar average results are obtained with the adoption of the coevolutionary optimization method, including also the set of training instances in the optimization process. In particular, there is a further improvement in AS2, which shows an accuracy of 91.96%, while a suboptimal result (98.2%) is achieved in AS3.

Table 4 aims to compare the results obtained by different HAR methods on MSR Action3D considering the cross-subject evaluation protocol and averaging the results on AS1, AS2, and

	AS1	AS2	AS3	Avg
Li et al. [38]	72.9	71.9	79.2	74.67
Chaaraoui et al. [68]	92.38	86.61	96.4	91.8
Lo Presti et al. [73]	90.29	95.15	93.29	92.91
Tao and Vidal [74]	89.81	93.57	97.03	93.5
Du et al. [75]	93.3	94.64	95.5	94.49
Temporal pyramid of key poses	95.24	90.18	100	95.4
Lillo et al. [76]	94.3	92.9	99.1	95.4
Xu et al. [77]	99.1	92.9	96.4	96.1
Liang et al. [78]	98.1	92.9	99.1	96.7
Shahroudy et al. [79]	–	–	–	98.2

Table 4. Results in terms of accuracy (%) obtained by main HAR algorithms evaluated on cross-subject tests.

AS3 [38]. Only the works in which the use of cross-subject test with actors 1-3-5-7-9 for training and the rest for testing is clearly stated are included in the table.

Some recently published works outperform the performance achieved by the method based on temporal pyramid of key poses. Lillo et al. [76] proposed an activity recognition method based on three levels of abstraction. The first level is dedicated to learning the most representative primitives related to body motion. The poses are combined to compose atomic actions at the mid-level, and more atomic actions are combined to create more complex activities at the top-level. As input data, the aforementioned proposal exploits angles and planes from segments extracted from joint coordinates, adding also histograms of optical flow calculated from RGB patches centered at the joint locations. Xu et al. [77] proposed the adoption of depth motion map (DMM), which is computed from the differences among consecutive maps, to describe the dynamic feature of an action. In addition to this method, the depth static model (DSM) can describe the static feature of an action. The so-called TPDM-SPHOG descriptor encodes DMMs and DSM represented by a temporal pyramid and histogram of oriented gradient (HOG) extracted using a spatial pyramid. DMM and multiscale HOG descriptors are also exploited by Liang et al. [78], and they are combined with local space-time auto-correlation of gradients (STACOG), which compensates the loss of temporal information. l_2-regularized collaborative representation classification (CRC) is adopted to take as inputs for the proposed descriptors and classify the actions. In Ref. [79], a joint sparse regression learning method, which models each action as a combination of multimodal features from body parts, is proposed. In fact, each skeleton is separated into a number of parts and different features, related to the movement and local depth information, are extracted from each part. A small number of active parts for each action class are selected through group sparsity regularization. A hierarchical mixed norm, which includes three levels of regularization over learning weights, is integrated into the learning and selection framework.

The comparison of the algorithm based on temporal pyramid of key poses to other approaches achieving higher accuracies on MSR Action3D allows to conclude that all the considered works exploit not only skeleton data but also RGB or depth information. One approach is based on the extraction of the most important postures considering skeleton joints and RGB data [76], DMM and HOG descriptors calculated from depth data are exploited by more papers [77, 78], and a heterogeneous set of depth and skeleton-based features has been considered in Ref. [79].

4. Conclusion

Human action recognition performed exploiting data collected by RGB-D devices has been an active research field and many researchers are developing algorithms exploiting the properties and characteristics of depth sensors. The main advantages in using this technology include unobtrusiveness and privacy preservation, differently from video-based solutions; additionally, it does not extract movements from interaction with objects, as environmental sensors do, and it does not require the subject to wear any device, differently from systems based on wearable technologies.

Among the HAR algorithms based on RGB-D data, the chapter provided a detailed discussion of a method exploiting a temporal pyramid of key poses that has been able to achieve state-of-the-art results on the well-known MSR Action3D dataset.

Author details

Enea Cippitelli*, Ennio Gambi and Susanna Spinsante

*Address all correspondence to: e.cippitelli@univpm.it

Department of Information Engineering, Polytechnic University of Marche, Ancona, Italy

References

[1] L. Chen, J. Hoey, C. D. Nugent, D. J. Cook, Z. Yu. Sensor-based activity recognition. IEEE Transactions on Systems, Man, and Cybernetics, Part C (Applications and Reviews). 2012;**42**(6):790-808. DOI: 10.1109/TSMCC.2012.2198883

[2] R. Poppe. A survey on vision-based human action recognition. Image and Vision Computing. 2010;**28**(6):976-990. DOI: 10.1016/j.imavis.2009.11.014

[3] A. Avci, S. Bosch, M. Marin-Perianu, R. Marin-Perianu, P. Havinga. Activity Recognition Using Inertial Sensing for Healthcare, Wellbeing and Sports Applications: A Survey. In: 23th International Conference on Architecture of Computing Systems. Hannover, Germany. 2010. pp. 1-10.

[4] T. D'Orazio, R. Marani, V. Renò, G. Cicirelli. Recent trends in gesture recognition: How depth data has improved classical approaches. Image and Vision Computing. 2016;**52**: 56-72. DOI: 10.1016/j.imavis.2016.05.007

[5] J. Shotton, A. Fitzgibbon, A. Blake, A. Kipman, M. Finocchio, R. Moore, T. Sharp. Real-time Human Pose Recognition in Parts from a Single Depth Image. In: CVPR; Colorado Springs, CO. June; 2011.

[6] Q. Ni, A. B. García Hernando, I. P. de la Cruz. The elderly's independent living in smart homes: A characterization of activities and sensing infrastructure survey to facilitate services development. Sensors. 2015;**15**(5):11312-11362. DOI: 10.3390/s150511312

[7] S. Wang, G. Zhou. A review on radio based activity recognition. Digital Communications and Networks. 2015;**1**(1):20-29. DOI: 10.1016/j.dcan.2015.02.006

[8] M. Shoaib, S. Bosch, O. D. Incel, H. Scholten, P. J. Havinga. A survey of online activity recognition using mobile phones. Sensors. 2015;**15**(1):2059-2085. DOI: 10.3390/s150102059.

[9] D. Lara, M. A. Labrador. A survey on human activity recognition using wearable sensors. IEEE Communications Surveys Tutorials. 2013;**15**(3):1192-1209. DOI: 10.1109/SURV.2012.110112.00192

[10] E. Munguia Tapia, S. S. Intille, K. Larson. Activity Recognition in the Home Using Simple and Ubiquitous Sensors. In: A. Ferscha, F. Mattern, editors. Pervasive Computing, Second International Conference, PERVASIVE 2004, Linz/Vienna, Austria, April 21-23, 2004. Proceedings. Lecture Notes in Computer Science ed. Springer Berlin Heidelberg; 2004. pp. 158-175. DOI: 10.1007/978-3-540-24646-6_10

[11] F. J. Ordóñez, P. de Toledo, A. Sanchis. Activity recognition using hybrid generative/discriminative models on home environments using binary sensors. Sensors. 2013;**13**(5):5460-5477. DOI: 10.3390/s130505460

[12] D. H. Wilson, C. Atkeson. Simultaneous Tracking and Activity Recognition (Star) Using Many Anonymous, Binary Sensors. In: H. W. Gellersen, R. Want, A. Schmidt, editors. Pervasive Computing: Third International Conference, Pervasive 2005, Munich, Germany, May 8-13, 2005. Proceedings. Lecture Notes in Computer Science ed. Springer Berlin Heidelberg; 2005. pp. 62-79. DOI: 10.1007/11428572_5

[13] S. Spinsante, E. Gambi, A. De Santis, L. Montanini, G. Pelliccioni, L. Raffaeli, G. Rascioni. Design and Implementation of a Smart Home Technological Platform for the Delivery of AAL Services: From Requirements to Field Experience. In: F. Florez-Revuelta, A. A. Chaaraoui, editors. Active and Assisted Living: Technologies and Applications. London (UK): The Institution of Engineering and Technology; 2016. pp. 433-456.

[14] L. Montanini, L. Raffaeli, A. De Santis, A. Del Campo, C. Chiatti, G. Rascioni, E. Gambi, S. Spinsante. Overnight Supervision of Alzheimer's Disease Patients in Nursing Homes - System Development and Field Trial. In: Proceedings of the International Conference on Information and Communication Technologies for Ageing Well and e-Health; 21-22 April 2016. Rome (IT); 2016. pp. 15-25. DOI: 10.5220/0005790000150025

[15] J. M. Sim, Y. Lee, O. Kwon. Acoustic sensor based recognition of human activity in everyday life for smart home services. International Journal of Distributed Sensor Networks. 2015;**11**(9) DOI: 10.1155/2015/679123

[16] S. Tremblay, D. Fortin-Simard, E. Blackburn-Verrault, S. Gaboury, B. Bouchard. Exploiting Environment Sounds for Activity Recognition in Smart Homes. In: 2nd AAAI Workshop on Artificial Intelligence Applied to Assistive Technologies and Smart Environments (ATSE '15); January 25-26; Austin (TX). 2015.

[17] E. L. Salomons, P. J. M. Havinga. A survey on the feasibility of sound classification on wireless sensor nodes. Sensors. 2015;**15**(4):7462-7498. DOI: 10.3390/s150407462

[18] L. Vuegen, B. Van Den Broeck, P. Karsmakers, H. Van hamme, B. Vanrumste. Energy Efficient Monitoring of Activities of Daily Living Using Wireless Acoustic Sensor Networks in Clean and Noisy Conditions. In: Signal Processing Conference (EUSIPCO), 2015 23rd European, Nice, France; 31 Aug.–4 Sept.; 2015. pp. 449-453. DOI: 10.1109/EUSIPCO.2015.7362423

[19] M. Salman Khan, M. Yu, P. Feng, L. Wang, J. Chambers. An unsupervised acoustic fall detection system using source separation for sound interference suppression. Signal Processing. 2015;**110**:199-210. DOI: 10.1016/j.sigpro.2014.08.021

[20] Y. Li, Z. Zeng, M. Popescu, K. C. Ho. Acoustic Fall Detection Using a Circular Microphone Array. In: 2010 Annual International Conference of the IEEE Engineering in Medicine and Biology; 31 Aug.–4 Sept; Buenos Aires, Argentina; 2010. pp. 2242-2245. DOI: 10.1109/IEMBS.2010.5627368

[21] Y. Wang, J. Liu, Y. Chen, M. Gruteser, J. Yang, H. Liu. E-eyes: Device Free Location-Oriented Activity Identification Using Fine-Grained Wifi Signatures. In: Proceedings of the 20th Annual International Conference on Mobile Computing and Networking; Maui, Hawaii, USA. 2014. pp. 617-628. DOI: 10.1145/2639108.2639143

[22] B. Çaglıyan, S. Z. Gürbüz. Micro-doppler-based human activity classification using the mote-scale bumblebee radar. IEEE Geoscience and Remote Sensing Letters. 2015;**12**(10):2135-2139. DOI: 10.1109/LGRS.2015.2452946

[23] R. M. Narayanan, M. Zenaldin. Radar micro-Doppler signatures of various human activities. IET Radar, Sonar & Navigation. 2015;**9**(9):1205-1215. DOI: 10.1049/iet-rsn.2015.0173

[24] S. Björklund, H. Petersson, G. Hendeby. Features for micro-Doppler based activity classification. IET Radar, Sonar & Navigation. 2015;**9**(9):1181-1187. DOI: 10.1049/iet-rsn.2015.0084

[25] R. Damaševičius, M. Vasiljevas, J. Šalkevičius, M. Woźniak. Human activity recognition in AAL environments using random projections. Computational and Mathematical Methods in Medicine. 2016;**2016**:Article ID 4073584, 17 pages. DOI: 10.1155/2016/4073584

[26] F. Attal, S. Mohammed, M. Dedabrishvili, F. Chamroukhi, L. Oukhellou, Y. Amirat. Physical human activity recognition using wearable sensors. Sensors. 2015;**15**(12):31314-31338. DOI: 10.3390/s151229858

[27] D. M. Karantonis, M. R. Narayanan, M. Mathie, N. H. Lovell, B. G. Celler. Implementation of a real-time human movement classifier using a triaxial accelerometer for ambulatory monitoring. IEEE Transactions on Information Technology in Biomedicine. 2006;**10**(1):156-167. DOI: 10.1109/TITB.2005.856864

[28] L. Atallah, B. Lo, R. King, G. Z. Yang. Sensor Placement for Activity Detection Using Wearable Accelerometers. In: International Conference on Body Sensor Networks, Singapore; 2010. pp. 24-29. DOI: 10.1109/BSN.2010.23

[29] J.-Y. Yang, J.-S.Wang, Y.-P. Chen. Using acceleration measurements for activity recognition: An effective learning algorithm for constructing neural classifiers. Pattern Recognition Letters. 2008;**29**(16):2213-2220. DOI: 10.1016/j.patrec.2008.08.002

[30] M. M. Hamdi, M. I. Awad, M. M. Abdelhameed, F. A. Tolbah. Lower Limb Gait Activity Recognition Using Inertial Measurement Units for Rehabilitation Robotics. In: International Conference on Advanced Robotics (ICAR); Istanbul. 2015. pp. 316-322. DOI: 10.1109/ICAR.2015.7251474

[31] L. Gao, A. Bourke, J. Nelson. Evaluation of accelerometer based multi-sensor versus single-sensor activity recognition systems. Medical Engineering & Physics. 2014;**36**(6):779-785. DOI: 10.1016/j.medengphy.2014.02.012

[32] E. Cippitelli, S. Gasparrini, E. Gambi, S. Spinsante, J. Wahslen, I. Orhan, T. Lindh. Time Synchronization and Data Fusion for Rgb-Depth Cameras and Inertial Sensors in AAL Applications. In: 2015 IEEE International Conference on Communication Workshop (ICCW); London. 2015. pp. 265-270. DOI: 10.1109/ICCW.2015.7247189

[33] J. R. Padilla-Lopez, A. A. Chaaraoui, F. Gu, F. Florez-Revuelta. Visual privacy by context: Proposal and evaluation of a level-based visualisation scheme. Sensors. 2015;**15**(6):12959-12982. DOI: 10.3390/s150612959

[34] J. K. Aggarwal, Q. Cai. Human motion analysis: A review. Computer Vision and Image Understanding. 1999;**73**(3):428-440. DOI: 10.1006/cviu.1998.0744

[35] P. Turaga, R. Chellappa, V. S. Subrahmanian, O. Udrea. Machine recognition of human activities: A survey. IEEE Transactions on Circuits and Systems for Video Technology. 2008;**18**(11):1473-1488. DOI: 10.1109/TCSVT.2008.2005594

[36] A. A. Chaaraoui, P. Climent-Perez, F. Florez-Revuelta. A review on vision techniques applied to human behaviour analysis for ambient-assisted living. Expert Systems with Applications. 2012;**39**(12):10873-10888. DOI: 10.1016/j.eswa.2012.03.005

[37] J. K. Aggarwal, L. Xia. Human activity recognition from 3D data: A review. Pattern Recognition Letters. 2014;**48**:70-80. DOI: 10.1016/j.patrec.2014.04.011

[38] W. Li, Z. Zhang, Z. Liu. Action Recognition Based on a Bag of 3d Points. In: 2010 IEEE Conference on Computer Vision and Pattern Recognition Workshops (CVPRW). 2010. San Francisco, CA; pp. 9-14. DOI: 10.1109/CVPRW.2010.5543273

[39] A. A. Chaaraoui, P. Climent-Perez, F. Florez-Revuelta. Silhouette-based human action recognition using sequences of key poses. Pattern Recognition Letters. 2013;**34**(15):1799-1807. DOI: 10.1016/j.patrec.2013.01.021

[40] L. Xia, J. K. Aggarwal. Spatio-temporal Depth Cuboid Similarity Feature for Activity Recognition Using Depth Camera. In: 2013 IEEE Conference on Computer Vision and Pattern Recognition; Portland. 2013. pp. 2834-2841. DOI: 10.1109/CVPR.2013.365

[41] A. Vieira, E. Nascimento, G. Oliveira, Z. Liu, M. Campos. STOP: Space-Time Occupancy Patterns for 3D Action Recognition from Depth Map Sequences. In: L. Alvarez, M. Mejail, L. Gomez, J. Jacobo, editors. Progress in Pattern Recognition, Image Analysis, Computer Vision, and Applications. Lecture Notes in Computer Science ed. Springer Berlin Heidelberg; 2012. pp. 252-259. DOI: 10.1007/978-3-642-33275-3_31

[42] O. Oreifej, Z. Liu. HON4D: Histogram of Oriented 4D Normals for Activity Recognition from Depth Sequences. In: 2013 IEEE Conference on Computer Vision and Pattern Recognition; Portland. 2013. pp. 716-723. DOI: 10.1109/CVPR.2013.98

[43] H. Rahmani, A. Mahmood, D. Q Huynh, A. Mian. HOPC: Histogram of Oriented Principal Components of 3D Pointclouds for Action Recognition. In: D. Fleet, T. Pajdla, B. Schiele, T. Tuytelaars, editors. Computer Vision - ECCV 2014. Lecture Notes in Computer Science ed. Springer International Publishing, Cham; 2014. pp. 742-757. DOI: 10.1007/978-3-319-10605-2_48

[44] M. Devanne, H. Wannous, S. Berretti, P. Pala, M. Daoudi, A. Del Bimbo. Space-Time Pose Representation for 3D Human Action Recognition. In: A. Petrosino, L. Maddalena, P. Pala, editors. New Trends in Image Analysis and Processing - ICIAP 2013. Lecture Notes in Computer Science ed. Springer, Berlin, Heidelberg; 2013. pp. 456-464. DOI: 10.1007/978-3-642-41190-8_49

[45] S. Gaglio, G. L. Re, M. Morana. Human activity recognition process using 3-d posture data. IEEE Transactions on Human-Machine Systems. 2015;**45**(5):586-597. DOI: 10.1109/THMS.2014.2377111

[46] I. Theodorakopoulos, D. Kastaniotis, G. Economou, S. Fotopoulos. Pose-based human action recognition via sparse representation in dissimilarity space. Journal of Visual Communication and Image Representation. 2014;**25**(1):12-23. DOI: 10.1016/j.jvcir.2013.03.008

[47] L. Gan, F. Chen. Human action recognition using apj3d and random forests. Journal of Software. 2013;**8**(9):2238-2245. DOI: 10.4304/jsw.8.9.2238-2245

[48] L. Xia, C.-C. Chen, J. Aggarwal. View Invariant Human Action Recognition Using Histograms of 3d Joints. In: 2012 IEEE Conference on Computer Vision and Pattern Recognition Workshops; 2012. Providence, Rhode Island; pp. 20-27. DOI: 10.1109/CVPRW.2012.6239233

[49] M. Firman. RGBD datasets: Past, present and future. CoRR. 2016;**abs/1604.00999**

[50] J. Zhang, W. Li, P. O. Ogunbona, P. Wang, C. Tang. RGB-D-based action recognition datasets: A survey. Pattern Recognition. 2016;**60**:86-105. DOI: 10.1016/j.patcog.2016.05.019

[51] J. Wang, Z. Liu, Y. Wu, J. Yuan. Mining Actionlet Ensemble for Action Recognition with Depth Cameras. In: 2012 IEEE Conference on Computer Vision and Pattern Recognition (CVPR); 2012. Providence, Rhode Island; pp. 1290-1297. DOI: 10.1109/CVPR.2012.6247813

[52] J. Sung, C. Ponce, B. Selman, A. Saxena. Unstructured Human Activity Detection from Rgbd Images. In: 2012 IEEE Conference on Robotics and Automation (ICRA); 2012. St. Paul, Minnesota; pp. 842-849. DOI: 10.1109/ICRA.2012.6224591

[53] H. S. Koppula, R. Gupta, A. Saxena. Learning human activities and object affordances from RGB-D videos. International Journal of Robotics Research. 2013;**32**(8):915-970. DOI: 10.1177/0278364913478446

[54] B. Ni, G. Wang, P. Moulin. RGBD-HuDaAct: A Color-Depth Video Database for Human Daily Activity Recognition. In: 2011 IEEE International Conference on Computer Vision Workshops; 2011. Barcelona, Spain; pp. 1147-1153. DOI: 10.1109/ICCVW.2011.6130379

[55] S. Fothergill, H. M. Mentis, P. Kohli, S. Nowozin. Instructing People for Training Gestural Interactive Systems. In: Proceedings of the SIGCHI Conference on Human Factors in Computing Systems; ACM, 2012. Austin, TX; pp. 1737-1746. DOI: 10.1145/2207676.2208303

[56] A. Kurakin, Z. Zhang, Z. Liu. A Real Time System for Dynamic Hand Gesture Recognition with a Depth Sensor. In: Proceedings of the 20th European Signal Processing Conference (EUSIPCO); 2012. Bucharest, Romania; pp. 1975-1979.

[57] F. Ofli, R. Chaudhry, G. Kurillo, R. Vidal, R. Bajcsy. Berkeley MHAD: A Comprehensive Multimodal Human Action Database. In: 2013 IEEE Workshop on Applications of Computer Vision (WACV); 2013. Clearwater, Florida; pp. 53-60. DOI: 10.1109/WACV.2013.6474999

[58] V. Bloom, D. Makris, V. Argyriou. G3D: A Gaming Action Dataset and Real Time Action Recognition Evaluation Framework. In: 2012 IEEE Conference on Computer Vision and Pattern Recognition Workshops (CVPRW); 2012. Providence, Rhode Island; pp. 7-12. DOI: 10.1109/CVPRW.2012.6239175

[59] L. Seidenari, V. Varano, S. Berretti, A. Del Bimbo, P. Pala. Recognizing Actions from Depth Cameras as Weakly Aligned Multi-part Bag-of-Poses. In: 2013 IEEE Conference on Computer Vision and Pattern Recognition Workshops (CVPRW); 2013. Portland, Oregon; pp. 479-485. DOI: 10.1109/CVPRW.2013.77

[60] Z. Cheng, L. Qin, Y. Ye, Q. Huang, Q. Tian. Human Daily Action Analysis with Multi-view and Color-Depth Data. In: A. Fusiello, V. Murino, R. Cucchiara, editors. Computer Vision - ECCV 2012. Workshops and Demonstrations. Lecture Notes in Computer Science ed. Springer, Berlin, Heidelberg; 2012. pp. 52-61. DOI: 10.1007/978-3-642-33868-7_6

[61] C. Wolf, J. Mille, E. Lombardi, O. Celiktutan, M. Jiu, M. Baccouche, E. Dellandréa, C.-E. Bichot, C. Garcia, B. Sankur. The LIRIS Human Activities Dataset and the ICPR 2012 Human Activities Recognition and Localization Competition. In: LIRIS Laboratory, Tech. Rep. RR-LIRIS-2012-004, March 2012.

[62] G. Yu, Z. Liu, J. Yuan. Discriminative Orderlet Mining for Real-Time Recognition of Human-Object Interaction. In: D. Cremers, I. Reid, H. Saito, M.-H. Yang, editors. Computer Vision – ACCV 2014: 12th Asian Conference on Computer Vision, Singapore, Singapore, November 1-5, 2014, Revised Selected Papers, Part V. Image Processing, Computer Vision, Pattern Recognition, and Graphics ed. Springer International Publishing, Cham; 2014. pp. 50-65. DOI: 10.1007/978-3-319-16814-2_4

[63] F. Negin, F. Özdemir, C. B. Akgül, K. A. Yüksel, A. Erçil. A Decision Forest Based Feature Selection Framework for Action Recognition from RGB-Depth Cameras. In: M. Kamel, A. Campilho, editors. Image Analysis and Recognition. Lecture Notes in Computer Science ed. Munich: Springer, Berlin, Heidelberg; 2013. pp. 648-657. DOI: 10.1007/978-3-642-39094-4_74

[64] C. Chen, R. Jafari, N. Kehtarnavaz. UTD-MHAD: A Multimodal Dataset for Human Action Recognition Utilizing a Depth Camera and a Wearable Inertial Sensor. In: 2015 IEEE International Conference on Image Processing (ICIP); 2015. Québec City, Canada; pp. 168-172. DOI: 10.1109/ICIP.2015.7350781

[65] M. Munaro, G. Ballin, S. Michieletto, E. Menegatti. 3D flow estimation for human action recognition from colored point clouds. Biologically Inspired Cognitive Architectures. 2013;**5**:42-51. DOI: 10.1016/j.bica.2013.05.008

[66] A. Shahroudy, J. Liu, T.-T. Ng, G. Wang. NTU RGB+D: A Large Scale Dataset for 3D Human Activity Analysis. In: 2016 IEEE Conference on Computer Vision and Pattern Recognition (CVPR); 2016. Las Vegas, NV; pp. 1010-1019. DOI: 10.1109/CVPR.2016.115

[67] E. Cippitelli, E. Gambi, S. Spinsante, F. Florez-Revuelta. Human Action Recognition Based on Temporal Pyramid of Key Poses Using RGB-D Sensors. In: J. Blanc-Talon, C. Distante, W. Philips, D. Popescu, P. Scheunders, editors. Advanced Concepts for Intelligent Vision Systems: 17th International Conference, ACIVS 2016, Lecce, Italy, October 24-27, 2016, Proceedings. Lecture Notes in Computer Science, Springer International Publishing; 2016. pp. 510-521. DOI: 10.1007/978-3-319-48680-2_45

[68] A. A. Chaaraoui, J. R. Padilla-López, F. Flórez-Revuelta. Fusion of Skeletal and Silhouette-Based Features for Human Action Recognition with RGB-D Devices. In: 2013 IEEE International Conference on Computer Vision Workshops; 2013. Sydney, Australia; pp. 91-97. DOI: 10.1109/ICCVW.2013.19

[69] E. Cippitelli, S. Gasparrini, E. Gambi, and S. Spinsante. A human activity recognition system using skeleton data from RGBD sensors. Computational Intelligence and Neuroscience. 2016;**2016**, Article ID 4351435, 14 pages. DOI: 10.1155/2016/4351435

[70] A. A. Chaaraoui, J. R. Padilla-Lopez, P. Climent-Perez, F. Florez-Revuelta. Evolutionary joint selection to improve human action recognition with RGB-D devices. Expert Systems with Applications. 2014;**41**(3):786-794. DOI: 10.1016/j.eswa.2013.08.009

[71] A. A. Chaaraoui, F. Florez-Revuelta. Optimizing human action recognition based on a cooperative coevolutionary algorithm. Engineering Applications of Artificial Intelligence. 2014;**31**:116-125. DOI: 10.1016/j.engappai.2013.10.003

[72] A. A. Chaaraoui, F. Florez-Revuelta. Adaptive human action recognition with an evolving bag of key poses. IEEE Transactions on Autonomous Mental Development. 2014;**6**(2):139-152. DOI: 10.1109/TAMD.2014.2315676

[73] L. Lo Presti, M. L. Cascia, S. Sclaroff, O. Camps. Hankelet-based dynamical systems modeling for 3d action recognition. Image and Vision Computing. 2015;**44**:29-43. DOI: 10.1016/j.imavis.2015.09.007

[74] L. Tao, R. Vidal. Moving Poselets: A Discriminative and Interpretable Skeletal Motion Representation for Action Recognition. In: 2015 IEEE International Conference on Computer Vision Workshop (ICCVW); 2015. Santiago, Chile; pp. 303-311. DOI: 10.1109/ICCVW.2015.48

[75] Y. Du, W. Wang, L. Wang. Hierarchical Recurrent Neural Network for Skeleton Based Action Recognition. In: 2015 IEEE Conference on Computer Vision and Pattern Recognition (CVPR); 2015. Boston, Massachusetts; pp. 1110-1118. DOI: 10.1109/CVPR.2015.7298714

[76] I. Lillo, J. C. Niebles, A. Soto. Sparse composition of body poses and atomic actions for human activity recognition in RGB-D videos. Image and Vision Computing. 2017;**59**:63-75. DOI: 10.1016/j.imavis.2016.11.004

[77] H. Xu, E. Chen, C. Liang, L. Qi, L. Guan. Spatio-Temporal Pyramid Model Based on Depth Maps for Action Recognition. In: 2016 IEEE 17th International Workshop on Multimedia Signal Processing (MMSP); 2015. Montreal, Canada; pp. 1-6. DOI: 10.1109/MMSP.2015.7340806

[78] C. Liang, L. Qi, E. Chen, L. Guan. Depth-Based Action Recognition Using Multiscale Sub-Actions Depth Motion Maps and Local Auto-Correlation of Space-Time Gradients. In: 2016 IEEE 8th International Conference on Biometrics Theory, Applications and Systems (BTAS); 2016. Niagara Falls, NY; pp. 1-7. DOI: 10.1109/BTAS.2016.7791167

[79] A. Shahroudy, T. T. Ng, Q. Yang, G. Wang. Multimodal multipart learning for action recognition in depth videos. IEEE Transactions on Pattern Analysis and Machine Intelligence. 2016;**38**(10):2123-2129. DOI: 10.1109/TPAMI.2015.2505295

Chapter 6

Gesture Recognition by Using Depth Data: Comparison of Different Methodologies

Grazia Cicirelli and Tiziana D'Orazio

Additional information is available at the end of the chapter

http://dx.doi.org/10.5772/68118

Abstract

In this chapter, the problem of gesture recognition in the context of human computer interaction is considered. Several classifiers based on different approaches such as neural network (NN), support vector machine (SVM), hidden Markov model (HMM), deep neural network (DNN), and dynamic time warping (DTW) are used to build the gesture models. The performance of each methodology is evaluated considering different users performing the gestures. This performance analysis is required as the users perform gestures in a personalized way and with different velocity. So the problems concerning the different lengths of the gesture in terms of number of frames, the variability in its representation, and the generalization ability of the classifiers have been analyzed.

Keywords: gesture recognition, feature extraction, model learning, gesture segmentation, human-robot interface, Kinect camera

1. Introduction

In the last decade, gesture recognition has been attracting a lot of attention as a natural way to interact with computer and/or robots through intentional movements of hands, arms, face, or body. A number of approaches have been proposed giving particular emphasis on hand gestures and facial expressions by the analysis of images acquired by conventional RGB cameras [1, 2].

The recent introduction of low cost depth sensors, such as the Kinect camera, allowed the spreading of new gesture recognition approaches and the possibility of developing personalized human computer interfaces [3, 4]. The Kinect camera provides RGB images together with depth information, so the 3D structure of the scene is immediately available. This allows us to easily manage many tasks such as people segmentation and tracking, body part recognition, motion estimation, and so on. Recently human activity recognition and motion analysis from 3D data have been reviewed in a number of interesting works [5–8].

At present, Gesture Recognition through visual and depth information is one of the main active research topics in the computer vision community. The launch on the market of the popular Kinect, by the Microsoft Company, influenced video-based recognition tasks such as object detection and classification and in particular allowed the increment of the research interest in gesture/activity recognition. The Kinect provides synchronized depth and color (RGB) images where each pixel corresponds to an estimate of the distance between the sensor and the closest object in the scene together with the RGB values at each pixel location. Together with the sensor some software libraries are also available that permit to detect and track one or more people in the scene and to extract the corresponding human skeleton in real time. The availability of information about joint coordinates and orientation has promoted a great impulse to research on gesture and activity recognition [9–14].

Many papers, presented in literature in the last years, use normalized coordinates of proper subset of skeleton joints which are able to characterize the movements of the body parts involved in the gestures [15, 16]. Angular information between joint vectors has been used as features to eliminate the need of normalization in Ref. [17].

Different methods have been used to generate gesture models. Hidden Markov Models (HMM) are a common choice for gesture recognition as they are able to model sequential data over time [18, 19]. Usually HMMs require sequences of discrete symbols, so different quantization schemes are first used to quantize the features which characterize the gestures. Support vector machines (SVM) reduce the classification problem into multiple binary classifications either by applying a one-versus-all (OVA-SVM) strategy (with a total of N classifiers for N classes) [20, 21] or a one-versus-one (OVO-SVM) strategy (with a total of $N \times (N-1)/2$ classifiers for N classes) [22, 23]. Artificial neural networks (ANNs) represent another alternative methodology to solve classification problems in the context of gesture recognition [24]. The choice of the network topology, the number of nodes/layers and the node activation functions depends on the problem complexity and can be fixed by using iterative processes which run until the optimal parameters are found [25].

Distance-based approaches are also used in gesture recognition problems. They use distance metrics for measuring the similarity between samples and gesture models. In order to apply any metric for making comparisons, these methods have to manage the problem related to the different length of feature sequences. Several solutions have been proposed in literature: Dynamic Time Warping technique (DTW) [26] is the most commonly used. It calculates an optimal match between two sequences that are nonlinearly aligned. A frame-filling algorithm is proposed in Ref. [27] to first align gesture data, then an eigenspace-based method (called Eigen3Dgesture) is applied for recognizing human gestures.

In the last years, the growing interest in automatically learning the specific representation needed for recognition or classification has fostered the recent emergence of deep learning architectures [28]. Rather than using handcrafted features as in conventional machine learning techniques, deep neural architectures are applied to learn representations of data at multiple levels of abstractions in order to reduce the dimensionality of feature vectors and to extract relevant features at higher level. Recently, several approaches have been proposed such as in Refs. [29, 30]. In Ref. [29], a method for gesture detection and localization based on multiscale and multimodel deep learning is presented. Both temporal and spatial scales are managed by employing a multimodel convolutional neural network. Similarly in Ref. [30], a multimodel gesture segmentation and recognition method, called deep dynamic neural networks, is presented. A semisupervised hierarchical dynamic framework based on a Hidden Markov Model is proposed for simultaneous gesture segmentation and recognition.

In this chapter, we compare different methodologies to approach the problem of Gesture Recognition in order to develop a natural human-robot interface with good generalization ability. Ten gestures performed by one user in front of a Kinect camera are used to train several classifiers based on different approaches such as dynamic time warping (DTW), neural network (NN), support vector machine (SVM), hidden Markov model (HMM), and deep neural network (DNN).

The performance of each methodology is evaluated considering several tests carried out on depth video streams of gestures performed by different users (diverse from the one used for the training phase). This performance analysis is required as users perform gestures in a personalized way and with different velocity. Even the same user executes gestures differently in separate video acquisition sessions. Furthermore, contrarily to the case of static gesture recognition, in the case of depth videos captured live the problem of gesture segmentation must be addressed. During the test phase, we apply a sliding window approach to extract sequences of frames to be processed and recognized as gestures. Notice that the training set contains gestures which are accompanied by the relative ground truth labels and are well defined by their start and end points. Testing live video streams, instead, involves several challenging problems such as the identification of the starting/ending frames of a gesture, the different length related to the different types of gestures and finally the different speeds of execution. The analysis of the performance of the different methodologies allows us to select, among the set of available gestures, the ones which are better recognized together with the better classifier, in order to construct a robust human-robot interface.

In this chapter, we consider all the mentioned challenging problems. In particular, the fundamental steps that characterize an automatic gesture recognition system will be analyzed: (1) feature extraction that involves the definition of the features that better and distinctively characterize a specific movement or posture; (2) gesture recognition that is seen as a classification problem in which examples of gestures are used into supervised and semisupervised learning schemes to model the gestures; (3) spatiotemporal segmentation that is necessary for determining, in a video sequence, where the dynamic gestures are located, i.e., when they start and end.

The rest of the chapter is organized as follows. The overall description of the problem and the definition of the gestures are given in Section 2. The definition of the features is provided in Section 3. The methodologies selected for the gesture model generation are described in Section 4. Section 6 presents the experiments carried out both in the learning and prediction stage.

Furthermore, details on gesture segmentation will be given in the same section. Finally, Section 7 presents the final conclusions and delineates some future works.

2. Problem definition

In this chapter, we consider the problems related to the development of a gesture recognition interface giving a panoramic view and comparing the most commonly used methodologies of machine learning theory. At this aim, the Kinect camera is used to record video sequences of different users while they perform predefined gestures in front of it. The OpenNI Library is used to detect and segment the user in the scene in order to obtain the information of the joints of the user's body. Ten different gestures have been defined. They are pictured in **Figure 1**. Throughout the chapter the gestures will be referred by using the following symbols G_1, G_2, G_3, ... G_N, where $N = 10$. Some gestures are quite similar in terms of variations of joint orientations; the only difference is the plane in which the bones of the arm rotate. This is the case, for example, of gestures G_9 and G_4 or G_1, and G_8. Furthermore, some gestures involve movements in a plane parallel to the camera (G_1, G_3, G_4, G_7) while others involve a forward motion in a plane perpendicular to the camera (G_2, G_5, G_6, G_8, G_9, G_{10}). In the last case, instability in detecting some joints can occur due to autoocclusions.

The proposed approaches for gesture recognition involve three main stages: a feature selection stage, a learning stage and a prediction stage. Firstly the human skeleton information, captured and returned by the depth camera, is converted into representative and discriminant

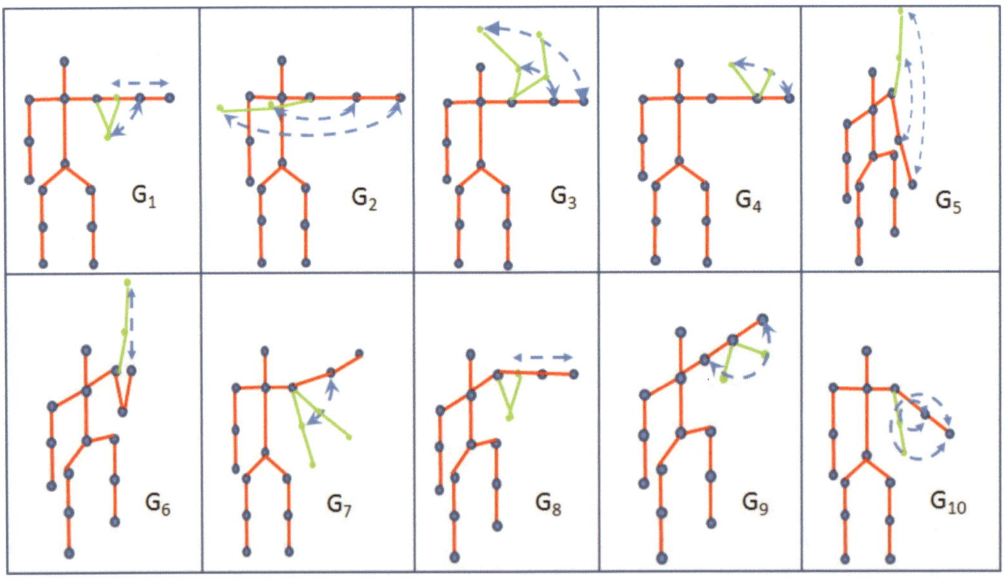

Figure 1. Ten different gestures are shown. Gestures G_1, G_3, G_4, and G_7 involve movements in a plane parallel to the camera. Gestures G_2, G_5, G_6, G_8, G_9, and G_{10} involve a forward motion in a plane perpendicular to the camera.

features. These features are used during the learning stage to learn the gesture model. In this chapter, different methodologies are applied and compared in order to construct the gesture model. Some methodologies are based on a supervised or semisupervised process such as neural network (NN), support vector machine (SVM), hidden Markov model (HMM), and deep neural network (DNN). Dynamic time warping (DTW) is a distance-based approach, instead. Finally, during the prediction stage new video sequences of gestures are tested by using the learned models. The following sections will describe in detail each stage previously introduced.

3. Feature selection

The complexity of the gestures strictly affects the feature selection and the choice of the methodology for the construction of the gesture model. If gestures are distinct enough, the recognition can be easy and reliable. So, the coordinates of joints, which are immediately available by the Kinect software platforms, could be sufficient. In this case a preliminary normalization is required in order to guarantee invariance with respect to the height of the users, distance and orientation with respect to the camera. On the other hand, the angular information of joint vectors has the great advantage of maximizing the invariance of the skeletal representation with respect to the camera position. In Ref. [31], the angles between the vectors generated by the elbow-wrist joints, and the shoulder-elbow joints, are used to generate the models of the gestures. The experimental results, however, prove that these features are not discriminant enough to distinguish all the gestures.

In our approach, we use more complex features that represent orientations and rotations of a rigid body in three dimensions. The quaternions of two joints (shoulder and elbow) of the left arm are used. A quaternion comprises a scalar component and a vector component in complex space and is generally represented in the following form:

$$q = a + bi + cj + dk \tag{1}$$

where the coefficients a, b, c, d are real numbers and i, j, k are the fundamental quaternion units. The quaternions are extremely efficient to represent three-dimensional rotations as they combine the rotation angles together with the rotation axes. In this work, the quaternions of the shoulder and elbow joints are used to define a feature vector V_i for each frame i:

$$V_i = [a_i^s, b_i^s, c_i^s, d_i^s, a_i^e, b_i^e, c_i^e, d_i^e] \tag{2}$$

where the index s stands for shoulder and e stands for elbow. The sequence of vectors of a whole gesture execution is defined by the following vector:

$$\overline{V} = [V_1, V_2, \ldots, V_n] \tag{3}$$

Where n is the number of frames during which the gesture is entirely performed.

4. Learning stage: gesture model construction

The learning stage regards the construction of the gesture model. As introduced in Section 1, machine learning algorithms are largely and successfully applied to gesture recognition. In this context, gesture recognition is considered as a classification problem. So, under this perspective, a number of gesture templates are collected, opportunely labeled with the class labels (*supervised learning*) and used to train a learning scheme in order to learn a classification model. The constructed model is afterwards used to predict the class label of unknown templates of gestures.

In this chapter, different learning methodologies are applied to learn the gesture model. For each of them, the best parameter configuration and the best architecture topology which assure the convergence of each methodology are selected. Artificial neural networks (ANNs), support vector machines (SVMs), hidden Markov models (HMMs), and deep neural networks (DNNs) are the machine learning algorithms compared in this chapter. Furthermore a distance-based method, the dynamic time warping (DTW), is also applied and compared with the aforementioned algorithms. The following subsections will give a brief introduction of each algorithm and some details on how they are applied to solve the proposed gesture recognition problem.

4.1. Neural network

A neural network is a computational system that simulates the way biological neural systems process information [32]. It consists of a large number of highly interconnected processing units (neurons) typically distributed on multiple layers. The learning process involves successive adjustments of connection weights, through an iterative training procedure, until no further improvement occurs or until the error drops below some predefined reasonable threshold. Training is accomplished by presenting couples of input/output examples to the network (*supervised learning*).

In this work, 10 different neural networks have been used to learn the models of the defined gestures. The architecture of each NN consists of an input layer, one hidden layer and an output layer with a single neuron. The back-propagation algorithm is applied during the learning process. Each training set contains the templates of one gesture as positive examples and those of all the others as negative ones. As each gesture execution lasts a different number of frames, a preliminary normalization of the feature vectors has been carried out by using a linear interpolation. Linear interpolation to resample the number of features is a good compromise between computational burden and quality of results. The length of a feature vector V, which describes one single gesture, has been fixed to $n = 60$. This length has been fixed considering the average time of execution of each type of gesture which is about 2 seconds and the sample rate of the Kinect camera which is 30 Hz.

4.2. Support vector machine

Support vector machine is a supervised learning algorithm widely used in classification problems [33]. The peculiarity of SVM is that of finding the optimal separating hyperplane between the negative and positive examples of the training set. The optimal hyperplane is defined as the maximum margin hyperplane, i.e., the one for which the distance between the hyperplane (decision surface) and the closest data points is maximum. It can be shown that the optimal hyperplane is fully specified by a subset of data called *support vectors* which lie nearest to it, exactly on the margin.

In this work, SVMs have been applied considering the one-versus-one strategy. This strategy builds a two-class classifier for each pair of gesture classes. In our case, the total number of SVMs is defined by:

$$M = \frac{N(N-1)}{2} \tag{4}$$

where N is the number of gesture classes. The training set of each SVM contains the examples of the two gesture classes for which the current classifier is built. As in the case of NNs, the feature vectors are preliminary normalized to the same length n.

4.3. Hidden Markov model

Hidden Markov model is a statistical model which assumes that the system to be modeled is a Markov process. Even if the theory of HMMs dates back to the late 1960s, their widespread application occurred only within the past several years [34, 35]. Their successful application to speech recognition problems motivated their diffusion in gesture recognition as well. An HMM consists of a set of unobserved (*hidden*) states, a state transition probability matrix defining the transition probabilities among states and an observation or emission probability matrix which defines the output model. The goal is to learn the best set of state transition and emission probabilities, given a set of observations. These probabilities completely define the model.

In this work, one discrete hidden Markov model is learnt for each gesture class. The feature vectors of each training set, which represent the observations, are firstly normalized and then discretized by applying a K-means algorithm. A fully connected HMM topology and the Baum-Welch algorithm have been applied to learn the optimal transition and emission probabilities.

4.4. Deep neural network

Deep learning is a relatively new branch of machine learning research [28]. Its objective is to learn features automatically at multiple levels of abstraction exploiting an unsupervised learning algorithm at each layer [36]. At each level a new data representation is learnt and used as input to the successive level. Once a good representation of data has been found, a supervised stage is performed to train the top level. A final supervised fine-tuning stage of the entire architecture completes the training phase and improves the results. The number of levels defines the deepness of the architecture.

In this work, a deep neural network with 10 output nodes (one for each class of gesture) is constructed. It comprises two levels of unsupervised autoencoders and a supervised top level.

The autoencoders are used to learn a lower dimensional representation of the feature vectors at a higher level of abstraction. An autoencoder is a neural network which is trained to reconstruct its own input. It is comprised of an encoder, that maps the input to the new representation of data, and a decoder that reconstruct the original input. We use two autoencoders with one hidden layer. The number of hidden neurons represents the dimension of the new data representation. The feature vectors of training set are firstly normalized, as described in Section 4.1, and fed into the first autoencoder. So the features generated by the first autoencoder are used as input to the second one. The size of the hidden layer for both the first and second autoencoder has been fixed to half the size of the input vector. The features learnt by the last autoencoder are given as input to the supervised top level implemented by using a softmax function trained with a scaled conjugate gradient algorithm [37]. Finally the different levels are stacked to form the deep network and its parameters are fine-tuned by performing backpropagation using the training data in a supervised fashion.

4.5. Dynamic time warping

DTW is a different technique with respect to the previously described ones as it is a distance-based algorithm. Its peculiarity is to find the ideal alignment (*warping*) of two time-dependent sequences considering their synchronization. For each pair of elements of the sequences, a cost matrix, also referred as local distance matrix, is computed by using a distance measure. Then the goal is to find the minimal cost path through this matrix. This optimal path defines the ideal alignment of the two sequences [38]. DTW is successfully applied to compare sequences that are altered by noise or by speed variations. Originally, the main application field of DTW was automatic speech processing [39], where variation in speed appears concretely. Successively DTW found its application in movement recognition, where variation in speed is of major importance, too.

In this work, DTW is applied to compare the feature vectors in order to measure how different they are for solving the classification problem. Differently from the previously described methodologies, the preliminary normalization of feature vectors is not required due to the warping peculiarity of DTW algorithm. For each class of gesture, one target feature vector is selected. This is accomplished by applying DTW to the set of training samples inside each gesture class. The one with the minimum distance from all the other samples of the same class is chosen as target gesture. Each target gesture will be used in the successive prediction stage for classification.

5. Prediction stage: gesture model testing

In prediction stage, also referred as testing stage, video sequences with unknown gestures are classified by using the learnt gesture models. This stage allows us to compare the recognition performance of the methodologies introduced in the learning stage. These methodologies have been applied by using different strategies as described in the following.

In the case of NN, 10 classifiers have been trained, one for each class. So the feature vector of a new gesture sample is inputted into all the classifiers and is assigned to the class with the maximum output value.

In the case of SVM, instead, a max-win voting strategy has been applied. The trained SVMs are 45 two-class classifiers. When each classifier receives as input a gesture sample, classifies it into one of the two classes. Therefore, the winning class gets one vote. When all the 45 votes have been assigned, the instance of the gesture is classified into the class with the maximum number of votes.

In the case of HMM, 10 HMMs have been learnt during the learning stage, one for each class of gesture. As introduced in Section 4.3 the model of each class is specified by the transition and emission probabilities learnt in the learning stage. When a gesture instance is given as input to the HMM, this computes the probability of that instance given the model. The class of the HMM returning the maximum probability is the winning class.

In the case of DNN, as described in Section 4.4, the deep architecture, constructed in the learning stage, has 10 output nodes. So, when a gesture sample is inputted in the network for prediction, the winning class is simply the one relative to the node with the maximum output value.

Finally, for what concerns the DTW case, the target gestures, found during the learning stage, are used to predict the class of new gesture instances. The distances between the unknown gesture sample and the 10 target gestures are computed. The winning class is that of the target gesture with minimum distance.

6. Experiments

In this section the experiments carried out in order to evaluate the performance of the analyzed methodologies will be described and the obtained results will be shown and compared. In particular, the experiments conducted in both the learning stage and the prediction stage will be detailed separately for a greater clarity of presentation.

Several video sequences of gestures performed by different users have been acquired by using a Kinect camera. Sequences of the same users in different sessions (e.g., in different days) have been also acquired in order to have a wide variety of data. The length of each sequence is about 1000 frames. The users have been requested to execute gestures standing in front of the Kinect, by using the left arm and without pause between one gesture execution and the successive one. The distance between Kinect and user is not fixed. The only constraint is that the whole user's body has to be seen by the sensor, so its skeleton data can be detected by using the OpenNi processing Library. These data are recorded for each frame of the sequence.

6.1. Learning stage

As described in Section 4, the objective of the learning stage is to construct or, more specifically, to *learn* a gesture model. In order to reach this goal, the first step is the construction of the training datasets. The idea of using public datasets has been discarded as they do not assure that real situations are managed. Furthermore, they contain sample gestures which are acquired mainly in the same conditions. We have decided to use a set of gestures chosen by us (see **Figure 1**), which have been selected from the "Arm-and-Hand Signals for Ground Forces" [40].

The video sequences of only one user (afterward referred as Training User) are considered for building the training sets. Each sequence contains several executions of the same gesture without idle frames between one instance and the other. In this stage, we manually segment the training streams into gesture instances in order to guarantee that each extracted subsequence contains exactly one gesture execution. Then each instance is converted in feature vector by using the skeleton data as described in Section 3. Notice that feature vectors V can have different lengths, because either gesture execution lasts a different number of frames or users execute gestures with different speeds. Part of the obtained feature vectors are used for training and the rest for validation.

The second step of the learning stage is the construction of the gesture model by using the methodologies described in Section 4. A preliminary normalization of feature vectors to the same length is needed in the cases of NN, SVM, HMM, and DNN. As described in Section 4.1, n has been fixed to 60. So each normalized feature vector V has 480 components which have been defined by using the quaternion coefficients of shoulder and elbow joints (see Eqs. (2) and (3)). In the case of DTW this normalization is not required.

For each methodology, different models can be learnt depending on the parameters of the methodology. These parameters can be structural such as the number of hidden nodes in the NN architecture or in the autoencoder or the number of hidden states in a HMM; or they can be tuning parameters as in the case of SVM. So, different experiments have been carried out for selecting the optimal parameters inside each methodology. Optimal parameters have to be intended as those which provide a good compromise between over-fitting and prediction error over the validation set.

6.2. Prediction stage

The prediction stage represents the recognition phase which allows us to compare the performance of each methodology. In this phase the class labels of feature vectors are predicted based on the learnt gesture model. Differently from the training phase that can be defined as an off-line phase, the prediction stage can be defined as an on-line stage. In this case the video sequences of six different users (excluded the Training-User) have been properly processed by using an approach that works when live video sequences have to be tested. Differently from the learning stage, where gesture instances were manually selected from the sequences and were directly available for training the classifiers, in the prediction stage the sequences need to be opportunely processed by applying a gesture segmentation approach. This process involves several challenging problems such as the identification of the staring/ending points of a gesture instance, the different length related to the different classes of gestures and finally the different speeds of execution.

In this work, the sequences are processed by using a sliding window approach, where a window slides forward over the sequence by one frame per time in order to extract subsequences. First, the dimension of the sliding window must be defined. As there are no idle frames among successive gesture executions, an algorithm based on Fast Fourier Transform (FFT) has been applied in order to estimate the duration of each gesture execution [41]. As each sequence contains several repetitions of the same gesture, it is possible to approximate the sequence of features as a periodic signal. Applying the FFT and by tacking the position of the fundamental harmonic component, the period can be evaluated as the reciprocal value of the peak position. The estimated period is then used to define the sliding window's dimension in order to extract subsequences of features from the original sequence. Each subsequence represents the feature vector which is then normalized (if required) and provided as input to the classifier which returns a prediction label for the current vector. In order to construct a more robust human computer interface, a further verification check has been introduced before the final decision is taken. This process has been implemented by using a max-voting scheme on 10 consecutive answers of the classifier obtained testing 10 consecutive subsequences. The final decision is that relative to the class label with the maximum number of votes.

6.3. Results and discussion

In **Figures 2–7**, the recognition rates obtained by testing the classifiers on a number of sequences performed by six different users are reported. For each user the plotted rates have been obtained by averaging the results over three testing sequences. As can be observed the classifiers behave in a very different way due to the personalized execution of gestures by the users. Furthermore, there are cases where some classifiers fail in assigning the correct class. This is, for example, the case of gestures G_2 and G_4 performed by User 6 (see **Figure 7**). DTW has 0% detection rate for G_2, whereas NN has 0% detection rate for G_4. The same happens for gesture G_9 performed by User 2 (see **Figure 3**) which is rarely recognized by all the classifiers, as well as G_3 performed by User 5 (see **Figure 6**).

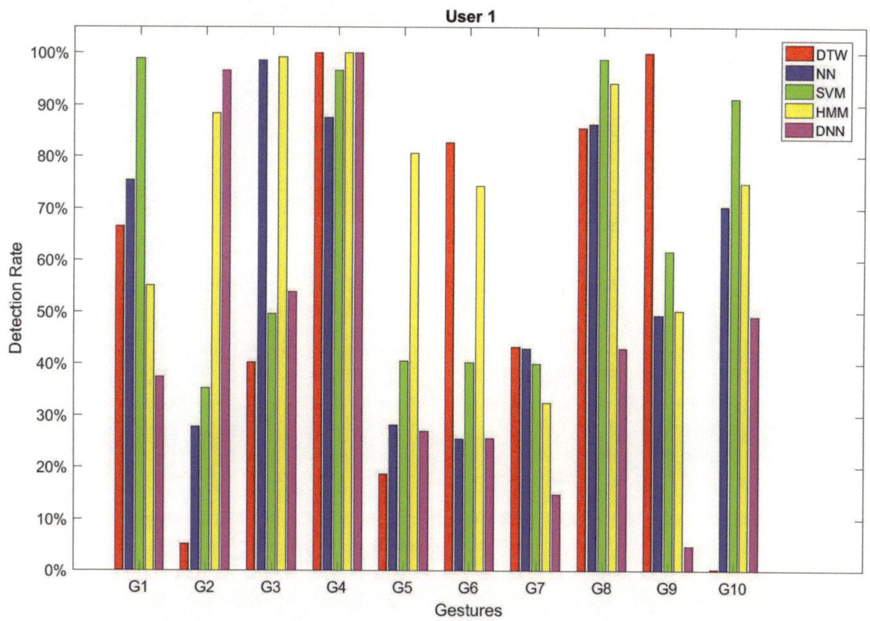

Figure 2. Recognition rates obtained by testing each method on sequences of gestures performed by User 1.

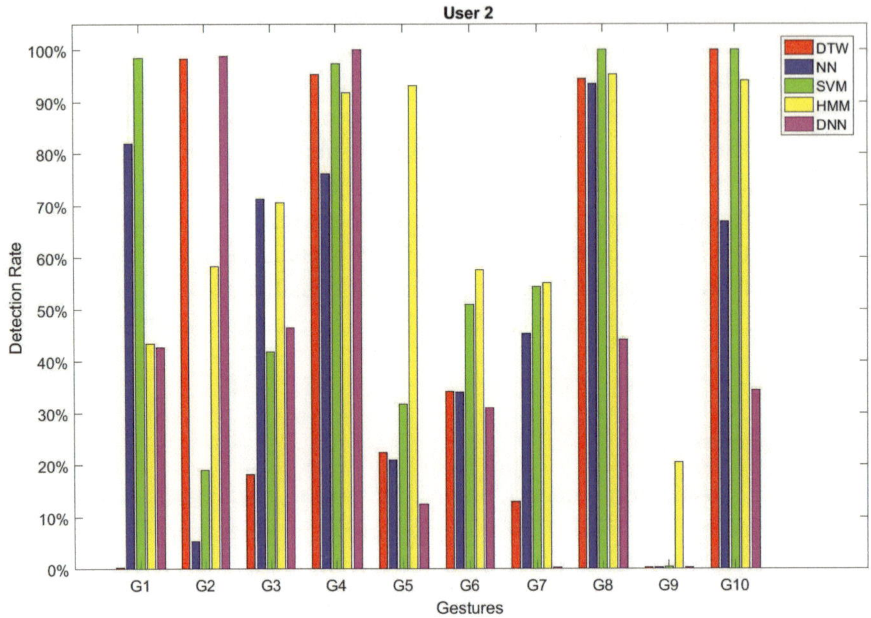

Figure 3. Recognition rates obtained by testing each method on sequences of gestures performed by User 2.

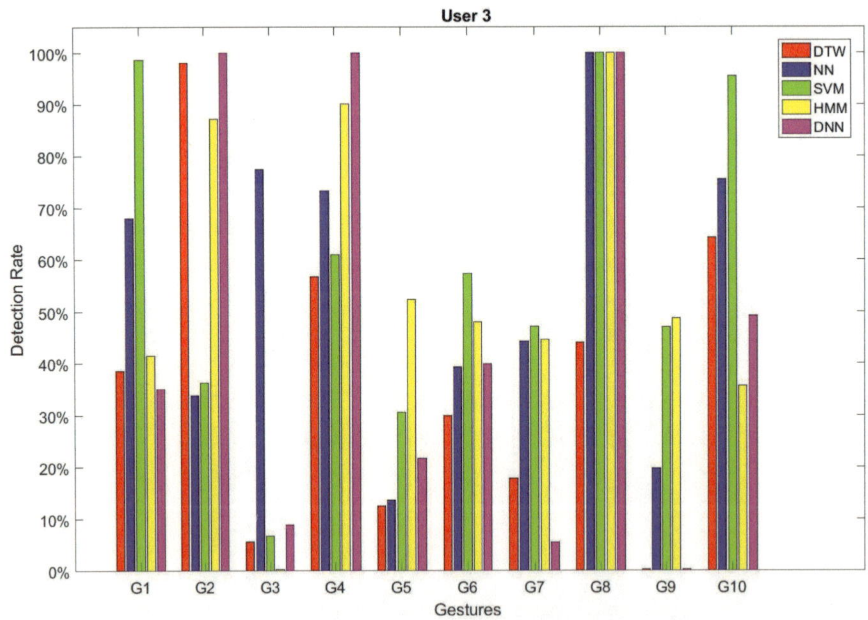

Figure 4. Recognition rates obtained by testing each method on sequences of gestures performed by User 3.

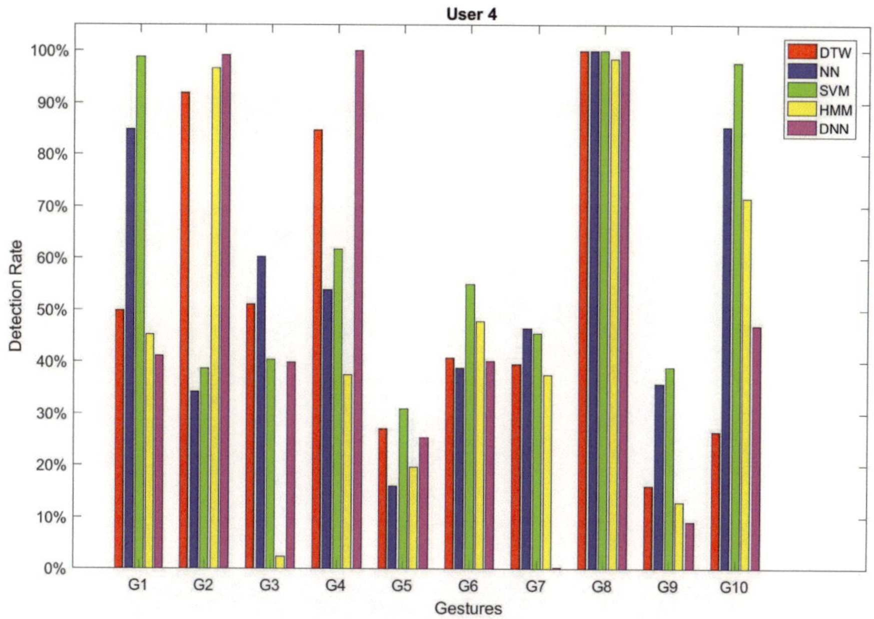

Figure 5. Recognition rates obtained by testing each method on sequences of gestures performed by User 4.

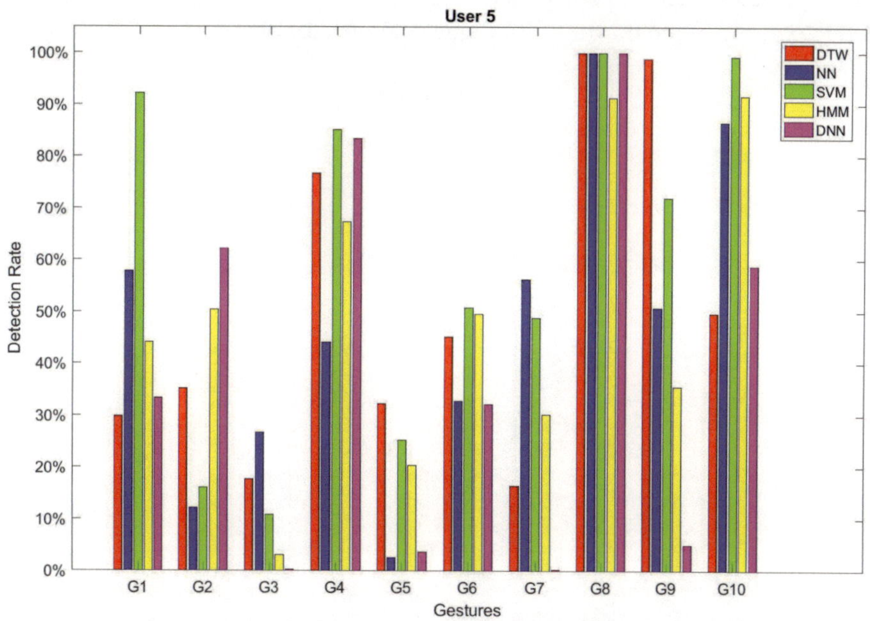

Figure 6. Recognition rates obtained by testing each method on sequences of gestures performed by User 5.

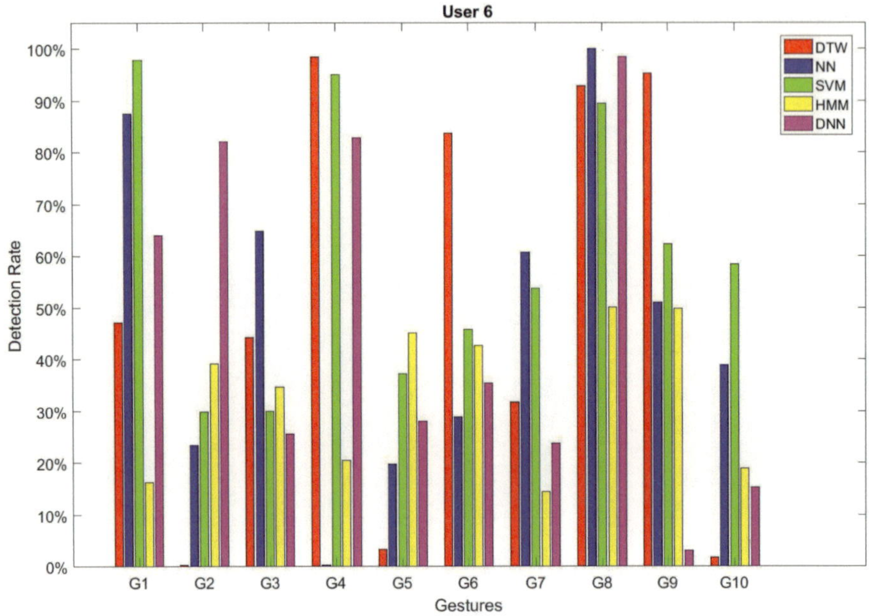

Figure 7. Recognition rates obtained by testing each method on sequences of gestures performed by User 6.

In order to analyze the performance of classifiers when the same user is used in the learning and prediction phases, an additional experiment has been carried out. So the Training User has been asked to perform again the gestures. **Figure 8** shows the obtained recognition rates. These

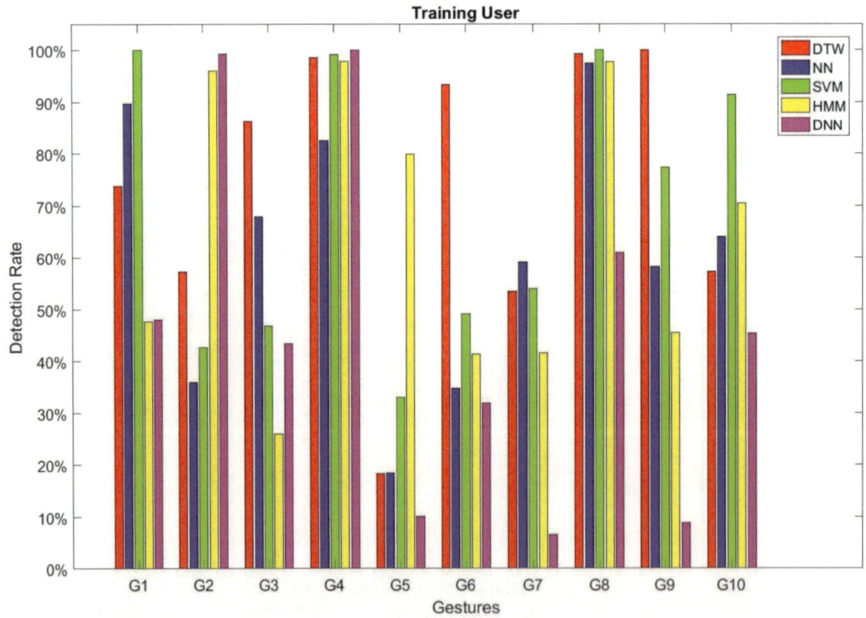

Figure 8. Recognition rates obtained by testing each method on sequences of gestures performed by the Training User in a session different from the one used for the learning phase.

results confirm the variability of classifiers performance even if the same user is used for training and testing the classifiers.

The obtained results confirm that it is difficult to determine the superiority of one classifier over the others because of the large number of variables involved that do not guarantee a uniqueness of gesture execution. These are for example: the different relative positions between users and camera, the different orientations of the arm, the different amplitude of the movement, and so on. All these factors can greatly modify the resulting skeletons and joint positions producing large variations in the extracted features.

Some important conclusions can be drawn from the experiments that have been carried out: the solution of using only one user to train the classifiers can be pursued as the recognition rates are quite good even if the gestures are performed in personalized way.

Another point concerns the complexity of the gestures used in our experiments. The results show that the failures are principally due either to the strict similarity between different gestures or to the fact that the gestures which involve a movement perpendicular with respect to the camera (not in the lateral plane) can produce false skeleton postures and consequently features affected by errors.

Moreover, some gestures have parts of the movement in common. **Figures 9** and **10** have been pictured to better explain these problems.

Figure 9 shows the results obtained by testing the first 1000 frames of a sequence of gesture G_3 executed by User 1. Each plot in the figure represents the output of each classifier DTW, NN, SVM, HMM, and DNN, respectively. As can be seen in the case of DTW, SVM, and DNN, gesture G_3 is frequently misclassified as gesture G_4. Both gestures are executed in a plane parallel to the camera: G_3 involves the rotation of the whole arm, whereas G_4 involves the rotation of the forearm only (as can be seen in **Figure 11**). Notice that the misclassification happens principally in the starting part of gesture G_3, which is very similar to the starting part of G_4; therefore, they can be easily mistaken.

Furthermore in **Figure 9**, it is worth to notice the good generalization ability of NN and HMM. As can be seen in these cases, both classifiers are always able to recognize the gesture even when the sliding windows cover the frames between two successive gesture executions.

An additional observation can be taken considering G_1 and G_8 as an example. In **Figure 12**, notice that gesture G_1 and gesture G_8 involve the same rotations of the forearm, but performed in different planes with respect to the camera (the lateral one in the case of G_1 and the frontal one in the case of G_8). It is evident that a slight different orientation of the user in front of the camera while performing gesture G_1 (risp. G_8), could generate skeletons quite similar to those obtained by performing gesture G_8 (risp. G_1). **Figure 10** shows the results relative to this case. As can be seen gesture G_8 is sometimes misclassified as gesture G_1 by DTW and SVM. A few misclassifications of gesture G_8 as G_6 are also present since G_8 and G_6 have some parts of movement in common.

6.4. Statistical evaluation

The analysis of the performance of the different methodologies, presented above, allows us to draw some important conclusions that must be considered in order to build a robust human-robot

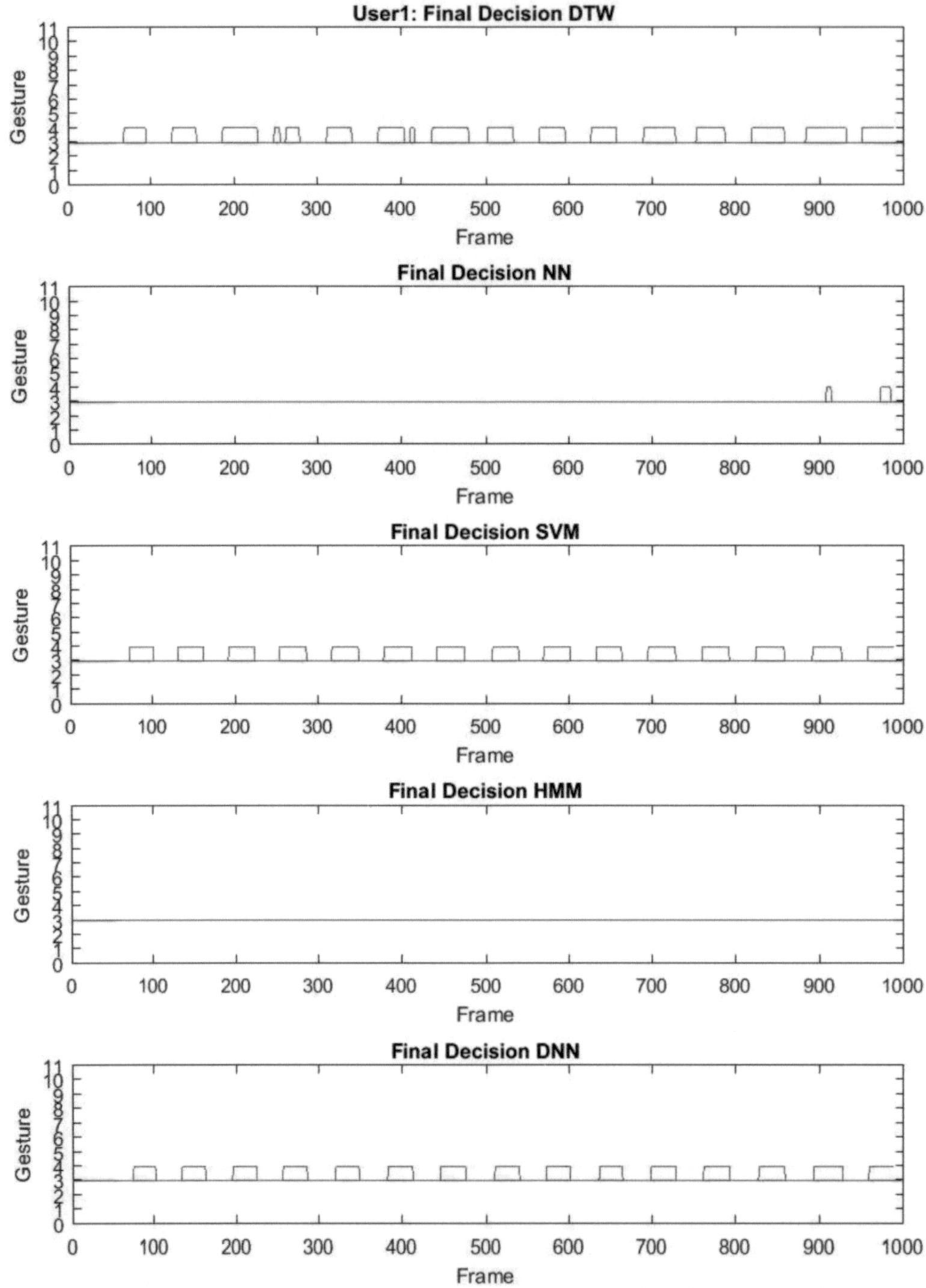

Figure 9. Recognition results relative to the first 1000 frames of a test sequence relative to gesture G_3 performed by User 1. The x-axis represents the frame number of the sequence and the y-axis represents the gesture classes ranging from 1 to 10 (the range 0–11 has been used only for displaying purposes). The red line denotes the ground truth label (G_3 in this case), whereas the blue one represents the predicted labels obtained from the classifiers.

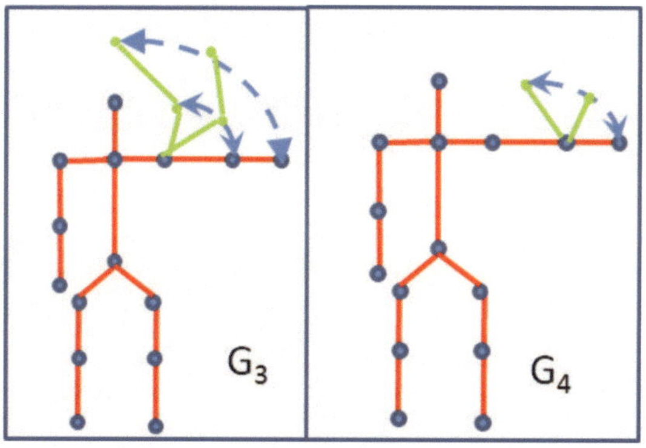

Figure 10. Gesture G_3 and G_4. Both gestures involve a rotation of the arm in a plane parallel to the camera.

interface. The recognition is highly influenced by the following elements: the subjectivity of the users, the complexity of the gestures, and the recognition performance of the applied methodology. In order to give an overall evaluation of the experimental results, a statistical analysis of the conducted tests has to be done. The F-score, also known as F-measure or F_1-score, has been considered as global performance metrics [42]. It is defined by the following equation:

$$F = \frac{2TP}{2TP + FP + FN} \tag{5}$$

where TP, FP, and FN are the true positives, false positives, and false negatives, respectively. The best values for the F-score are those close to 1, whereas the worst are those close to 0. This measure captures information mainly on how well a model handles positive examples.

Figure 13 shows the F-score values obtained for each methodology and for each gesture, averaged over all users. As can be seen each methodology behaves differently among the set of available gestures: SVM, for example, has an F-score close to 1 for G_1 and G_8, whereas DNN has maximum F-score in the case of G_2 or G_4. **Figure 13** highlights another important aspect: some gestures are better recognized instead of others. This is the case, for example of G_8 or G_4 for which the F-scores reaches high values whatever methodology is applied. On the contrary, gestures such as G_5 or G_7 are generally badly recognized by each methodology. These considerations are very useful as allows us to select a subset of gestures and for each of them the best methodology in order to build a robust human robot interface. To this aim, a threshold $(= 0.85)$ can be fixed for the F-score values and the gestures that have at least one classifier with F-score above this threshold can be selected. By seeing **Figure 13**, these gestures are: G_1, G_2, G_4, G_8, G_9, and G_{10}. For each selected gesture the classifier with the maximum F-score can be chosen: so SVM for G_1, DNN for G_2 and G_4, SVM for G_8, DTW for G_9, and finally SVM for G_{10}. These set of gestures with the relative best classifiers can be used to build the human-robot interface.

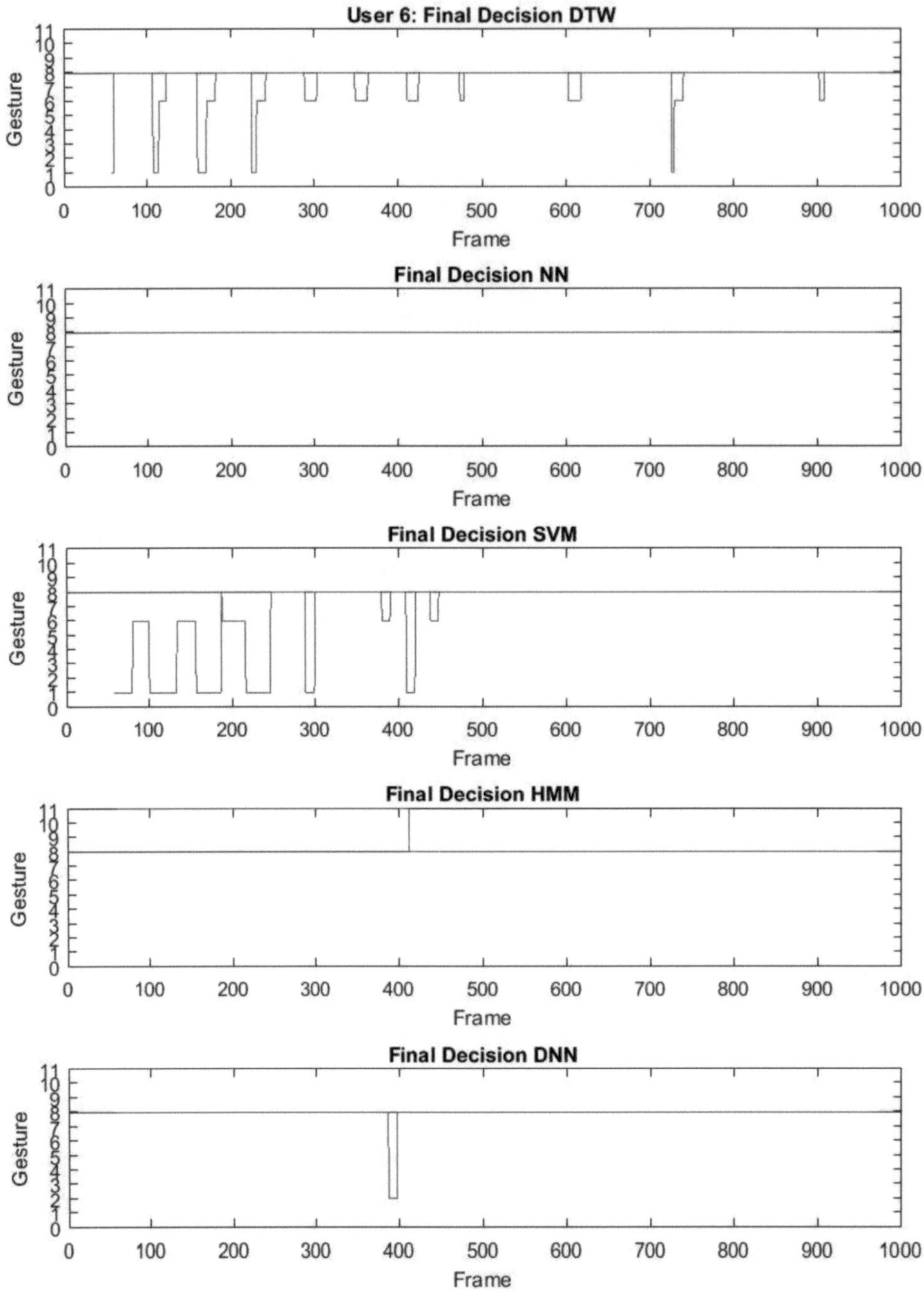

Figure 11. Recognition results relative to the first 1000 frames of a test sequence relative to gesture performed by User 6. The x-axis represents the frame number of the sequence and the y-axis represents the gesture classes ranging from 1 to 10 (the range 0 -11 has been used only for displaying purposes). The red line denotes the ground truth label (in this case), whereas the blue one represents the predicted labels obtained from the classifiers.

http://dx.doi.org/10.5772/68118

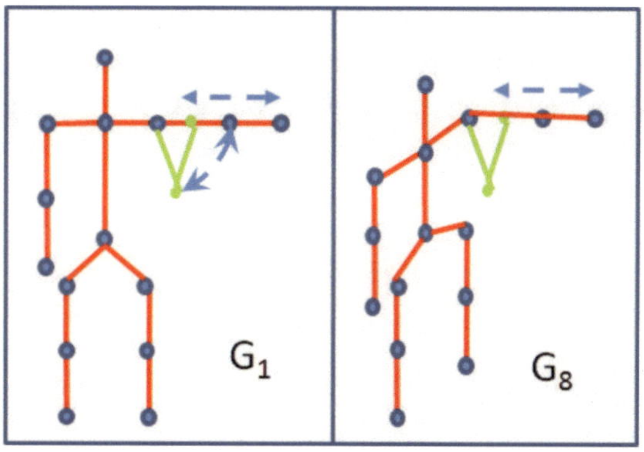

Figure 12. Gestures G_1 and G_8. Gesture G_1 involves a movement in a plane parallel to the camera, whereas gesture G_8 involves a movement in a plane perpendicular to the camera.

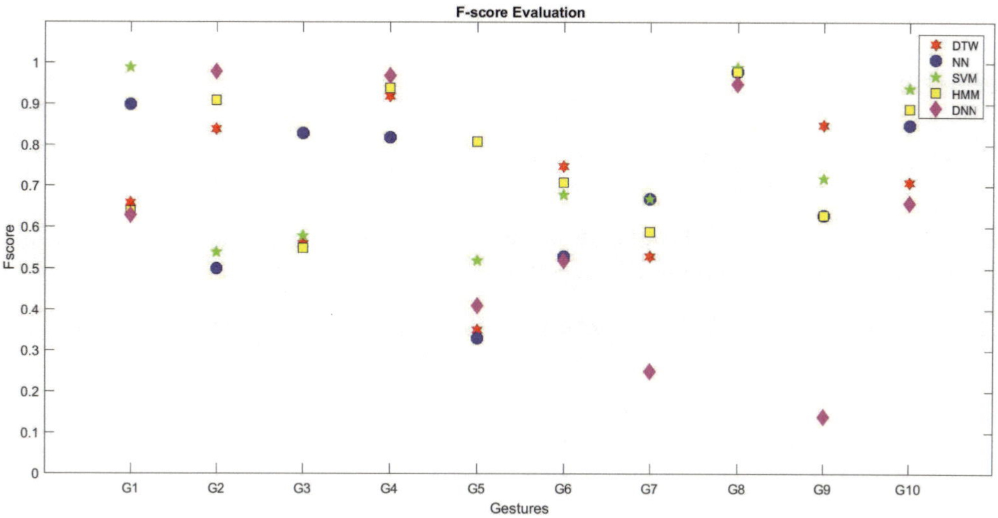

Figure 13. F-score values of all methodologies for each gesture averaged over all users.

7. Conclusions

In this chapter the problem of Gesture Recognition has been considered. Different methodologies have been tested in order to analyze the behaviors of the differently obtained classifiers. In particular, neural network (NN), support vector machine (SVM), hidden Markov model (HMM), deep neural network (DNN), and dynamic time warping (DTW) approaches have been applied.

The results obtained during the experimental phase prove the great heterogeneity of tested classifiers. In this work, the majority of problems arise in part from the complexity of the gestures and in part from the variations coming from the users. The classifiers perform differently often preserving complementarity and redundancy. These peculiarities are very important for fusion. So, encouraged by these observations, we will concentrate our further investigations on the fusion of different classifiers in order to improve the overall performance and reduce the total error.

Author details

Grazia Cicirelli* and Tiziana D'Orazio

*Address all correspondence to: cicirelli@ba.issia.cnr.it

Institute of Intelligent Systems for Automation, National Research Council of Italy, Bari, Italy

References

[1] Habib Z, Bux A, Angelov P. Vision Based Human Activity Recognition: A Review. Vol. 513. Cham: Springer; 2017. pp. 341-371

[2] Hassan MH, Mishra PK. Hand gesture modeling and recognition using geometric features: A review. Canadian Journal on Image Processing and Computer Vision. 2012;**3**(1):12-26

[3] Jang F, Zhang S, Wu S, Gao Y, Zhao D. Multi-layered gesture recognition with kinect. Journal of Machine Learning Research. 2015;**16**:227-254

[4] Traver VJ, Latorre-Carmona P, Salvador-Balaguer E, Pla F, Javidi B. Three-dimensional integral imaging for gesture recognition under occlusions. IEEE Signal Processing Letters. 2017;**24**(2):171-175

[5] D'Orazio T, Marani R, Renó V, Cicirelli G. Recent trends in gesture recognition: How depth data has improved classical approaches. Image and Vision Computing. 2016;**52**:56-72

[6] Presti LL, Cascia ML. 3D skeleton-based human action classification: A survey. Pattern Recognition. 2016;**53**:130-147

[7] Cheng H, Yang L, Liu Z. Survey on 3d hand gesture recognition. IEEE Transactions on Circuits and Systems for Video Technology. 2016;**26**(9):1659-1673

[8] Aggarwal JK and Xia L. Human activity recognition from 3D data: A review. Pattern Recognition Letters. Oct. 2014;**48**:70-80

[9] Cruz L, Lucio F, Velho L. Kinect and RGBD images: Challenges and applications. In: Proceedings of 25th SIBGRAPI IEEE Conference on Graphics, Patterns and Image Tutorials, pp. 36-49, IEEE Computer Society, Los Alamitos, USA, 2012

[10] Almetwally I, Mallem M. Real-time tele-operation and tele-walking of humanoid robot Nao using Kinect depth camera. In: Proceedings of 10th IEEE International Conference

on Networking, Sensing and Control (ICNSC), pp. 463-466, IEEE Computer Society, Los Alamitos, 2013

[11] Jacob MG, Wachs JP. Context-based hand gesture reognition for the operating room. Pattern Recognition Letters. 2014;**36**:196-203

[12] Wang C, Liu Z, Chan SC. Superpixel-based hand gesture recognition with kinect depth camera. IEEE Transactions on Multimedia. 2015;**17**(1):29-39

[13] Plouffe G, Cretu A-M. Static and dynamic hand gesture recognition in depth data using dynamic time warping. IEEE Transactions on Instrumentation and Measurement. 2016;**65** (2):305-316

[14] Venkataraman V, Turaga P. Shape distributions of nonlinear dynamical systems for video-based inference. IEEE Transactions on Pattern Analysis and Machine Intelligence. 2016;**38**(12):2531-2543

[15] Lai K, Konrad J, Ishwar P. A gesture-driven computer interface using kinect. In: Proceedings of the IEEE Southwest Symposium on Image Analysis and Interpretation (SSIAI); IEEE Computer Society, Los Alamitos, USA, April 2012; 2012. pp. 185-188

[16] Oh J, Kim T, Hong H. Using binary decision tree and multiclass SVM for human gesture recognition. In: Proc. of the IEEE International Conference on Information Science and Applications (ICISA); IEEE Computer Society, Los Alamitos, USA, June 2013; 2013; pp. 1-4

[17] Pal M, Saha S, Konar A. Distance matching based gesture recognition for healthcare using microsoft's kinect sensor. In: Proc. of International Conference on Microelectronics, Computing and Communications (MicroCom); IEEE Computer Society, Los Alamitos, USA, 23–25 June 2016, pp. 1-6

[18] Deo N, Rangesh A, Trivedi M. In-vehicle hand gesture recognition using hidden markov models. In: Proceedings of the 19th IEEE International Conference on Intelligent Transportation Systems (ITSC); IEEE Computer Society, Los Alamitos, USA, 1–4 November 2016; 2016. pp. 2179-2184

[19] Song Y, Gu Y, Wang P, Liu Y, Li A. A kinect based gesture recognition algorithm using GMM and HMM. In: Proceedings of the 6th International Conference on Biomedical Engineering and Informatics (BMEI); 16-18 December 2013, IEEE Computer Society, Los Alamitos, USA, pp. 750-754

[20] Miranda L, Vieira T, Martinez D, Lewiner T, Vieira A, Campos M. Online gesture recognition from pose kernel learning and decision forests. Pattern Recognition Letters. April 2014;**39**:65-73

[21] Ghosh DK, Ari S. Static hand gesture recognition using mixture of features and SVM classifier. In: Proceedings of the 5th IEEE International Conference on Communication Systems and Network Technologies; IEEE Computer Society, Los Alamitos, USA, 4–6 April 2015; 2015. pp. 1094-1099

[22] Bhattacharya S, Czejdo B, Perez N. Gesture classification with machine learning using kinect sensor data. In: 3rd International Conference on Emerging Applications of Information

Technology (EAIT); November 30- December 01, 2012, IEEE Computer Society, Kolkata, India, pp. 348-351

[23] Althloothi S, Mahoor MH, Zhang X, Voyles RM. Human activity recognition using multi-features and multiple kernel learning. Pattern Recognition. 2014;**47**:1800-1812

[24] Ibraheem NA, Khan RZ. Vision based gesture recognition using neural networks approaches: A review. International Journal of Human Computer Interaction. 2012;**3**(1):1-14

[25] Cicirelli G, Attolico C, Guaragnella C, D'Orazio T. A kinect-based gesture recognition approach for a natural human robot interface. International Journal of Advanced Robotic Systems. 2015;**12**(3).

[26] Ruan X, Tian C. Dynamic gesture recognition based on improved DTW algorithm. In: Proceedings of IEEE International Conference on Mechatronics and Automation (ICMA); IEEE Computer Society, Los Alamitos, USA, 2–5 August 2015; 2015. pp. 2134-2138

[27] Ding IJ, Chang CW. An eigenspace-based method with a user adaptation scheme for human gesture recognition by using Kinect 3D data. Applied Mathematical Modelling. 2015;**39**(19):5769-5777

[28] LeCun Y, Bengio Y, Hinton G. Deep learning. Nature. 2015;**521**(7553):436-444

[29] Neverova N, Wolf C, Taylor G, Nebout F. Mod drop: Adaptive multi-modal gesture recognition. IEEE Transactions on Pattern Analysis and Machine Intelligence. August 2016;**38**(8):1692-1706

[30] Wu D, Pigou L, Kindermans PJ, Le N, Shao L, Dambre J, Odobez JM. Deep dynamic neural networks for multimodal gesture segmentation and recognition. IEEE Transactions on Pattern Analysis and Machine Intelligence. August 2016;**38**(8):1583-1597

[31] D'Orazio T, Attolico C, Cicirelli G, Guaragnella C. A neural network approach for human gesture recognition with a kinect sensor. In International Conference on Pattern Recognition Applications and Methods (ICPRAM); March 2014; Angers, France. SCITEPRESS - Sience and Technology Publications, Setubal, Portugal, pp. 741-746

[32] Haykin S. Neural Networks-A Comprehensive Foundation. 2nd ed. Prentice Hall PTR Upper Saddle River, NJ, USA, 1998

[33] Vapnik V. The Nature of Statistical Learning Theory. Berlin: Spinger; 1995

[34] Rabiner LR. A tutorial on Hidden Markov Models and selected applications in speech recognition. Proceedings of the IEEE. February 1989;**77**(2):257-286

[35] Ghahramani Z. An introduction to Hidden Markov Models and Bayesian Networks. International Journal of Pattern Recognition and Artificial Intelligence. 2001;**15**(1):9-42

[36] Hinton GE, Salakhutdinov RR. Reducing the dimensionality of data with neural networks. Science. July 2006;**313**:504-507

[37] Møller MF. A scaled conjugate gradient algorithm for fast supervised learning. Neural Networks. 1993;**6**(4):525-533

[38] Müller M. Dynamic Time Warping, Information Retrieval for Music and Motion, Springer-Verlag Berlin Heidelberg, 2007, pp. 69-84

[39] Rabiner L, Juang B-H. Fundamentals of Speech Recognition. Englewood Cliffs, NJ: Prentice Hall PTR; 1993

[40] Headquarters Department of the Army. Visual Signals: Arm-and-Hand Signals for Ground Forces. Field Manual FM 21-60, Washington, DC, September 1987. This report is downloadable at: http://www.apd.army.mil/epubs/DR_pubs/DR_a/pdf/web/fm21_60.pdf

[41] Attolico C., Cicirelli G., Guaragnella C., D'Orazio T. (2015) A Real Time Gesture Recognition System for Human Computer Interaction. In: Schwenker F., Scherer S., Morency LP. (eds) Multimodal Pattern Recognition of Social Signals in Human-Computer-Interaction. MPRSS 2014. Lecture Notes in Computer Science, vol 8869. Springer, Cham

[42] Powers DMW. Evaluation: From Precision, Recall and F-Factor to ROC, Informedness, Markedness and Correlation. Technical report SIE-07-001, School of Informatics and Engineering Flinders University, Adelaide, Australia, December 2007

Chapter 7

Gait Recognition

Jiande Sun, Yufei Wang and Jing Li

Additional information is available at the end of the chapter

http://dx.doi.org/10.5772/68119

Abstract

Gait recognition has received increasing attention as a remote biometric identification technology, i.e. it can achieve identification at the long distance that few other identification technologies can work. It shows enormous potential to apply in the field of criminal investigation, medical treatment, identity recognition, human-computer interaction and so on. In this chapter, we introduce the state-of-the-art gait recognition techniques, which include 3D-based and 2D-based methods, in the first part. And considering the advantages of 3D-based methods, their related datasets are introduced as well as our gait database with both 2D silhouette images and 3D joints information in the second part. Given our gait dataset, a human walking model and the corresponding static and dynamic feature extraction are presented, which are verified to be view-invariant, in the third part. And some gait-based applications are introduced.

Keywords: gait recognition, gait dataset, 2D-based, 3D-based, view invariant

1. Introduction

Gait recognition has been paid lots of attention as one of the biometric identification technologies. There have been considerable theories supporting that person's walking style is a unique behavioural characteristic, which can be used as a biometric. Differing from other biometric identification technologies such as face recognition, gait recognition is widely known as the most important non-contactable, non-invasive biometric identification technology, which is hard to imitate. Since these advantages, gait recognition is expected to be applied in scenarios, such as criminal investigation and access control. Usually gait recognition includes the following five steps, which are shown in **Figure 1**.

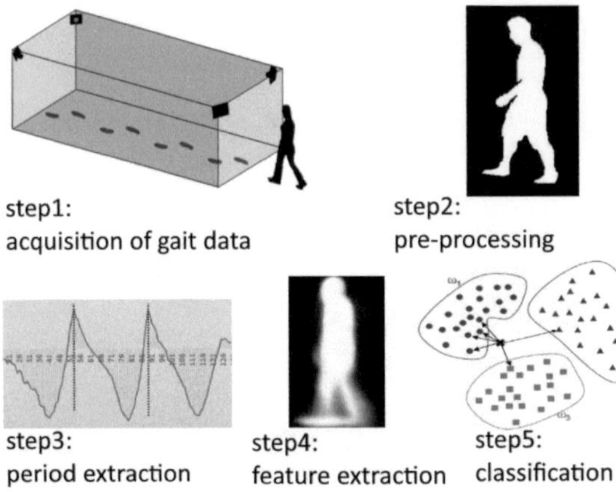

Figure 1. The steps in gait recognition.

Step 1: acquisition of gait data

The ways of acquiring the original gait data depend on how to recognize the gait. Usually the gait is acquired by single camera, multiple cameras, professional motion capture system (e.g. VICON) and camera with depth sensor (e.g. Kinect).

Step 2: pre-processing

The methods of pre-processing are quite different corresponding to the terms of acquiring gait. For instance, in some single camera-based methods, the pre-processing is usually the background subtraction, which is to get the body silhouette of walking people. However, in Kinect-based methods, the pre-processing is to filter the noise out of the skeleton sequences.

Step 3: period extraction

Since human gait is a kind of periodic signal, a gait sequence may include several gait cycles. Gait period extraction is helpful to reduce the data redundancy because all the gait features can be included in one whole gait cycle.

Step 4: feature extraction

Various gait features are used in different kinds of gait recognition methods and they influence the performance of gait recognition. Gait features can be divided into hand-crafted and machine-learned features. The hand-crafted ones are easy to be generalized to different datasets, while the machine-learned ones are usually better for the specific dataset.

Step 5: classification

Gait classification, i.e. gait recognition, is to use the classifiers based on the gait features. The classifiers range from the traditional one, such as kNN (k-nearest neighbour), to the modern one, such as deep neural network, which has achieved success in face recognition, handwriting recognition, speech recognition, etc.

Generally, gait recognition methods can be divided into 3D-based and 2D-based ones. The 2D-based gait recognition methods depend on the human silhouette captured by one 2D camera, which is the normal situation of the video surveillance. The 2D-based gait recognition methods are dominant in this field of gait recognition and they are usually divided into model-based and model-free methods.

The model-based methods extract the information of the shape and dynamics of the human body from video sequences, establish the suitable skeleton or joint model by integrating the information and classify the individuals based on the variation of the parameters in such a model. Cunado et al. [1] modelled gait as an articulated pendulum and extracted the line via the dynamic Hough transform to represent the thigh in each frame, as shown in **Figure 2a**. Johnson et al. [2] identified the people based on the static body parameters recovered from the walking action across multiple views, which can reduce the influence introduced by variation in view angle, as shown in **Figure 2b**. Guo et al. [3] modelled the human body structure from the silhouette by stick figure model, which had 10 sticks articulated with six joints, as shown in **Figure 2c**. Using this model, the human motion can be recorded as a sequence of stick figure parameters, which can be the input of BP neural network. Rohr [4] proposed a volumetric model for the analysis of human motion, using 14 elliptical cylinders to model the human body, as shown in **Figure 2d**. Tanawongsuwan et al. [5] projected the trajectories of lower body joint angles into walking plane and made them time-normalized by dynamic time warping (DTW). Wang et al. [6] made a fusion between the static and dynamic body features. Specifically, the static body feature is in a form of a compact representation obtained by Procrustes shape analysis. The dynamic body feature is extracted via a model-based approach, which can track the subject and recover joint-angle trajectories of lower limbs, as shown in **Figure 2e**. Generally, the model-based gait recognition methods have better invariant properties and are better at handling occlusion, noise, scaling and view-variation. However, model-based methods usually require a high resolution and a heavy computational cost.

On the other hand, model-free methods generate gait signatures directly based on the silhouettes, which are extracted from the video sequences, without fitting a model. Gait energy image (GEI) [7] is the most popular gait representation, which represents the spatial and temporal gait information in a grey image. GEI is generated by averaging silhouettes over a complete gait cycle and represents human motion sequence in a single image while preserving

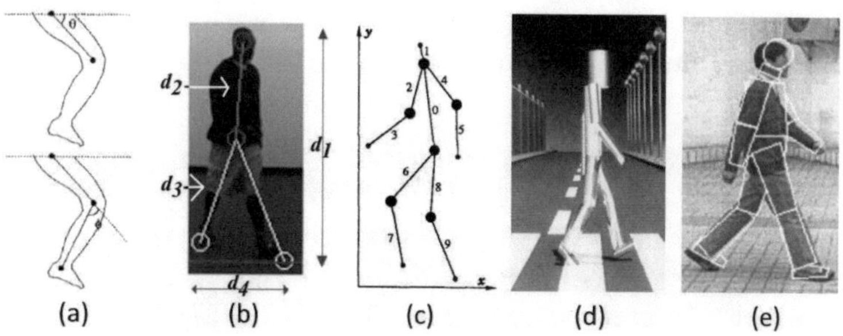

Figure 2. Examples of model-based methods.

the temporal information, as shown in **Figure 3a**. Motion silhouette image (MSI) [8] is like GEI and is a grey image too. The intensity of an MSI is determined by a function of the temporal history of the motion of each pixel, as shown in **Figure 3b**. The intensity of an MSI represents motion information during one gait cycle. Because GEI and MSI represent both motion and appearance information, they are sensitive to the changes in various covariate conditions such as carrying and clothing. Shape variation-based (SVB) frieze pattern is proposed in [9], as shown in **Figure 3c**, to improve their robustness against these changes. SVB frieze pattern projects the silhouettes horizontally and vertically to represent the gait information, and uses key frame subtraction to reduce the effects of appearance changes on the silhouettes. Although it has been shown that SVB frieze pattern can get better results when there are significant appearance changes, it does not outperform in the case of no changes, and it requires temporal alignment pre-processing for each gait cycle, which brings more computation load. Gait entropy image (GEnI) [10] is another gait representation, which is based on Shannon entropy. It encodes the randomness of pixel values in the silhouette images over a complete gait cycle, and it is more robust to appearance changes, such as carrying and clothing, as shown in **Figure 3d**. Wang et al. [11] propose the Chrono-Gait image (CGI), as shown in **Figure 3e**, to compress the silhouette images without losing too much temporal relationship between them. They utilize a colour mapping function to encode each gait contour image in the same gait sequence, and average over a quarter gait cycle to one CGI. It is helpful to preserve more temporal information of a gait cycle.

The methods mentioned above are all convert the gait sequence into a single image/template. There are other methods to keep temporal information of gait sequences, which have good performance too. Sundaresan et al. [12] propose the gait recognition methods based on hidden Markov models (HMMs) because the gait sequence is composed of a sequence of postures, which is suitable for HMM representation. In this method, the postures are regarded as the states of the HMM and are identical to individuals, which provide a means of discrimination. Wang et al. [13] apply principal component analysis (PCA) to extract statistical spatio-temporal features from the silhouette sequence and recogniz gait in the low-dimensional eigenspace via supervised pattern classification techniques. Sudeep et al. [14] utilize the correlation of sequence pairs to preserve the spatio-temporal relationship between the galley and probe sequences, and use it as the baseline for gait recognition.

The advantages of model-free methods are computational efficiency and simplicity; however, the robustness against the variations of illumination, clothing, scaling and views still needs to be improved. Here, we focus on the view-invariant gait recognition methods.

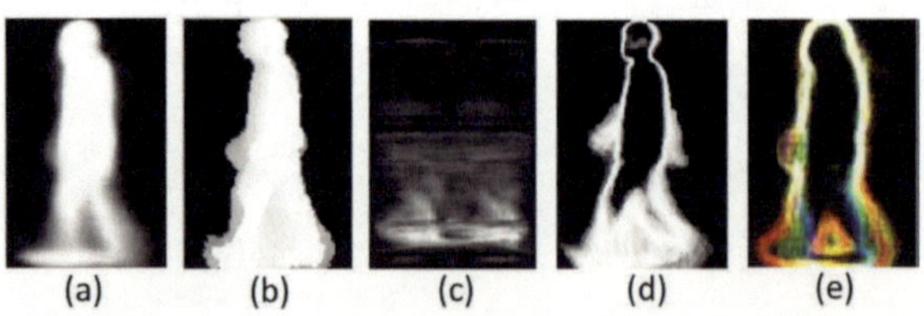

Figure 3. Examples of model-free methods.

Up to date, 2D-based view-invariant gait recognition methods can be divided into pose-free and pose-based ones. The pose-free methods aim at extracting the gait parameters independent from the view angle of the camera. Johnson et al. [2] present a gait recognition method to identify people based on static body parameters, which are extracted from the walking across multiple views. Abdelkader et al. [15] propose to extract an image template corresponding to the person's motion blob from each frame. Subsequently, the self-similarity of the obtained template sequence is computed. On the other hand, the pose-based method aims at synthesizing the lateral view of the human body from an arbitrary viewpoint. Kale et al. [16] show that if the person is far enough from the camera, it is possible to synthesize a side view from any of the other arbitrary views using a single camera. Goffredo et al. [17] use the human silhouette and human body anthropometric proportions to estimate the pose of lower limbs in the image reference system with low computational cost. After a marker-less motion estimation, the trends of the obtained angles are corrected by the viewpoint-independent gait reconstruction algorithm, which can reconstruct the pose of limbs in the sagittal plane for identification. Muramatsu et al. [18] propose an arbitrary view transformation model (AVTM) for cross-view gait matching. 3D gait volume sequences of training subjects are constructed, and then 2D gait silhouette sequences of the training subjects are generated by projecting the 3D gait volume sequences onto the same views as the target views. Finally, the AVTM is trained with gait features extracted from the 2D sequences. In the latest work [19], the deep convolutional neural networks (CNNs) is established and trained with a group of labelled multi-view human walking videos to carry out a gait-based human identification via similarity learning. The method is evaluated on the CASIA-B, OU-ISIR and USF dataset and performed outstanding comparing with the previous state-of-the-art methods.

It can be seen from the above-mentioned methods that the main idea of 2D view-invariant methods is to find the identical gait parameters that are independent from the camera point of view or can be used to synthesize a lateral view with arbitrary viewpoint.

2. 3D-based gait recognition and dataset

2.1. 3D-based gait recognition

3D-based methods have the instinctive superiority in the robustness against view variation. Generally, multiple calibrated cameras or cameras with depth sensors are used in 3D-based methods, which is necessary to extract gait features with 3D information. Zhao et al. [20] propose to build the 3D skeleton model based on 10 joints and 24 degrees of freedom (DOF) captured by multiple cameras, and the 3D information provides robustness to the changes of viewpoints, as shown in **Figure 4a**. Koichiro et al. [21] capture the dense 3D range gait from a projector-camera system, which can be used to recognize individuals at different poses, as shown in **Figure 4b**. Krzeszowski et al. [22] build a system with four calibrated and synchronized cameras, estimate the 3D motion using the video sequences and recognize the view-variant gaits based on marker-less 3D motion tracking, as shown in **Figure 4c**.

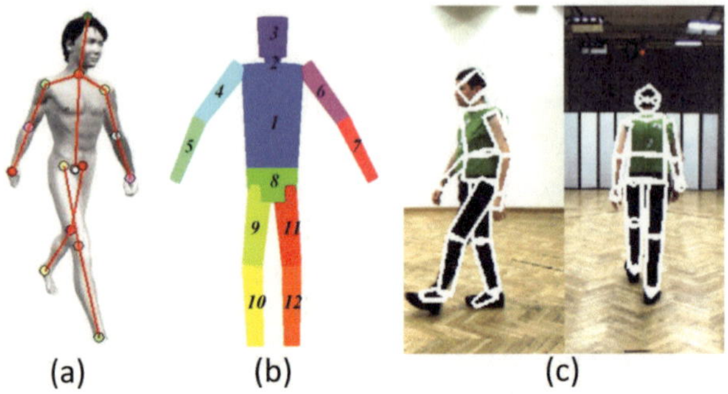

Figure 4. Examples of 3D-based methods.

3D-based methods are usually better than 2D-based view-invariant approaches in not only the recognition accuracy but also the robustness against view changing. However, these methods have high computational cost due to the calibration of multiple cameras and fusion of multiple videos.

The Microsoft Kinect brought about new strategies upon the traditional 3D-based gait recognition methods because it is a consumable RGB-D (Depth) sensor, which can provide depth information easily. So far, there are two generations of Kinect, which are shown in **Figure 5a** and **b**. Sivapalan et al. [23] extend the concept of the GEI from 2D to 3D with the depth images captured by Kinect. They average the sequences of registered three-dimensional volumes over a complete gait cycle, which is called gait energy volume (GEV), as shown in **Figure 6**. In Ref. [24], the depth information, which is represented by 3D point clouds, is integrated in a silhouette-based gait recognition scheme.

Another characteristic of Kinect is that it can precisely estimate and track the 3D position of joints at each frame via machine learning technology. **Figure 7a** and **b** shows the differences of tracking points between the first and second generation of Kinect.

Araujo et al. [25] calculate the length of the body parts derived from joint points as the static anthropometric information, and use it for gait recognition.Milovanovic et al. [26] use the coordinates of all the joints captured by Kinect to generate a RGB image, combine such RGB images into a video to represent the walking sequence, and identify the gait based on the

Figure 5. The first and second generation kinects.

http://dx.doi.org/10.5772/68119

Figure 6. Gait energy volume (GEV).

spirit of content-based image retrieval (CBIR) technologies. Preis et al. [27] select 11 skeleton features captured by Kinect as the static feature, use the step length and speed as dynamic feature and integrate both static and dynamic features for recognition. Yang et al. [28] propose a novel gait representation called relative distance-based gait features, which can reserve the periodic characteristic of gait comparing with anthropometric features. Ahmed et al.[29] propose a gait signature using Kinect, which a sequence of joint relative angles (JRAs) is calculated over a complete gait cycle. They also introduce a new dynamic time warping (DTW)-based kernel to complete the dissimilarity measure between the train and test samples with JRA sequences. Kastaniotis et al. [30] propose a framework for gait-based recognition using Kinect. The captured pose sequences are expressed as angular vectors (Euler angles) of eight selected limbs. Then the angular vectors are mapped in the dissimilarity space resulting into a vector of dissimilarities. Finally, dissimilarity vectors of pose-sequences are modelled via sparse representation.

2.2. Dataset

Gait dataset is important to gait recognition performance improvement and evaluation. There are lots of gait datasets in the current academia and their purposes and characteristics

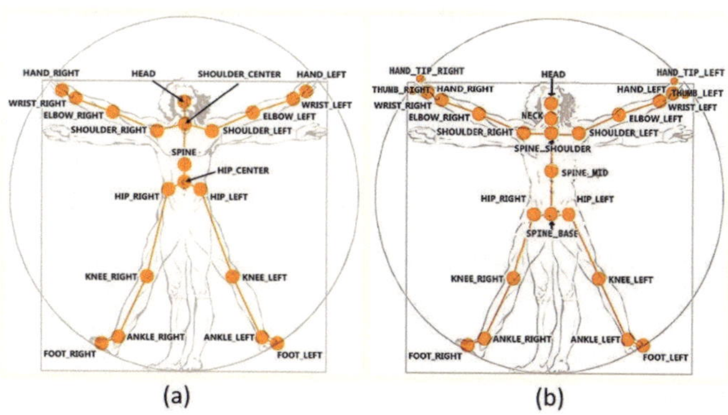

Figure 7. (a) The 20 joints tracked by first generation Kinect and (b) 25 joints tracked by second generation Kinect.

are different from each other. The differences among these datasets are mainly on the number of subjects, number of video sequences, covariate factors, viewpoints and environment (indoor or outdoor). Though the number of subjects in gait datasets is much smaller than that in the datasets of other biometrics (e.g. face, fingerprint, etc.), the current dataset can still satisfy the requirement of gait recognition method design and evaluation. Here, we give a brief introduction about several popular gait datasets. **Table 1** summarizes the information of these datasets.

SOTON Large Database [31] is a classical gait database containing 115 subjects, who are observed from side view and oblique view, and walk in several different environment, including indoor, treadmill and outdoor.

SOTON Temporal [32] contains the largest variations about time elapse. The gait sequences are captured monthly during 1 year with controlled and uncontrolled clothing conditions. It is suitable for purely investigating the time elapse effect on the gait recognition without regarding clothing conditions.

USF HumanID [14] is one of the most frequently used gait datasets. It contains 122 subjects, who walk along an ellipsoidal path outdoor, as well as contains a variety of covariates, including view, surface, shoes, bag and time elapse. This database is suitable for investigating the influence of each covariate on the gait recognition performance.

CASIA gait database contains three sets, i.e. A, B and C. Set A, also known as NLPR, is composed of 20 subjects, and each subject contains 12 sequences, which includes three walking directions, i.e. 0, 45 and 90°. Set B [33] contains large view variations from the front view to the rear view with 18° interval. There are 10 sequences for each subject, which are six normal sequences, two sequences with a long coat and two sequences with a backpack. Set B is suitable for evaluating cross-view gait recognition. Set C contains the infrared gait data of 153 subjects captured by infrared camera at night under 4 walking conditions, which are walk with normal speed, walk fast, walk slow and walk with carrying backpack.

OU-ISIR LP [34] contains the largest number of subjects, i.e. over 4000, with a wide age range from 1 year old to 94 years old and with an almost balanced gender ratio, although it does

Name	Subject	Sequence	Covariates	Viewpoints	In/Outhoor	Device
SOTON	115	2128	Yes	2	In/Outdoor	Camera(2D)
USF HumanID	122	1870	Yes	2	Outdoor	Camera(2D)
CASIA B	124	1240	Yes	11	Indoor	Camera(2D)
OU-ISIR,LP	4007	7842	No	2	Indoor	Camera(2D)
TUM-GAID	305	3370	Yes	1	Outdoor	Multimedia
KinectREID	71	483	yes	3	Indoor	Kinect

Table 1. List of popular gait datasets.

http://dx.doi.org/10.5772/68119

not contain any covariate. It is suitable for estimating a sort of upper bound accuracy of the gait recognition with high statistical reliability. It is also suitable for evaluating gait-based age estimation.

TUM-GAID [35] is the first multi-model gait database, which contains gait audio signals, RGB gait images and depth body images obtained by Kinect.

KinectREID [36] is a Kinect-based dataset that includes 483 video sequences of 71 individuals under different lighting conditions and 3 view directions (frontal, rear and lateral). Although the original motivation is for person re-identification, all the video sequences are taken for each subject by using Kinect, which contains all the information Kinect provided and is convenient for other Kinect SDK-based applications.

According to the overview [37] about the gait dataset, most of datasets are based on 2D videos or based on 3D motion data captured by professional camera, such as VICON. To our best knowledge, there are a few gait datasets containing both 2D silhouette images and 3D joints position information. Such a dataset can make the joint position-based methods, such as the method in Ref. [17] directly use the joint positions captured by Kinect, which can make use of both advantages of 2D- and 3D-based methods and bring improvement to the recognition performance. Meanwhile, the Kinect-based method such as in Refs. [25–28] will have a uniform platform to compare with each other. Therefore, a novel database based on Kinect is built, whose characteristics are following:

1. Two Kinects are used for simultaneously obtaining the 3D position of 21 joints (excluding 4 finger joints) and the corresponding binarized body silhouette images of each frame, as shown in **Figure 8**;

2. There are 52 subjects in the dataset, where each subject has 20 gait sequences and totally 1040 gait sequences;

3. Each subject has in six fixed and two arbitrary walking directions, which can be used to investigate the influence of view variation on the performance of gait recognition;

4. There are 28 males and 24 females with an average age of 22 in the dataset. There is no limitation for wearing, though most subjects wear shorts and T-shirts, and few females wear dress and high-heeled shoes, which is recorded in a basic information file.

The reason we choose Kinect V2 is that Kinect V2 has the comprehensive improvement over its first generation, such as broader field of view, higher resolution of colour and depth image, and more joints recognition ability. The 3D data and 2D RGB images are recorded, as shown in **Figure 8**. The upper area in **Figure 8** shows the 3D position of 21 joints, which means each joint will have a coordinate like (x, y, z) at each frame. We record all these original 3D position data at each frame during whole walking cycle. The lower area shows the corresponding binary silhouette image sequence after subtracting the subject from background.

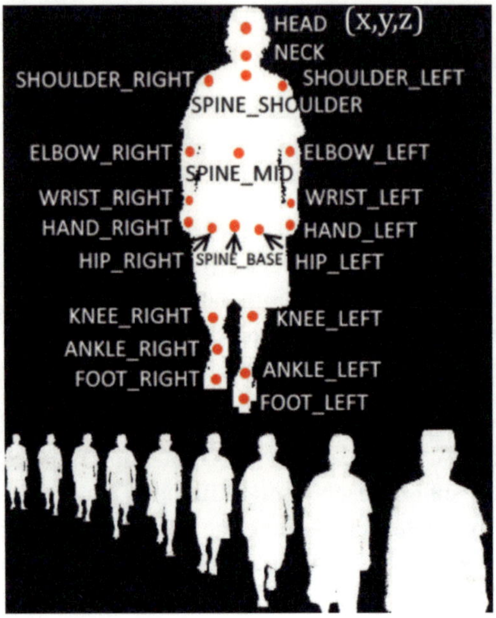

Figure 8. Two kinds of data in our database: 3D position of 21 joints in the upper area and the corresponding binarized silhouette images in the lower area.

The experimental environment is shown in **Figure 9**. Two Kinects are located mutually perpendicular at the distance of 2.5 m to form the biggest visual field, i.e. walking area. Considering the angle of view, we put two Kinects at 1 m height on the tripod. The red dash lines are the maximum and minimum deep that Kinect can probe. The area enclosed by the black solid lines is the available walking area.

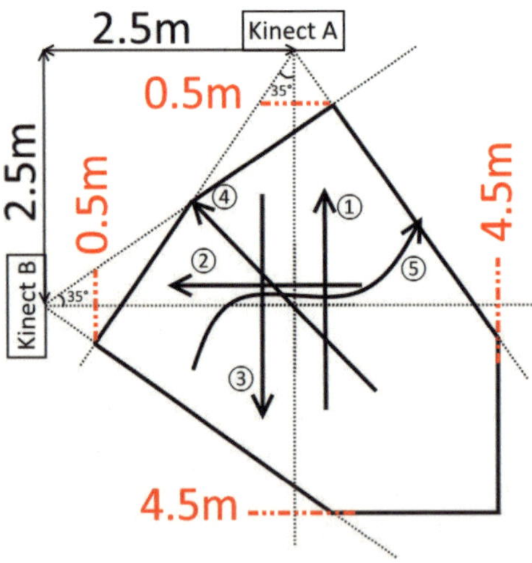

Figure 9. The top view of the experimental environment.

Before we record the data of each subject, we collect the basic information, such as name, sex, age, height, wearing (e.g. the high-heeled shoes, dress for female volunteers) and so on, for potential analysis and data mining. Each subject is asked to walk twice on the predefined directions shown as the arrows ①–⑤ in **Figure 9**, particularly ⑤ means the subjects walk in a straight line on an arbitrary direction. We can treat all the data as recorded by one Kinect since the two Kinects are the same, so that each subject has 20 walking sequences, and the walking duration on each predefined direction is shown in **Figure 10**. The dataset can be accessed at the website, https:/sites.google.com/site/sdugait/, and it can be downloaded with application.

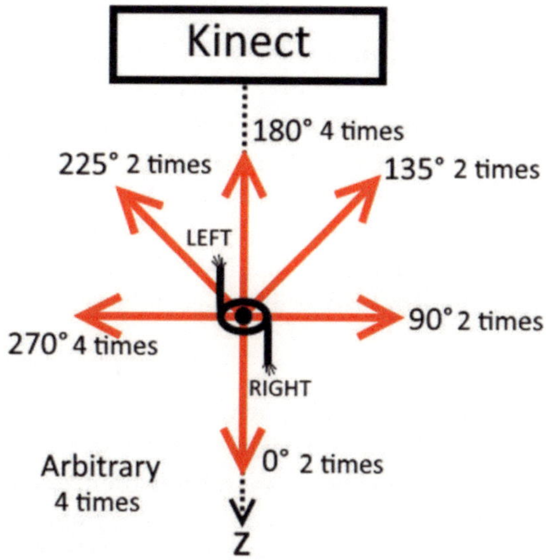

Figure 10. Walking directions and the corresponding walking duration.

3. Kinect-based gait recognition

3.1. The Kinect-based gait recognition

The gait features extracted from Kinect captured data contain the static and dynamic features. In this part, we will firstly introduce how to extract the static and dynamic features and demonstrate the properties of these two kinds of features. And then we will show how to extract a walking period from the sequence. Finally, we make a feature fusion of these two kinds of features for gait recognition.

A static feature is a kind of feature that can barely change during the whole walking process, such as height, the length of skeletons and so on. Given the knowledge of anthropometry, the person can be recognized based on static body parameters to some extent. Here, we choose the length of some skeletons as the static features, including the length of legs and arms. Considering the symmetry of human body, the length of limbs on both sides is usually treated to be equal. The static feature is defined as an eight-dimension vector, i.e. $(d_1, d_2, d_3, d_4, d_5, d_6, d_7, d_8)$, where d_i is a space distance between Joint_1 and Joint_2 listed in **Table 2**. Here, the Euclidean distance is chosen to measure the space distance referring to the research experiences in Refs. [37, 38].

We can acquire the 3D coordinate of the joints listed in **Table 2** in each frame and calculate each component of the static feature vector.

$$d_i = \sqrt{(x_1 - x_2)^2 + (y_1 - y_2)^2 + (z_1 - z_2)^2} \quad (1)$$

where (x_1, y_1, z_1) and (x_2, y_2, z_2) represent 3D positions of the corresponding joints listed as Joint_1 and Joint_2, respectively.

When we evaluate the estimation on the position of joints obtained by Kinect, we find that the accuracy will change along with the depth range. Given the empirical results, we discover that more stable data can be acquired when the depth is between 1.8 and 3.0 m. Hence, we propose a strategy to automatically choose the frames in that range. We choose the depth information of HEAD joint to represent the depth of whole body, because it can be detected stably and keep monotonicity in depth direction during walking. Then we set two depth thresholds, i.e. the distance in the Z-direction, as the upper and lower boundaries, respectively. The frames between the two boundaries are regarded as the reliable frames.

$$\{f_a\} = \{ H_f \mid H_{f,z>1.8} \cap H_{f,\, z<3.0} \} \quad (2)$$

where H_f denotes the frames of the HEAD, f_a denotes the reliable frames and $H_{f,\,z}$ represents the frame(s) that obtained when the coordinate of HEAD joint is z. We reserve the 3D coordinates of all the joints during the period when the reliable frames can be obtained. Finally, we calculate the length of the skeleton we need at each reliable frame, and take their average to calculate the components of the static feature vector.

The subjects are required to walk along the same path for seven times, which can make subjects walk more naturally later. For each subject, Kinect is turned for 5° started from −15° to

Component	Joint_1	Joint_2
d_1	HIP_RIGHT	KNEE_RIGHT
d_2	KNEE_RIGHT	ANKLE_RIGHT
d_3	SHOULDER_RIGHT	ELBOW_RIGHT
d_4	ELBOW_RIGHT	WRIST_RIGHT
d_5	SPINE_SHOULDER	SPINE_BASE
d_6	SHOULDER_RIGHT	SHOULDER_LEFT
d_7	SPINE_SHOULDER	NECK
d_8	NECK	HEAD

Table 2. Components of the static feature vector.

+15°, and the static feature vector on each direction is recorded. These directions are denoted by $n15, n10, n5, 0, p5, p10$ and $p15$, where '0' denotes the front direction, and 'n' and 'p' denote anticlockwise and clockwise, respectively. Totally 10 volunteers are randomly selected to repeat this experiment, and all the results prove that the static feature we choose is robust to the view variation. We show an example in **Figure 13a**, in which each component of these static vectors on the seven directions and the average values of these vectors are plotted.

The dynamic feature is a kind of feature that any change along with time during walking, such as speed, stride, variation of barycentre, etc. Given many researches [5, 39, 40], the angles of swing limbs during walking are remarkable dynamic gait features. For this reason, four groups of swing angles of upper limbs, i.e. arm and forearm, and lower limbs, i.e. thigh and crus, are defined as shown in **Figure 11**, and denoted as $a1, \ldots, a8$. Here, $a2$ is taken as the example for illustration. The coordinate at KNEE_RIGHT is denoted as (x, y, z), and coordinate at ANKLE_RIGHT is denoted as (x', y', z'), so $a2$ can be calculated as

$$\tan\angle a2 = \left(\frac{x - x'}{y - y'}\right) \; a2 = \tan^{-1}\left(\frac{x - x'}{y - y'}\right) \tag{3}$$

Each dynamic angle can be regarded as an independent dynamic feature for recognition. Given the research results in Ref. [41] and our comparison experiments on these dynamic angles, angle $a2$ on the right side or $a4$ on the left side is selected as the dynamic angle, according to the side near to the Kinect.

The value of $a2$ and $a4$ at each frame can be calculated, and the whole walking process can be described, as shown in **Figure 12**. We carried out the verification experiments similar to what for the static feature to prove its robustness against the invariant of views, the result shown in **Figure 13b** indicates that the proposed dynamic feature is also robust to the view variation.

Gait period extraction is an important step in gait analysis, because gait is a periodical feature and majority features could be captured within one period. Silhouette-based methods usually analyse the variation of silhouette width alone with time to obtain the period information. Some methods apply the signal processing to analyse the dynamic feature for period extraction, such as peak detection and Fourier transform. Different from them, we propose to extract periodicity by combining the data of left limb and right limb together, which can be shown in **Figure 12**. $a2$ and $a4$ sequences represent the right and left signals, respectively.

It can be concluded that the crossing points between left and right signals can segment the gait period appropriately. We use the crossing point between the left and right signals to extract

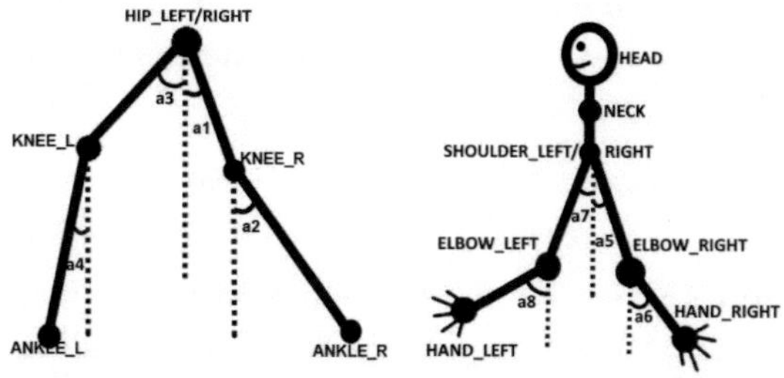

Figure 11. Side view of the walking model.

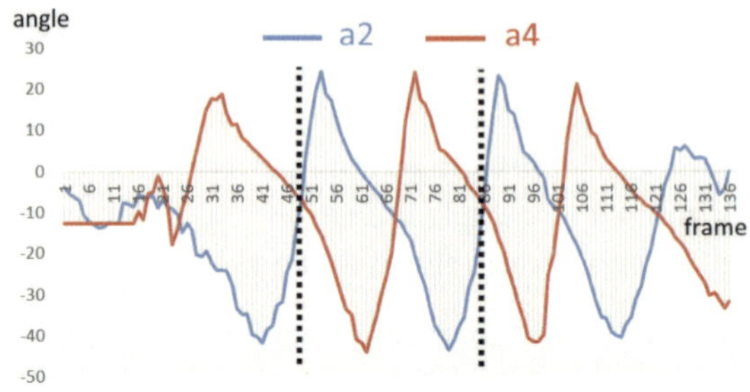

Figure 12. Period extracted based on dynamic features.

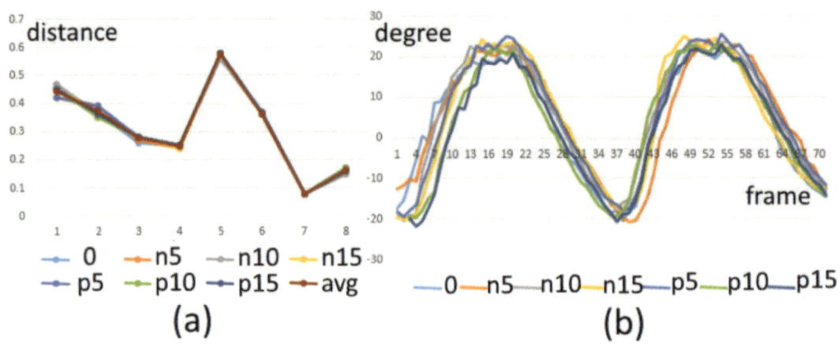

Figure 13. (a) Static feature and (b) dynamic feature of one subject on seven directions.

the gait period. After cutting off the noisy part at the beginning of the signal, we make the subtraction on the left and right signals, obtain the crossing point as the zero point and extract the period between two interval zero points. The black dash lines show the detected period.

The static and dynamic features have their own advantages and disadvantages, respectively. These two kinds of features are fused in the score-level. Two different kinds of matching scores are normalized onto the closed interval [0,1] by the linear normalization.

$$\hat{\mathbf{s}} = \frac{s - \min(\mathbf{S})}{\max(\mathbf{S}) - \min(\mathbf{S})} \tag{4}$$

Where **S** is the matrix before normalization, whose component is s, here represent the score, $\hat{\mathbf{S}}$ is the normalized matrix, whose component is $\hat{s}$. The two kinds of features are weighted fused as

$$F = \sum_{i=1}^{R} \omega_i \hat{s}_i, \quad \omega_i = \frac{C_i}{\sum_{j=1}^{R} C_i} \tag{5}$$

where F is the score after fusion, R is the number of features used for fusion, ω_i is the weight of ith classifier, $\hat{s}_i$ is the score of ith classifier, here which is our distance. C_i is the CCR (correct classification rate) of ith feature used to recognize separately, so the weight can be set according to the level of CCR.

3.2. Comparisons

The cross-view recognition abilities of the static feature, dynamic feature and their fusion are analysed. Four sequences on 180° are used as the training data since both body sides of the subjects can be recorded. The sequences on the other directions are used as the testing data. Because the sequences acquired on the nearer side to Kinect have more accuracy, the data on the nearer body side is selected automatically for the calculation at each direction.

The static feature is extracted from the right body side on 0, 225 and 270°, and the left body side on 90 and 135°. Due to the symmetry, the skeleton lengths on the two sides of the body are regarded to be equal. The static feature is calculated as Eq. (1), and NN classifier is used for recognition. The results are shown in the first row of **Table 3**.

The dynamic feature, *a2*, is calculated from the right side of the limb on 0, 225 and 270°, and the dynamic feature, *a4*, is calculated on 90 and 135°, from the left side of the limb. As we can extract both *a2* and *a4* on the direction of 180°, either of them can be used as the dynamic feature on the training set. The results are shown in the second row of **Table 3**.

The static feature and dynamic feature are fused in the score-level as we discussed before, and the results are tested after feature fusion in situation under view variation. Given the CCR of dynamic feature and static feature obtained from different directions, we redistribute the weight, get the final score for different subjects and use the NN classifier to get the final recognition results as shown in the third row of **Table 3**. The comparison in **Table 3** shows that the feature fusion can improve the recognition rate on each direction.

Preis et al. [27] proposed a Kinect-based gait recognition method, in which 11 lengths of limbs are extracted as the static feature, and step length and speed are taken as the dynamic feature. Their method was tested on their own dataset including nine persons and the highest CCR can reach to 91%. The gait feature they proposed is also based on 3D position joint, so it is possible to rebuild their method on our database. In this chapter, we rebuilt their method and test on our database with 52 persons and make a comparison with our proposed method. As their dataset only include frontal walking sequences, we compare two methods in our database only on 180° (frontal) directions. We randomly choose three sequences on 180° directions as training data and the rest are treated as testing data. The CCR results of both methods are shown in **Table 4**. Our proposed method has about 10% accuracy improvement.

The proposed method is evaluated another Kinect-based gait dataset, i.e. KinectREID dataset in Ref. [36]. Four recognition rate curves are shown in **Figure 14**, which are front_VS_front, rear_VS_rear, front_VS_rear and front_VS_lateral, because there are only three directions in

Static Feature	0°	90°	135°	225°	270°
	88.46	84.61	82.69	84.61	88.46
Dynamic Feature	0°	90°	135°	225°	270°
	88.46	86.5	84.61	84.61	90.38
Feature Fusion	0°	90°	135°	225°	270°
	94.23	90.38	90.38	88.46	92.31

Table 3. CCR (%) results of the static feature, dynamic feature, and feature fusion on each walking direction.

	CCR
Method in [27]	82.7%
Our method	92.3%

Table 4. Comparison on CCR between the proposed methodand the method in [27].

KinectREID dataset, i.e. front, rear and lateral. It can be seen from **Figure 14** that the cross-view recognition rate of the propose method is slightly worse than that on the same directions, which demonstrates that the robustness of the proposed method against view variation, though the recognition rate, decreases with the increasing of the amount of test subjects.

Given the experimental results we have discussed above, we can say that the static relation and dynamic moving relation among joints are very important features that can represent the characteristic of gait. In many 2D-based methods, many researchers also tried to get the relation among joints, but the positions of joints have to be calculated from the 2D video with all kinds of strategies in advantage. Goffredo et al. proposed a view-invariant gait recognition method in Ref. [17]. They only make use of 2D videos obtained by one single camera. After extracting the walking silhouette from the background, they estimate the position of joints according to the geometrical characteristics of the silhouette and calculate the angle between the shins and the vertical axis and the angle between thigh and the vertical axis as the dynamic feature, and finally make a projection transformation to project these features into the sagittal plane using their viewpoint rectification algorithm. Actually, Goffredo's

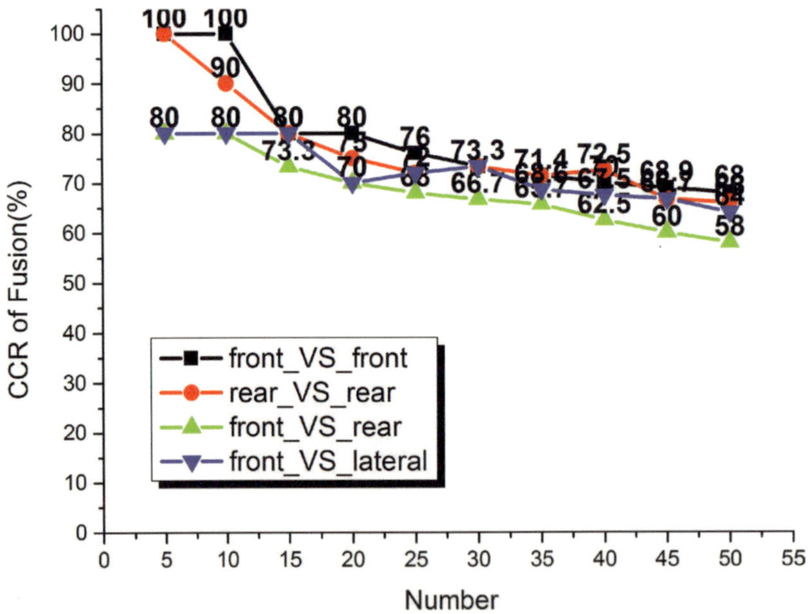

Figure 14. Gait recognition performance on KinectREID dataset.

http://dx.doi.org/10.5772/68119

method has a lot of similar gait features comparing with our method in logically. As we mentioned before, our database not only have the 3D position data but also the 2D silhouette images at each frame. Take advantage of our database, we can rebuild their method using the 2D silhouette image sequences; meanwhile, we use the 3D joint position data of the same person. We compare this method with our method with the varying views on three directions. The comparison results in **Table 5** show that our proposed method has 14–19% accuracy improvement.

3.3. Applications

Gait research is still at an exploring stage rather than a commercial application stage. However, we have confidence to say that the gait analysis is promising given its recent development. The unique characteristics of gait, such as unobtrusive, non-contactable and non-invasive, have a powerful potential to apply in the scenarios including criminal investigation, access security and surveillance. For example, face recognition will become unreliable if there is a larger distance between the subject and camera. Fingerprint and iris recognition have proved to be more robust, but they can only be captured by some contact or nearly contact equipment.

For instance, gait biometrics has already been used as the evidence for forensics [42]. In 2004, a perpetrator robbed a bank in Denmark. The Institute of Forensic Medicine in Copenhagen (IFMC) was asked to confirm the perpetrator via gait analysis, as they thought the perpetrator had a unique gait. The IFMC instructed the police to establish a covert recording of the suspect from the same angles as the surveillance recordings for comparison. The gait analysis revealed several characteristic matches between the perpetrator and the suspect, as shown in **Figure 15**. In **Figure 15**, both the perpetrator on the left and the suspect on the right showed inverted left ankle, i.e. angle b, during left leg's stance phase and markedly outward rotated feet. The suspect was convicted of robbery and the court found that gait analysis is a very valuable tool.

Another similar example is in the intelligent airport, where the Kinect-based gait recognition is used during the security check. Pratik et al. [43] established a frontal gait recognition system using RGB-D camera (Kinect) considering a typical application scenario of airport security check point, as shown in **Figure 16a**. In their further work [44], they addressed the occlusion problem in frontal gait recognition via the combination of two Kinects, which is demonstrated in **Figure 16b**.

In addition, gait analysis plays an important role in medical diagnosis and rehabilitation. For example, assessment of gait abnormalities in individuals affected by Parkinson's disease

	0°	90°	135°
Method in [17]	80.8	71.15	73.08
Our method	94.23	90.38	90.38

Table 5. CCR (%) result comparing on three directions.

Figure 15. Bank robbery identification.

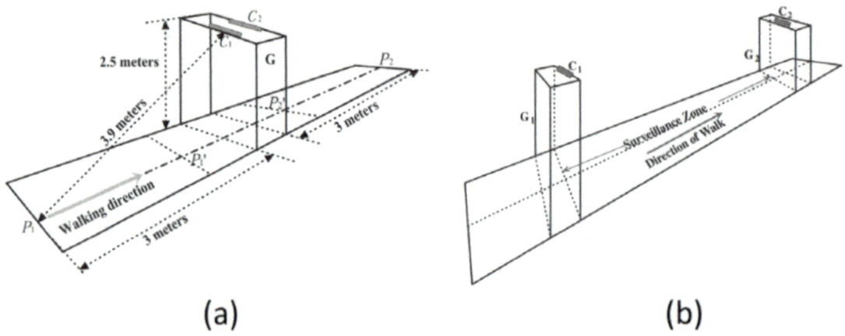

Figure 16. Gait-based airport security check system with (a) single and (b) double Kinects.

(PD) is essential to determine the disease progression, the effectiveness of pharmacologic and rehabilitative treatments. Corona et al. [45] investigate the spatio-temporal and kinematics parameters of gait between lots of elderly individuals affected by PD and normal people, which can help clinicians to detect and diagnose the Parkinson's disease.

Author details

Jiande Sun[1,2]*, Yufei Wang[1] and Jing Li[3]

*Address all correspondence to: jiandesun@hotmail.com

1 School of Information Science and Engineering, Shaodong Normal University, Jinan, Shandong Province, China

2 Institute of Data Science and Technology, Shandong Normal University, Jinan, Shandong Province, China

3 School of Mechanical and Electrical Engineering, Shandong Management University, Jinan, Shandong Province, China

http://dx.doi.org/10.5772/68119

References

[1] Cunado D, Nixon MS, Carter JN. Using gait as a biometric, via phase-weighted magnitude spectra. In: International Conference on Audio- & Video-Based Biometric Person Authentication (AVBPA 1997); 12-14 March 1997; Crans-Montana, Switzerland. Berlin: Springer; 1997. pp. 93-102

[2] Johnson AY, Bobick AF. A multi-view method for gait recognition using static body parameters. Audio- & Video-Based Biometric Person Authentication (AVBPA 2001); 6-8 June 2001; Halmstad, Sweden. Berlin: Springer; 2001. pp. 301-311

[3] Guo Y, Xu G, Tsuji S. Understanding human motion patterns. In: International Conference on Pattern Recognition (ICPR 1994); 9-13 October 1994; Jerusalem, Israel. New York: IEEE. 1994;**2**:325-329

[4] Rohr K. Towards models-based recognition of human movements in image sequences. CVGIP. 1994;**59**(1):94-115

[5] Tanawongsuwan R, Bobick A. Gait recognition from time-normalized joint-angle trajectories in the walking plane. In: IEEE Computer Society Conference on Computer Vision & Pattern Recognition (CVPR 2001); 8-14 December 2001; Kauai, HI, USA. New York: IEEE. 2001;**2**:726

[6] Wang L, Ning H, Tan T, Hu W. Fusion of static and dynamic body biometrics for gait recognition. IEEE Transactions on Circuits & Systems for Video Technology. 2003;**14**(2):149-158

[7] Han J, Bhanu B. Individual recognition using gait energy image. IEEE Transactions on Pattern Analysis & Machine Intelligence. 2006;**28**(2):316-322

[8] Lam THW, Lee RST. A new representation for human gait recognition: Motion silhouettes image (MSI). In: International Conference on Advances in Biometrics (ICB 2006); 5-7 January 2006; Hong Kong, China. Berlin: Springer. 2006;**3832**:612-618

[9] Lee S, Liu Y, Collins R. Shape variation-based frieze pattern for robust gait recognition. In: IEEE Computer Society Conference on Computer Vision & Pattern Recognition (CVPR 2007); 18-23 June 2007; Minneapolis, Minnesota, USA. New York: IEEE; 2007. pp. 1-8

[10] Bashir K, Xiang T, Gong S. Gait recognition using gait entropy image. In: International Conference on Imaging for Crime Detection & Prevention (ICDP 2009); 3 December 2009; London, United Kingdom. IET; 2010. pp. 1-6

[11] Wang C, Zhang J, Pu J, Yuan X, Wang L. Chrono-gait image: A novel temporal template for gait recognition. In: European Conference on Computer Vision (ECCV 2010); 5-11 September 2010; Crete, Greece. Berlin: Springer. 2010;**6311**:257-270

[12] Sundaresan A, Roychowdhury R, Chellappa R. A hidden Markov model based framework for recognition of humans from gait sequences. In: International Conference on Image Processing (ICIP 2003); 14-18 September 2003; Barcelona, Catalonia, Spain. New York: IEEE. 2003;**2**:93-96

[13] Wang L, Tan T, Ning H, Hu W. Silhouette analysis-based gait recognition for human identification. IEEE Transactions on Pattern Analysis & Machine Intelligence. 2004;**25**(12):1505-1518

[14] Sudeep S, Phillips PJ, Liu Z, Isidro RV, Patrick G, Bowyer KW. The human ID gait challenge problem: Data sets, performance, and analysis. IEEE Transactions on Pattern Analysis & Machine Intelligence. 2005;**27**(2):162-177

[15] Abdelkader CB, Davis L, Cutler R. Motion-based recognition of people in Eigen gait space. In: IEEE International Conference on Automatic Face and Gesture Recognition (FG 2002); 20-21 May 2002; Washington, DC, USA. New York: IEEE; 2002. pp. 267-272

[16] Kale A, Chowdhury AKR, Chellappa R. Towards a view invariant gait recognition algorithm. In: IEEE Conference on Advanced Video & Signal Based Surveillance (AVSS 2003); 21-22 July 2003; Miami, FL, USA. New York: IEEE; 2003. pp. 143-150

[17] Goffredo M, Bouchrika I, Carter JN, Nixon MS. Self-calibrating view-invariant gait biometrics. IEEE Transactions on Systems Man & Cybernetics Part B Cybernetics A Publication of the IEEE Systems Man & Cybernetics Society. 2010;**40**(4):997-1008

[18] Muramatsu D, Shiraishi A, Makihara Y, Uddin MZ, Yagi Y. Gait-based person recognition using arbitrary view transformation model. IEEE Transactions on Image Processing. 2014;**24**(1):140-154

[19] Wu Z, Huang Y, Wang L, Wang X, Tan T. A comprehensive study on cross-view gait based human identification with deep CNNs. IEEE Transactions on Pattern Analysis & Machine Intelligence. 2017;**39**(2):209-226

[20] Zhao G, Liu G, Li H, Pietikainen M. 3D gait recognition using multiple cameras. In: International Conference on Automatic Face and Gesture Recognition (FG 2006); 10-12 April 2006; Southampton, UK. New York: IEEE; 2006. pp. 529-534

[21] Yamauchi K, Bhanu B, Saito H. Recognition of walking humans in 3D: Initial results. In: IEEE Computer Society Conference on Computer Vision & Pattern Recognition Workshops (CVPR 2009); 20-25 June 2009; Miami, Florida, USA. New York: IEEE; 2009. pp. 45-52

[22] Krzeszowski T, Michalczuk A, Kwolek B, Switonski A, Josinski H. Gait recognition based on marker-less 3D motion capture. In: IEEE International Conference on Advanced Video and Signal Based Surveillance (AVSS 2013); 27-30 August 2013; Krakow, Poland. New York: IEEE; 2013. pp. 232-237

[23] Sivapalan S, Chen D, Denman S, Sridharan S, Fookes C. Gait energy volumes and frontal gait recognition using depth images. In: International Joint Conference on Biometrics (IJCB 2011); 11-13 October 2011; Washington, DC, USA. New York: IEEE; 2011. pp. 1-6

[24] Nambiar AM, Correia PL, Soares LD. Frontal gait recognition combining 2D and 3D data. In: Proceedings of the on Multimedia and Security; 6-7 September 2012; Coventry, United Kingdom. New York: ACM; 2012. pp. 145-150

[25] Araujo RM, Graña G, Andersson V. Towards skeleton biometric identification using the Microsoft Kinect sensor. In: ACM Symposium on Applied Computing; 18-22 March 2013; Coimbra, Portugal. New York: ACM; 2013. pp. 21-26

[26] Milovanovic M, Minovic M, Starcevic D. Walking in colors: Human gait recognition using Kinect and CBIR. Multimedia IEEE. 2013;**20**(4):28-36

[27] Preis J, Kessel M, Linnhoff-Popien C, Werner M. Gait recognition with Kinect. In: Workshop on Kinect in Pervasive Computing; 18-22 June 2012; Newcastle, UK

[28] Yang K, Dou Y, Lv S, Zhang F, Lv Q. Relative distance features for gait recognition with Kinect. Journal of Visual Communication & Image Representation. 2016;**39**(C):209-217

[29] Ahmed F, Paul PP, Gavrilova M. Kinect-based gait recognition using sequence of the most relevant joint relative angles. Journal of WSCG. 2015;**23**(2):147-156

[30] Kastaniotis D, Theodorakopoulos I, Theoharatos C, Economou G, Fotopoulos S. A framework for gait-based recognition using Kinect. Pattern Recognition Letters. 2015;**68**(P2):327-335

[31] Shutler JD, Grant MG, Nixon MS, Carter JN. On a large sequence-based human gait database. Applications and Science in Soft Computing. 2004;**24**:66-71

[32] Hadid A, Ghahramani M, Bustard J, Nixon MS. Improving gait biometrics under spoofing attacks. In: Image Analysis and Processing (ICIAP 2013); 9-13 September 2013; Naples, Italy. Berlin: Springer; 2013. pp. 1-10

[33] Yu S, Tan D, Tan T. A framework for evaluating the effect of view angle, clothing and carrying condition on gait recognition. In: International Conference on Pattern Recognition (ICPR 2006); 20-24 August 2006; Hong Kong, China. New York: IEEE. 2006;**4**:441-444

[34] Iwama H, Okumura M, Makihara Y, Yagi Y. The OU-ISIR gait database comprising the large population dataset and performance evaluation of gait recognition. IEEE Transactions on Information Forensics & Security. 2012;**7**(5):1511-1521

[35] Hofmann M, Geiger J, Bachmann S, Schuller B, Rigoll G. The TUM Gait from Audio, Image and Depth (GAID) Database: Multimodal recognition of subjects and traits. Journal of Visual Communication & Image Representation. 2014;**25**(1):195-206

[36] Pala F, Sata R, Fumera G, Roli F. Multimodal person reidentification using RGB-D cameras. IEEE Transactions on Circuits & Systems for Video Technology. 2016;**26**(4):788-799

[37] Makihara Y, Matovski DS, Nixon MS, Carter JN, Yagi Y. Gait recognition: Databases, representations, and applications. Wiley Encyclopedia of Electrical and Electronics Engineering. Wiley; 2015. DOI: 10.1002/047134608X.W8261

[38] Andersson VO, Araujo RM. Person identification using anthropometric and gait data from Kinect sensor. In: AAAI Conference on Artificial Intelligence; 25-30 January 2015; Austin, Texas, USA. Menlo Park, CA: AAAI Press; 2015. pp. 425-431

[39] Dan IS, Toth-Tascau M. Influence of treadmill velocity on joint angles of lower limbs during human gait. In: E-Health and Bioengineering Conference (EHB 2011); 24-26 November 2011; Iasi, Romania. IEEE; 2011. pp. 1-4

[40] Tech SXMYM, Larsen PK, Alkjær T, Simonsen EB, Lynnerup N. Variability and similarity of gait as evaluated by joint angles: Implications for forensic gait analysis. Journal of Forensic Sciences. 2014;**59**(2):494-504

[41] Pfster A, West AM, Bronner S, Noah JA. Comparative abilities of Microsoft Kinect and Vicon 3D motion capture for gait analysis. Journal of Medical Engineering & Technology. 2014;**38**(5):274-280

[42] Bouchrika I, Goffredo M, Carter J, Nixon MS. On using gait in forensic biometrics. Journal of Forensic Sciences. 2011;**56**(4):882-889

[43] Chattopadhyay P, Sural S, Mukherjee J. Frontal gait recognition from incomplete sequences using RGB-D camera. IEEE Transactions on Information Forensics & Security. 2014;**9**(11):1843-1856

[44] Chattopadhyay P, Sural S, Mukherjee J. Frontal gait recognition from occluded scenes. Pattern Recognition Letters. 2015;**63**:9-15

[45] Corona F, Pau M, Guicciardi M, Murgia M, Pili R, Casula C. Quantitative assessment of gait in elderly people affected by Parkinson's disease. In: IEEE International Symposium on Medical Measurements and Applications (MeMeA 2016); 15-18 May 2016; Benevento, Italy. IEEE; 2016. pp. 1-6